THE DIVINITY OF SEX

THE DIVINITY
OF SEX

The Search for Ecstasy in a Secular Age

Charles Pickstone

St. Martin's Press ❧ New York

THE DIVINITY OF SEX. Copyright © 1996 by Charles
Pickstone. All rights reserved. Printed in the United
States of America. No part of this book may be used
or reproduced in any manner whatsoever without
written permission except in the case of brief
quotations embodied in critical articles or reviews.
For information, address St. Martin's Press,
175 Fifth Avenue, New York, N.Y. 10010.

Library of Congress Cataloging-in-Publication Data

Pickstone, Charles.
    The divinity of sex : the search for ecstasy in a
secular age / Charles Pickstone.
        p.   cm.
    ISBN 0-312-15516-6
    1. Sex—Religious aspects—Christianity.   I. Title.
BT708.P49   1997
233'.5—dc21   97-12809
                                                   CIP

First published in Great Britain by Hodder and
Stoughton, a division of Hodder Headline PLC, as
For Fear of the Angels: How Sex Has Usurped Religion

First U.S. Edition: August 1997

10   9   8   7   6   5   4   3   2   1

for Helen

(although these are only words
and for others to read)

Contents

THE DIVINITY OF SEX

Introduction

Landscapes of Desire

France is divided from Spain by a narrow chain of mountains. Travellers approaching the Pyrenees from the French side always remark on the strikingly abrupt change in landscape they present. After the endless flatness of Les Landes, that part of western France which runs along the coast and which is so flat that it looks almost as if it is still part of the sea, suddenly the foothills of the Pyrenees emerge with hardly even a warning ripple. And then, almost immediately, there in the distance are visible the peaks of the mountains themselves, that alarming band of dark, jagged rock only a few miles across which breaks through the attractive greenness of the foothills – a world of hostile precipices and inaccessible glaciers. You do not need to know much about geology to realise that the soft, fertile, secondary rocks have been torn apart by a breaking out of the hard, primary, igneous rock which normally lies beneath it. Pressure from the Alps hundreds of miles away has pushed it up. The earth's surface has been torn open, and the area is rich in thermal springs where water heated on the rocks of the earth's core bubbles up through the fault-line, often still warm and with healing properties that have been known about for centuries. The spring at Lourdes is a recent example.

Sexuality is the direct expression of the life-force within all human beings. It is the fuel that drives nature, a flammable petrol that can be a source of energy or destruction. It is so powerful and abundant that it tends to overflow its natural channels and ends up giving form and meaning to quite neutral objects, throwing up the whole gamut of phallic and feminine symbols without which life would be immensely dull. It adds zest to conversation and relish to observation and somehow it always finds a way of managing to evade the careful barriers society puts up in defence against it. In this respect, its force is similar to the Alpine folding responsible for the dark peaks of the Pyrenees. In film after play after novel, time and again sex causes someone's dark, primary nature to push up through the affable and rational everyday self that people display most of the time.

However, for most of human history this eruption of the primitive bedrock of human nature has been seen as terrifying and sinful, and has had to be fought against with an entire apparatus of social and religious taboos, not to mention the whole comic *batterie de cuisine* of cold showers, flagellation, fasting, iron chains about the loins and other mortifications that the human mind has devised for this purpose. Even today, for some people this threatened loss of control to the fury and the mire of human veins is not to be borne and must be blocked off or else channelled into some other, more acceptable obsession. But for most, sexual repression is a mediaeval nonsense which can be safely disregarded with amusement.

Even so, the power of sex upon the Western mind could hardly be stronger. Many theories exist as to why this is so: the excitement of breaking an anachronistic taboo; cynical exploitation of the consumer by the media; the search for relief from unbearable stress in daily life; titillation for jaded palates in a society grown stale and decadent . . . A new theory is put forward every week.

But these theories on their own cannot really do justice to our all-consuming interest in sex. There must be some other, underlying source for this fascination. It need not have been so; many writers argue that the Western concept of 'sexuality' is an artificial construction foisted on to a simple biological fact. So why have we gone to such lengths, why have we invested so much of our psychological capital in building so grand and imposing an

2

edifice? Everywhere one looks, there are people writing about, reading about, talking about, making films and documentaries about, fantasising about – sex.

In this book, I am going to suggest that there is an underlying common thread: namely that sex has taken on many of the functions once performed by religion. In particular, sex has become a path to an encounter with primordial mystery. It is this encounter which is the subject of this book.

But more than this, in our present condition sex is not only one possible route to the encounter with mystery, it is also the most popular. This is the primary reason why sex is so important and why it is invested with such extraordinary power: it is one of the main modes of access, for those of us who are not nuclear scientists, astrophysicists or cell biologists, to the mystery of life itself; access that can be found almost nowhere else in our world, given the general lack of interest in religion, the traditional path to the mystery of life. From this point of view, sex has become the religion of the Western world, the bearer of most people's hopes of encountering something truly 'other'.

This may seem an extraordinary statement to make. But how else are we fully to explain the extraordinary hopes, fears and fantasies people have of sex – the time and energy we invest in it, the unrealistic expectations we have of it, the celestial aspirations and profound yearnings, the diffuse projections and strange nightmares with which we endow what is, after all, a simple biological function? So many of these aspects of sex are normally associated with religion that in the end no other explanation will do.

Sexuality: a touch of heaven

The link between sex and religion is in one sense well known and well documented. For hundreds of years, religious writers and

3

poets have used sexual imagery to describe their relationship with their particular god. For example, the Islamic poet Sana'i saw Allah as his beloved, and wrote him passionate love poems: 'Every breath which my body breathes/Is a sigh of desire', or 'Under your gaze my limbs go weak,/And I fall into delicious slumber.'[1] There are similar passages in the Old Testament Song of Songs.

On the other side, lovers have always used the language of religious ecstasy to describe their passion. At its most trivial we have 'Having sex is a wonderful experience; making love to someone you cherish is a touch of heaven.'[2] On a more sophisticated level is John Donne teasing his mistress on going to bed:

> *Now off with those shoes, and then safely tread*
> *In this love's hallow'd temple, this soft bed.*
> *In such white robes, heaven's angels us'd to be*
> *Received by men; thou angel bring'st with thee*
> *A heaven like Mahomet's paradise; and though*
> *Ill spirits walk in white, we easly know*
> *By this these angels from an evil sprite,*
> *Those set our hairs, but these our flesh upright.*[3]

His mistress's white underwear makes her look like an angel in the Muslim paradise (where the righteous feast with a thousand beautiful women) and a practical test reveals that she is a good angel and not an evil spirit.

More recently, many writers on sex of very different persuasions have discussed the link between sex and religion. For example, the right-wing philosopher Roger Scruton remarks at the beginning of his book *Sexual Desire: A Philosophical Investigation*: 'At many points in what follows, my discussion will make contact with religion, . . . because – as has been frequently observed – erotic and religious sentiments show a peculiar isomorphism.'[4]

A completely different kind of writer, the French anthropologist Georges Bataille, in his classic book on sex, *L'Érotisme*, confesses how in his youth he was obsessed with the image of God; and how, even now, in 'the abandoned world which we are exploring in this

4

book, human passion has only one object [i.e. God]. It is the ways along which we approach him which vary.' He concludes, 'I insist on the fact that, in this book, the energies of the Christian religion and those of the erotic life appear in their unity.'[5]

For another example, the well-known academic sociologist Anthony Giddens speaks of the connection between sex and religion in his seminal work *The Transformation of Intimacy.* Sexual ecstasy, he argues, 'has echoes of the "ethical passion" which transcendental symbolism [i.e. religion] used to inspire, and, of course, cultivated eroticism – as distinct from sexuality in the service of reproduction – has long been associated with religiosity'.[6]

The great French thinker Michel Foucault regarded sex as an excuse for continuing 'the ancient [art]form . . . of preaching.' 'A great sexual sermon,' he claims, 'has swept through our societies over the last decades', reminding him of Franciscan preaching. He wonders how so trivial a subject as sex has come to have such importance, asking himself in mock disbelief, 'And we might wonder how it is possible that the lyricism and religiosity that long accompanied the revolutionary project have, in Western industrial societies, been largely carried over to sex.'[7]

At its bluntest the connection between sex and religion is encapsulated in a quotation from the theologian Jim Cotter in a contemporary book for schoolchildren: 'Through our experience of sexuality, there is the possibility of our becoming more open to the Beyond whom we call God.'[8] Or even more blatantly, as another theologian puts it, 'The man who knocks on the door of a brothel is really looking for God.'

And yet, despite all these statements about the close link between religion and sex, there is very little concrete evidence offered for it by these writers or by others who write about sex, and there is surprisingly little discussion as to why this should be the case – especially today. Everyone is agreed on the importance of the topic. As a North London priest I interviewed for this book, someone who probably has as much experience of either as anyone I have come across, put it, 'We are talking about two sorts of ecstasy. The relationship between them is crucial.' And yet there is surprisingly little systematic research available on this extremely important issue.

Perhaps the reason for this is that even though some spiritual writers have not been afraid to use sexual imagery, nor, when it suits them, writers on sex the language of religion, this is a deeply uncomfortable area. Sex and religion are traditionally so far apart. It has always been assumed that 'religion' is so opposed to sex, so contrary to the lubricious or pneumatic pleasures of this world, that it has such a prurient distaste for the juices and bodily secretions of reproduction, that it can make little use of the business of sex or vice versa, except insofar as naughty nuns and bloated bishops may feature in a certain sort of pornography, or else insofar as the alleged sexual practices of 'Oriental' religions are turned into books and videos such *The Tao of Sex* or *The Kama Sutra for Today* – the latter a rather prim exercise of the '101 varieties' genre.

The reason for this will be explored in succeeding chapters. But there is still something rather puritanical about our notions of religion, and even for devout non-believers the notion of sex and religion coming together (in copulation, one might say) always elicits a certain *frisson* – the contamination of the pure by the impure, the heavenly by the earthly. This sense of blasphemy can be highly stimulating, as Georges Bataille points out in *L'Érotisme*, where he regards the breaking of taboos as the basis of the erotic quest. But for most people it is a matter of distaste. So we must tread carefully.

Sex and secularisation

The basic thesis of this book is that in an affluent society such as ours, people are actually no less religious than in a poor one. People still have the same religious instinct, the same heightened experiences, the same sense of something 'beyond' as they have ever had. However, this basic religious sense is expressed today in highly variegated and more subtle ways than in the past.

In a poor community, religion is in one sense relatively straightforward, an essential part of the highly important business of the survival of the community, of warding off the forces over which its members are powerless. An impoverished community's religion is its soul, into which are absorbed the individual labours and fates of the people who make it up, and which gives them in return their sense of identity and purpose. It can be a magnificent construction, a thing of power and great beauty; it can equally be mean-spirited and enslaving.

In an affluent society, however, the corporate tyranny of such a unidimensional religion is generally shed with a sigh of relief, although not without a certain nostalgia, as individuals emerge into importance. Religion, now, is not so much a question of the community being united in the observances of certain necessary rituals that give it its identity in the face of suffering, as of individuals having heightened experiences.

In the last hundred years we have seen the final development along these lines, with the transformation of religion into what one might call spirituality. God can be found in art, in music, in warm feelings in the heart experienced by individuals rather than communities. Of course, the great rituals of the ancient Churches still exist. But for the majority, the ancient God, while deeply attractive for nostalgic reasons, does not seem to be of much help in the daily compromises and complex decisions that must be made when living in an affluent world, nor altogether to fulfil the contemporary desire for a rich and nuanced religious experience. In the modern world, religion becomes spirituality, and, as life becomes increasingly secular, spirituality becomes culture.

Another implication of this is that whereas it used to be the corporate, communal aspects of religion which were important (although there were, of course, always occasional hermits and mystics, of wide influence), increasingly in a society where people have less need to gather formally, it is individual experience which is important, and large gatherings, expressing corporate or communal identity, the exception.

However, strange survivals of what one might call peasant religion persist. This form of religion was based firmly on the existence of another world – whether the world of superstition, of ghoulies and ghosties, or of heaven, of God and eternal life – above, beyond or after the present one. Affluent religion is likely to have much less imaginative energy invested in another world – after all, the present world is very comfortable for many people. But even the most sensate and hard-headed among us just occasionally have a glimpse of something beyond the normal – from the mundane experience of seeing a ghost to an unearthly coincidence, from a sense of benign providence to the subtlest tragic ecstasy of a Mozart string quintet. How better to explain these heightened experiences than by suggesting that they are in some sense 'otherworldly' – even if the concept of an 'other' world is no longer very coherent?

The historical process I have been describing is known by the rather formidable term 'secularisation'. The process of secularisation describes how the secular world outside the Church takes over the sacred world of heaven. To draw an analogy, one might imagine a great flood blotting out all civilisation except for small, scattered communities up in the mountains. The religion of the mountains, where life was short, brutish and nasty, where people were entirely at the mercy of chance events and uncontrollable forces, would be very different from that of the large, sheltered communities who would have lived in the plains. In the history of Europe, a similar process has taken place in reverse. The great mediaeval Church was highly appropriate to a primitive peasant society just emerging from the Dark Ages; today, a more affluent and developed culture generates more sophisticated channels for expressing religious instincts and desires. 'Secularisation' is the word that describes the religion of the mountain peaks giving way to the religion of the plains. It is a momentous process which should not be underestimated.

It was at the end of the Victorian period that what had been a gradual process finally gathered speed; a number of things came together which were definitively to tip the balance away from the other world and towards this one. Let us take, for example, the coming of the railways. The 'iron horse' is an excellent example of all the different aspects of affluence which led by an inexorable process to the secularisation of religion. We have here democracy (railway travel was available to all); rapidly advancing technology (for most people, it was their first experience of going faster than running pace); the rise of leisure for all; social and cultural mobility; the efficient distribution of goods (leading to increased living standards) – all symbolised by a great man-made monster, the steam engine. Given that horses had featured so prominently in English life heretofore, this man-made horse was a potent symbol, remarked upon regularly at the time, of how God and nature were yielding their place to technology and capital.

A hundred years later, the railway train would in turn yield to that lesser half-monster, the private motor car, but cars would never really be able to compete mythologically with steam trains. The religion of the motor car – individualistic, domestic, uniform and competitive in a trivial sort of way – is an excellent example of the further progress of secularisation. The heroic initial phase of secularism degenerates into the tawdry, mass-produced and symbolically flat.

Other contributing factors to the secularisation of religion in the Victorian period and beyond need briefly to be spelt out. Decent sanitation and proper nutrition, better public health and a declining birth-rate made healthy urban living more possible, even though there were plenty of slums. Education was increasingly available.

Thus, on the one hand, material progress and mass production made life more comfortable, less prone to mischance, and therefore perhaps diminished the necessity for religious belief among the wealthier – even though many of the population had to exist still in grinding poverty, although this urban poverty did not prevent vast numbers heading for the cities from the country and abandoning their rural and semi-rural roots and the parish churches that went with them. And on the other hand, the very foundations of the Christian faith were under attack, and thanks to generally increasing literacy, everyone knew it. (Voltaire, the eighteenth-century French philosopher, would not declare himself an atheist in front of his maid, fearing a decline in standards of service, but now his maid could learn to read his works for herself.)

For example, Darwin had attacked the authority of the Bible by providing a this-worldly explanation of human evolution which obviated the need for God. The new science of biblical criticism began to treat the Bible as any other human document and to reveal its very human origins – it was increasingly difficult to see God literally dictating such a variegated and self-contradictory document. Knowledge of other religions – particularly, for example, in India, where British scholars went out with the Empire and unearthed large numbers of fascinating religious texts with their own rival narratives of creation and redemption – began to bring an aspect of relativity to Christianity. (It has been argued that what today is known as Hinduism was in fact a British invention.) From being a universal faith, Christianity became one religion among many. Church history studies began to show that the Church herself was a very human institution.

Thus both the intellectual and social foundations of the Christian Church were under attack at the same time as large numbers of working-class people moved into the cities away from their rural communities and conspicuously failed to develop any sort of religious roots in their new urban environment, where they adopted a very different lifestyle from before, and intellectual discoveries provided the middle class with weapons with which to express their sense of alienation from the Church.

As a result, there developed a feeling, very common in industrial societies, that God was no longer to be found. Just as the motor car does not have the mythological power of the gloriously uneconomic steam train, so, people felt, the developed, industrialised world of mass production did not have the materials available for God to be adequately represented; it was as if the increasingly materialistic world somehow could not contain God, that God had lost his natural habitat – hence the overwhelming attraction, in the Victorian period, of the 'Gothic', a nostalgia partly responsible for the biggest religious revival of the century, the Oxford Movement.

The spirituality of sex

What happens, then, to people's religious instincts as the ecclesiastical channels for the expression of religious energies begin to silt up and fewer and fewer pointers are available to the realm of the other world? From the dawn of time, most people some of the time, and a few people most of the time, have had what might be called religious experiences – some sense of a transcendent world, of the workings of providence, of some external moral foundation to their lives and actions. But increasingly in the late Victorian period, there was a general sense that the traditional metaphors, the usual signposts or bridges to the world beyond, were drawing a blank. The riches of Europe's first affluent society for 1500 years were paralleled by an increasing religious and aesthetic poverty. So how was religious experience to be expressed?

There were any number of answers. New cults, small religions, social utopias, the arts, some sciences, foreign travel, education, archaeology – all provided partial answers. But for the vast majority of people, there were more democratic and easily accessible means: the locus of the sacred came to repose increasingly in such everyday institutions as childhood, marriage and the family, and in easily available experiences such as of the grandeur of nature – and in sexuality.

The majority of people, especially as the nineteenth century turned into the twentieth, began to turn to the mysterious, forbidden, private, ritualised world of sex both for experience of another world and for the language in which to express that experience. In succeeding chapters, we look at the various aspects of life that were contaminated by these quasi-religious expectations of sex, particularly in this crucial period of late Victorian and early Edwardian England, when secularisation finally came of age. We see that for many people their religious energies were entirely rerouted in this direction.

The process continues today. Sex is a major source of spirituality. In a sense, although the parallel is not very strong, what the Gothic revival was to the Victorian world, the world of sex is today

– an outlet for natural instincts, a displacement of religious energies.

It used to be said that religion was for those who do not get enough sex. This book aims to show, by contrast, that today we have reached the point where the opposite is true: that on the sunny beaches of a society bathed in a warm, shallow tide of spirituality – a society that has, of course, immensely strong dikes in place to keep out the ocean swell – sex has become a rather strange religion substitute. Where once religion could be seen as the sublimation of people's natural but repressed sexual impulses, today it is clear that our investment in the copious mythology of sex is, in fact, the result of our natural religious instincts being diverted, rechannelled. It might be argued that there are few other outlets available.

Not that sex is a particularly good religion substitute. There will be plenty of sport to be had in the ensuing pages, as we consider some of the more extreme forms of nonsense that people come up with when they are being religious about sex, or sexy about religion. A great deal of this spirituality of sex turns out to be spurious. Much of the confusion of modern life is precisely because of the extraordinary and unrealistic expectations that people have of sex. Do-it-yourself spirituality provides the best possible breeding ground for obfuscation, manipulation and deceit. There is a great deal of bogus mythology around, much of which is potentially harmful. Throughout the book, therefore, we shall be concerned to try to distinguish the genuine 'religious' experiences of sex from the mass-produced peddling of sexual fantasies in the name of religion but for the greater good of the church of commerce.

Most of these pseudo-spiritualities are potentially dangerous, especially in that they create false expectations or are unrealistic about basic human psychology; also, some tend to represent rather antiquated middle-class aspirations, and in the new, even flatter world in which we live (the tide of poverty has gone out even further) this sexual orthodoxy is already under attack.

And yet there is also an element of truth here as well. It is paradoxical that despite all the press coverage and media attention given to sex, it is still enormously difficult for rational and down-to-earth human beings to admit to these strange geological faults in their make-up which sex pushes up. The exposed primary matter of the soul is too embarrassing and painful, its igneous passions, sulphurous odour and basal deformities too apparent and ugly, to make acceptance as easy as the glossy magazines suggest it ought to be. On the other hand, it is in precisely these areas of geological fault that the interface between this world and the other world, the passage to the underworld, the tunnel to the centre of the earth, is located. Boundary areas are always by far the most interesting to explore; and in our culture it is especially through sex that the two worlds meet and that the everyday world encounters a world that is beneath it and beyond it.

There are a huge variety of these encounters – as one might expect when dealing with human creativity in all its multifaceted variety – from a white wedding service in a city church to a crowd of sailors outside a Turkish brothel in Istanbul, from the back room in a Manhattan gay bar to the secret garden of mediaeval legend. All of these are in one sense or another boundary or sacred places, the gates to Paradise or Hell. And together they yield unique and unparalleled insight into the range and diversity of human life, despite all the attempts of advertisers and others to shrink sex into a narrow range. Sex may, in fact, despite the hype, be an embarrassing or awkward topic – but it is generally at the unfashionable sidelines of culture that the most interesting discoveries are to be made.

So, finally, this book is an exploration of other worlds in encounter with our world. We explore some of the particular locations at which such sexual encounters take place, those thin points on the earth's crust, but also the strange concept of the 'other' itself and the important role it plays in an increasingly standardised world.

The ultimate 'other world' is that of death, and the relationship between sex and death is also important. The mystics have always claimed that glimpses of the other world return us to the present world refreshed and remade – and, in a strange way, readier for death. The great cycle of birth and death cannot be escaped and paradoxically it is generally those who have been surest of their hold on life who pass most easily into mysticism and death.

For evidence, we shall use a wide range of materials, from men's and women's magazines to the writings of philosophers and psychologists, and particularly works of art and novels. It is very difficult to pin down the general feelings, thoughts and emotional states of ordinary people. Two sorts of evidence are available: one can either ask people what they think, or else draw conclusions from the books they read, the pictures they buy. Since sex is such a carnal business, it is conveyed as well by the visual as the verbal; and so we shall be looking at works of art and advertisements, for example. Advertisers may sell fantasies, but they themselves have to be masters of the real, of what works, if they wish to sell their clients' products.

I shall not be relying very heavily upon the endless barrage of statistics that most books about sex delight in. The works of such as Kinsey and Desmond Morris are all very interesting in their way, but the domain of the poets and artists is a much richer, more human terrain. Novels and poems are 'laboratories of the spirit' where the depths of the human psyche can be explored in a more revealing way – much more interesting than the rather infantile pursuit of information about where men and women put (or don't put) their sexual organs and how often.

Inevitably, the more popular works of D.H. Lawrence will feature regularly, not because they are necessarily especially good (or bad), but because they have been so very influential. It was Lawrence's particular genius to have expressed – perhaps even to have created – the way of thinking that has become the secular spirituality of sex which is the subject of this book, and of which he therefore is the best-known prophet. There are many other similar prophets, whose works we will look at, but Lawrence provides the best distillation of the pseudo-religion of sexuality.

Many today read Lawrence with a sense of despair. Sex today is so much taken for granted that it is difficult to sympathise with his pioneering and impassioned worship of its power. But at the time, the effect was electrifying.

For fear of the angels

Like all mysteries worthy of the name, any approach to the mystery of life is fraught with danger. As long ago as the first century AD, in a post-modern society remarkably similar, in some ways, to our own, St Paul strictly admonished the young Christian Church in Corinth (one of the red-light districts of the ancient world) that women should wear veils in church to cover their glorious hair 'out of respect for the men and *for fear of the angels*'. This curious turn of phrase stems from an old Jewish tradition recorded in Genesis 6: 'And it came to pass, when men began to multiply on the face of the earth, and daughters were born unto them, that the sons of God saw the daughters of men that they were fair; and they took them wives of all which they chose.'

These mysterious 'sons of God' are generally identified with angels. Angels, it seems, can control themselves less easily even than men when it comes to being tempted by a glamorous woman in church. Such a woman, St Paul warns, is putting herself at risk from more than human dangers unless she is modestly apparelled.

St Paul's advice may appear quaint, and yet it contains an element of truth. Sex can evoke forces that are in one sense or another superhuman or demonic, in that they can take over the whole of one's life or personality (as is regularly attested in literature, film and drama). This is a dangerous area, where mistakes are easily made and their consequences severe – ruined lives and burnt-out victims. But then it can also be a source of quasi-religious ecstasy without parallel. Take a supremely powerful biological force, add religious expectations, and stand well back! This book chronicles some of the ensuing fireworks.

I offer here a couple of definitions of words that will recur regularly. One is 'mythology', or 'myth', a complex idea which I use to indicate patterns of (apparently) deep meaning that cannot be easily analysed and are often expressed by stories – in other words, something that gives sense or purpose to life; whereas 'mythical' I tend to use in the more popular sense of spurious or nonsensical. Since many a mythology turns out to be mythical, 'demythologisation' is what happens when a myth is shown to be spurious, and loses its power.

A 'sacrament' is an object or institution in this world which gives access to an 'other' world – originally one of seven sacraments defined by the Church, but today, thanks to its use as a metaphor, we have reached the point where anything will do.

1

Entering the Garden
Sex and Childhood

Eventually we will reach the Turkish brothel and the back room
of the Manhattan bar. But we begin this exploration of sex and
spirituality at the sacred place where we first learn to be carnal. A
child's bodily contact with his or her mother or carer is their first
introduction to the sensual delights of relating to someone through
touch. It is our entry to the garden of paradise, and therefore that
this embrace should be invested with religious allure, as it so often
is, is highly significant. At the earliest stages of our existence, sex
and religion are intimately linked.

In this chapter, I shall show how it has been argued that
the Victorians and Edwardians not only invented our notion
of childhood, but did so that it might do service as a religion
substitute as conventional church-going began to decline. If God
was to be found neither in church nor in the nasty world outside,
then in the protected realm of childhood the Victorian middle
classes were able to imagine a quasi-religious peace. This was
at least in part because children were seen as pure and innocent,
especially of sex: the Victorian religious Arcadia, their childhood
paradise, was a sex-free zone.

It would not be long before Freud would incur a great deal of
hostility for puncturing this myth and reminding the Edwardians

that children are not innocent of sex, not in an unhealthy way but simply in terms of their natural development. But that the Victorians needed to project these fantasies on to their children demonstrates that conventional religious practices were no longer able to supply what was needed, and that the world of childhood had become a (bogus) religion substitute. (The reality was that Victorian sexual abuse of children probably exceeded anything dreamt of today.)

Nowadays, children's sexual development is far better understood and documented, and the Victorian middle-class world no longer exists. Nonetheless, that sense of a protected realm which the Victorians (and the Romantic poets) projected on to childhood still exists. But now, I shall suggest, we have a new myth about its origins. It has been pushed earlier into children's development. Psychologists suggest that the baby's earliest bodily experiences of comfort and feeding at its mother's breast (or bottle) are both the basis of *sexual gratification* in later life and are also the origin of the experience of the *'sacred space'* – the very foundation of religious experience in adult life. In other words, in early childhood sex and religion are inseparable and in adult life they continue to interact.

This myth, too, is not without its problems. But we begin in the remarkable sex-free zone of late Victorian and early Edwardian children's literature – a walled garden of powerful fantasy.

Religion in decline: the discovery of Arcadia

In his book *Secret Gardens: A Study of the Golden Age of Children's Literature*, Humphrey Carpenter examines most of the classic books of English childhood literature from Kingsley's *Water Babies* to A.A. Milne's *Winnie the Pooh*. Carpenter sets himself the task of discovering what unites these stories.

As he writes in his preface, he had long been convinced that this entire genre of nominally children's fiction – from *The Wind in the Willows* to *Alice in Wonderland*, from *Peter Pan* to *Peter Rabbit* – had something in common, 'formed some sort of discernible pattern of ideas and themes' with 'a web of connections, influences and common purposes'. 'What was it that possessed the late Victorians and Edwardians to create a whole new genre of fiction?'[1]

He identifies their common ground as follows: these books are the product of a crisis of faith. Their authors were disillusioned with the established Christianity of their time, and thus what these books have in common is that they substituted a secular sacred place for the world of Christian belief. They created an Arcadia – originally the bucolic paradise that the ancient Romans located in a mythical kingdom in southern Greece. They set their novels and stories in an other world – whether the underwater world of Kingsley's *Water Babies* or the river bank of *Wind in the Willows*, whether the Enchanted Forest of A.A. Milne or J.M. Barrie's Never-Never-Land in *Peter Pan*, or Mrs Burnett's *Secret Garden*. They attempted to create not a Christian paradise in which they could no longer believe but a secular paradise (or secular hell, in the case of *Alice in Wonderland* and Edward Lear). More than that: partly through the popularity of these very influential stories, the whole world of childhood became for the late Victorians a sacred space.

For example, A.A. Milne's early masterpiece 'Vespers', in which a little boy kneels by his bed to say his prayers at the end of the day, is for many people a deeply religious poem despite being written by an agnostic. It is not religious in the conventional sense (the little boy is hardly attentive to his prayers and much more interested in himself, a common situation, as those who say prayers with their children will recognise). Rather, Milne has sketched the world of security most of his adult readers remember from their own childhoods, security of the type granted by simple trust in the sort of protecting God generally abandoned at adolescence. The child is sufficiently at home within this security to be able to play within its frame – secure despite the awful and possibly terrifying disorder most children experience when they step outside the familiar bounds of home, family and friends.

Even if this childhood paradise is hardly religious in the conventional sense, it is a recognisably religious space and was immensely attractive to Milne's sophisticated adult readers. In fact, as Carpenter points out, most of these stories and poems are enjoyed more by adults than by their children, presumably because children find their topsy-turvy world and often difficult language hard to grasp. Even Beatrix Potter, 'the ironist', deliberately (Carpenter claims) uses language that the most articulate child will find difficult to follow; while children never fail to be embarrassed at their parents' inevitably bursting into tears halfway through the last story in *The House at Pooh Corner*, 'Farewell to the Forest'.

One or two of his authors, Carpenter suggests, have even briefly peered into the terrifying Nietzschean world that ensues when not only religious belief is given up, but also any principle of order or foundation of reason or morality. This howling abyss, which even today in the post-modern 1990s very few have the courage to contemplate, proved too much for Edward Lear and Charles Dodgson (Lewis Carroll's real name). 'Having peered into the abyss of nothingness and anti-religion in *Alice in Wonderland* ... Dodgson stepped back hastily and turned to safer stuff.'[2] As a result, several of these pioneers retreated into alcohol or conventional children's literature.

The secret garden that Carpenter describes as being common to all these stories (except the Nietzschean ones) is 'an enchanted place in which all shall be well once more'. This place in fact consisted not only of the topography of children's literature but also of the whole world of childhood itself. As social historians such as Asa Briggs relate, the Victorians sentimentalised village life[3] and they sentimentalised children. At a time when the consolations of traditional Christianity were failing for all the reasons previously outlined, increasing affluence enabled middle-class children to be cocooned for the first time against the world of work, and childhood could become a 'Golden Age', a secular Paradise, a 'credible Arcadia'.

This is a pattern we shall find repeated throughout this book:

increasing affluence runs in parallel with a decline in traditional religious practices and in consequence people's religious needs and instincts flow into other areas. A small example might be the extraordinary vogue for fairies in Edwardian England after the success of J.M. Barrie's *Peter Pan*; quite clearly they take the place of the guardian angels that are now no longer credible. Carpenter's authors consciously or unconsciously 'rejected, or had doubts about conventional religious teaching . . . and their search for an Arcadia, a Good Place, a Secret Garden, was to a very large extent an attempt to find something to replace it'.[4] And very often, sexuality (or in this case, sexual innocence) will turn out to have an important role to play in defining these 'other areas' of pseudo-religious activity.

If this is true, and if these books represent the genuine sentiment of the Victorian middle classes, then we can conclude that for the Victorian adult, the garden of childhood was a protected space peopled with fantasy creations; protected, of course, not just from sex but from money, responsibility and adult cares in general. Adults themselves might feel they had been expelled from this Garden of Eden whose entrance was now barricaded by a seraph with a fiery torch, and that they were only permitted brief return visits to these forbidden Arcadian worlds which banishment made sublime. But through their children, they might still have a vicarious access.

Today, adult fantasies about children appear rather sick – correctly so. For the Victorians and Edwardians, these fantasies had a sinister shadow side which led not only to half-hidden sexual overtones in children's literature (as we shall see shortly) but also to incest and child sexual abuse on a scale that is only now becoming frighteningly clear. The repressed contents of the imagination inevitably emerge sooner or later, and the contrast between the protection lavished upon the children of fiction, dwelling in their middle-class protected garden, their sacred space, and the appalling things to which children – especially working-class children – had in reality to submit, is extraordinary.

For example, a recent television documentary interviewed six octogenarian women all of whom had been abused in the respectable Edwardian era, and whose treatment was, they claimed, entirely typical. The Society for the Protection of Children, the forerunner of the NSPCC, was founded in 1884: in its first year it dealt with five million cases of abuse (though clearly not all of them sexual). Steven Marcus, in his now-famous *The Other Victorians*, catalogues the underground corollary to superficial Victorian sexual purity, the childhood discipline (such as severe flogging at the larger public schools) which surfaced later in life in adult fantasies of beating and flogging. The very real agonies suffered by those who have been sexually abused by an adult in whom they trusted cannot any longer be denied; it is an experience that often blights their whole life, making their childhood the complete antithesis of the secret garden, a place of banishment rather than an echoing green on which children play, a secret hell which as a child they can share with no one but the abuser (the serpent). When they reach adult years, access to the creative springs has often dried up.

And even more appalling consequences followed when the Victorians attempted to make nature actually fit the fantasies of sexual purity they had dreamt up for her. Peter Gay, in his ground-breaking survey of the Victorian middle classes, *The Bourgeois Experience*, written to dispel some of the myths about Victorian 'hypocrisy', retails some of the devices anxious doctors and parents employed to deter their children (of both sexes) from the 'vicious habit' of masturbating (mechanical restraints, metal contrivances, chastity belts, penile rings, special waistcoats . . .). The most terrible example is that of a nervous seven-year-old girl who persisted in masturbating. 'All else failing, she was subjected to a clitoridectomy. The little girl stopped masturbating; a few weeks after the operation, making one final attempt, she admitted defeat: "You know that there is nothing there now," she said with heart-rending reasonableness, "so of course I could do nothing".'[5]

Today, thanks to a more realistic understanding of childhood, it is appreciated not only how easily children can be hurt, but also how the quasi-religious mystique projected on to children is largely a sentimental adult fantasy. As a result, children are now not only better protected from inappropriate sexual experience, thanks to the awareness of the damage caused by child sexual abuse, but also better instructed from an early age, in enlightened circles at least, about sex and their bodies thanks to sex education at school.

This is borne out by Carpenter's commenting, at the end of his book, that the prevailing style of children's novels has changed dramatically since his Golden Age of children's literature. Now, children's novels may still be concerned with secret gardens, but even so, 'if Arcadia is visited, the journey is made for the benefit of present and future';[6] the 'realisation that you can't "make it stop now" dominates English children's book of the modern period . . . The past exists as an enrichment of the present.' He ascribes this partly to demographic changes, and 'a loss of interest in that age group' (7–12s);[7] today parents tend to focus their attention mainly on toddlers' and pre-school children's books. But no doubt it is partly too because children's books are actually written for children, who in reality find life outside and inside the garden hard to prise apart and for whom, at times, even if they have not been abused, the garden is more like hell than paradise.

I want to digress for a moment, before beginning to move towards a more positive approach to childhood spirituality and sexuality (which are indeed linked), by bringing the story of childhood up to date.

The theme of the 'end of childhood', by which people seem to mean that the vision of childhood invented by the Victorians no longer exists, has become a particularly dominant one at present on television and in the press. There are a number of theories advanced for this development.

Firstly, thanks to child psychologists and novelists, we have a much more realistic view of children's development. Books such as the now ubiquitous *Toddler Taming* by Dr Christopher Green treat even very young children not as angels nor as demons, but simply as skilled game players whom their parents must learn to control not by violence or threats but by beating them at their own games. It is difficult to turn a sturdy toddler such as Green describes into a mystical angel or demon.

The seventeenth century held a view diametrically opposed to the Victorian one, namely that rather than being little angels children were the unreformed victims of original sin, who required intensive indoctrination and meticulous supervision. 'The Calvinist ideal embraced the notions of ingrained infantile depravity and juvenile frivolity . . . the aim of child training was to break the recalcitrant will of the infant,' as Bryan Turner puts it in his sociological study of the body through the ages, *The Body and Society*.[8] But today, thanks to children's psychologists, not to mention novels such as *Lord of the Flies* and *A High Wind in Jamaica*, it is no longer possible to imagine children as little innocents, untouched angels, as did the Victorians, nor as little demons, as did the Calvinists. The complete antidote to the myth of the protected child is a novel such as Iain Banks's *Wasp Factory*, which has been hailed with grateful sighs of relief from those surfeited on the sentimentality of the *Little Lord Fauntleroy* school of children's stories, as the young hero efficiently despatches several other children to their deaths in a matter-of-fact sort of way ('It was just a stage I was going through').

Even the baby at the breast, according to one theory, is trying to destroy the breast on which he or she feeds in order to test its reality (and thereby to establish his or her own separate identity). The child is no little Lord Fauntleroy, not even a half-angel or half-devil. If children experience feelings of wonder or awe, they are rarely important to them at the time.

Secondly, there is the rise of commercialisation and of the convenient popularity of the myth of the family. The pace of economic change since 1914 has been quite extraordinary: western Europe has seen the most radical redistribution of wealth ever known. If the rapid growth of affluence in the Victorian period enfranchised the burgeoning middle classes who constituted the Victorian and Edwardian bourgeoisie, who had the time and leisure to read the golden stories of childhood to their children, a further widening of the economic franchise has ensued, and the middle classes have, in their turn, yielded up their place to the enriched working classes who control colossal sums of money, of which the National Lottery is the perfect symbol.

Just a tiny ripple in this sea of wealth is worth forty million pounds.

Tim Gardom, who was part of the design team for the award-winning dinosaur gallery at the Natural History Museum and of the hands-on exhibition at the National Maritime Museum at Greenwich, explains the consequences as follows. Even august establishments such as the Natural History Museum and the Victoria and Albert Museum have discovered the huge sums of money that many families have at their disposal and are prepared to hand over for entertainment (the Natural History Museum ranks number four in the tourist league tables, and even the child-unfriendly Royal Academy is at number ten). They are therefore gearing their exhibitions to be family-friendly in contrast to the serious and austere aura of the Victorian museum (which was often built to look like a cathedral and demanded a similar decorum). Everything must be as accessible to as many people as possible. If feasible, they must have interactive displays where children can use computers, CD-ROMs or videos to learn about the museum's objects and the world in which they live. The myth of the protected child is in today's world as uneconomic as is the middle-class lifestyle that generated it in the first place (as our crisis-stricken public schools are discovering). In the Victorian period, the middle classes constituted the mass market. Today, everything, from the childhood stories to church services, must be geared to a much wider spectrum of users.

Thirdly, the dominance of working-class culture means that the 'classic' middle-class books for children, which often contained a very rigid hierarchical class system in disguise (for example, *Wind in the Willows*, where the aristocratic Badger despairs of the wastrel Toad), are no longer important. Working-class culture has traditionally always been less protective of children. For one thing, economically there was always less possibility of cosseting children; and secondly the television, the working-class medium *par excellence*, one always mistrusted at some level by middle-class families, tends to be left on all day. Carpenter refers to Neil Postman's theory that television, because it makes no distinction between childhood and adulthood, has largely eroded the idea of the former. As a result, 'the walls that formerly surrounded childhood – protection from the issues that dominate the adult world – are broken down'.

At one level, this prospect of more realistic children's story-telling is exciting; on the other hand, the Disneyfication of traditional children's stories means that local cultural variations are inevitably levelled out into different degrees of fancy dress clothing a pan-American world view. For example, the Disney version of *Winnie the Pooh and Tigger Too* bears almost no relation to A.A. Milne's original stories, nor *Quasimodo* to that of Victor Hugo.

Mass-marketing and the consequent flattening out of society is another reason why the world of childhood can no longer be a sacred place. Sacred places depend upon exclusion, but today the old patriarchy has broken down. Today the child has rights and so the gap between child and adult is not wide enough to make the world of children a separate sacred place. We are too familiar with this world, and like the Garden of Eden it is now deprived of power. If a myth is going to compel, it must be able to conjure up a differential, an other world. A bland myth has no power. A democratic, theme-park Eden is a great place to take the kids on a summer Sunday, but not much good as a religious symbol. Similarly, it is difficult to project a secret garden on to Grange Hill or Byker Grove!

The sexuality of children

Let us take stock. The Victorian and Edwardian world of child-hood was an Arcadian paradise, a world of innocence, especially sexual innocence. Affluent middle-class parents could afford to have their children cocooned against the real world of money, violence and sex. This paradise was, it is suggested, a sort of religion substitute for an age that was increasingly disenchanted with the formalistic observances that constituted the Victorian

Church, and was itself cocooned from the raw suffering that might have made religion a necessity. Today, by contrast, we have recovered a more realistic notion of childhood, thanks partly to changing economic circumstances. However, there is now, I want to suggest, a genuine spirituality of childhood unlike the bogus Victorian vision with its appalling consequences. In order better to approach it, we need to spend some time looking at how our understanding of the sexuality of children has changed.

Perhaps the best illustration of the Victorian and Edwardian attitude to childhood is Frances Hodgson Burnett's *The Secret Garden* of 1911. Of all the elegies to Old Europe that were being penned during this momentous era on the brink of the cataclysm of World War I, there is none more unsophisticated than this, the one story that almost everyone remembers from their own childhood, and which even now is possibly as popular with adults as with children.

Five years after Einstein published the special theory of relativity, and in the year in which Germany began to mobilise its armies and thus take an axe to the roots of the intellectual and moral fabric of Victorian Europe, Mrs Burnett heard (mistakenly) that the walled garden of a country house she regularly rented in England was to be destroyed. She was thus inspired to write a eulogy to the magic powers of nature which is also a farewell to an era: an era of innocence, privilege and security (for some), in which childhood could be protected from adult concerns (including, of course, sex) as securely as by a garden wall, where children lived in a world apart.

Today, looking back, now that the stately homes and their walled gardens have been turned into car parks and theme parks and safari parks, the book still has an extraordinarily nostalgic effect – stimulating a nostalgia for a state of childhood innocence closely allied in the imagination to the culture of privilege of Old Europe, a veritable land of lost content.

The Secret Garden is the story of a young orphan, Mary Lennox, brought up and then orphaned in India. She is sent to be looked after by her uncle, himself grieving for the loss of his wife ten years previously. He lives in a large and rambling country house on the

Yorkshire moors, although absent abroad most of the year. He has 'crooked shoulders' and his only son, Colin, is an invalid confined to bed for fear of the same thing, hidden away in a far recess of the large house. The heroine herself, unlike the children in Mrs Burnett's previous novels, notably *Little Lord Fauntleroy*, is a spoilt and awkward girl, and not pretty. On wet days, when not allowed out, she explores the rambling house, and one day discovers the invalid Colin. While outside in the grounds, thanks to an alluring robin, she comes across a mysterious key – and then the door into which it fits, which leads into a walled rose garden. This had been the pride and joy of Colin's mother, but had been left to go wild after her death. Mary tends her secret garden with the help of a local wild boy, Dickon (described by Humphrey Carpenter as a 'Heathcliff gone right'), and as the garden recovers its former beauty so Colin, once introduced to it, is cured of his psychosomatic illness. The book ends with Mary (now herself transformed into an outgoing young person) bringing about the cure of Colin's father's depressive illness.

The garden and the characters in the book are closely connected. Mary tends the garden; she is herself restored and Colin is also cured as he comes out into the garden. The author explains the connection as magical ('She always said that what happened to her at that moment was magic'), and for a child reader magic is as good an explanation as any. While for adults magic is enjoyable and unthreatening, mild entertainment for an idle half-hour's television, for a child (as adults tend to forget) magic can be terrifying. Since for a child the world is not a coherent whole where everything can be fitted into place, so magic represents things beyond his or her control or comprehension.

For adults, however, 'magic' requires a more sophisticated level of analysis, and this is where childhood sexuality comes in. The twentieth century has, after all, made the systematic analysis of the non-rational forces that operate on human beings its speciality. If the eighteenth was the century of reason, the twentieth century must be the century of the irrational, and so there are plenty of tools at our disposal with which to analyse this magic.

Perhaps the best way of analysing the connection between the secret garden and the characters in the story is to see it as a symbolic account of Mary's discovery of her sexuality. In the story she is almost ten, the age of most of her readers. For a child, a large, rambling house with hidden rooms can be a symbol of oneself, the many rooms signifying different aspects of one's personality, many of them as yet unknown to the pre-adolescent child. The dependent, crippled child hidden away in one of the rooms may represent a buried childhood memory – a symbol, perhaps, of Mary's stultified emotional development caused by the death of her parents – remedied through friendship and the discovery of the garden.

But on another level, a house can also be a symbol of logic, structure or will, and a garden a place of nature, reproduction and growth. The symbol of the walled rose garden has been associated with maturing female sexuality ever since the Middle Ages. In other words, Mary's learning to relate and care is bound up with the development of her own sexuality.

In the crucial passage in which Mary discovers the door to the lost walled garden, there is a veritable plethora of blatant and yet apparently unselfconscious sexual imagery – in the display of the robin who lures her to the key, in the symbolism of wall, door, key, lock, keyhole, fronds of ivy, knob, pocket, roses and the secrecy attached to it all. This barely concealed imagery makes it clear that it is through her own sexual development and maturation that the young girl finds healing, so that at the end of the book her uncle – the absent male whose obscure presence hangs over the book – can be allowed back into the garden, with the girl transformed from moody prepubescent adolescent into a developing sexual being.

In a sense it is rather shooting a sitting duck to undertake a psychological analysis of *The Secret Garden* in that the attraction of the book is precisely its innocence, its imagery entirely on the surface. But perhaps this explains why the story is attractive both to child and adult readers: the child can enjoy it at face value, as making sense of his or her chaotic world and uncontrollable bodily and hormonal developments, of that sense of bereavement, of ugliness, of aloneness and uselessness characteristic of many children at this stage of their development; while the adult can use it to escape from the all-too-real world. For the adult, the book is a sort of sexual holiday, precisely a secret garden, a return to Paradise, where one can take off all one's sophisticated adult clothes without having to adopt a sexual persona and walk around naked like Adam and Eve, without shame.

Generalising to other major works of childhood literature from this period, one could show how often the childhood Arcadia depicted is bound up symbolically with children's sexual development. In other words, many of the classic childhood stories (which, if Carpenter is right, create an alternative quasi-religious paradise for adults) are also about sex. For the creators of the best English childhood literature, sexual imagery is intimately allied to religious sacred space. This is an important conclusion, about which a great deal has been written, as we shall see. But first, we need to look at another example of childhood stories, stories that appeal to a much younger age group and which also reveal a great deal about children's sexual development.

This much older tradition of childhood literature also deals with sex in a magical or religious context. This is the world of fairy tales and folk stories, stories of great antiquity which, because they have been passed down through generations, have (at their best) acquired the hallmark of earthy realism uncontaminated with genteel niceties concerning sex and death.

Moreover, they are stories that young children have chosen themselves. Out of the thousands of folk tales that have been told over the years, some have survived precisely because they are popular with their listeners, who use the stories to get a handle on the strange and contradictory forces at whose mercy they largely find themselves by dressing them up in fancy clothes – as seductive wolves, kindly grandmothers, helpful birds, wicked ogres, valiant young men and women, beautiful daughters, handsome sons. The world of folk stories is certainly a religious world in any sense, featuring powerful beings with god-like powers, miracles, unexpected reversals, all underscored by a basic sense of justice and fairness with everything turning out for the best in the end.

A classic analysis of fairy tales in human developmental terms can be found in Bruno Bettelheim's much-acclaimed book *The*

Uses of Enchantment. He has performed the remarkable feat of decoding the meaning of many of the best-known fairy tales for a developing child through years of working with children with learning difficulties and emotional problems. He uses the language of Freudian psychoanalysis, and so, for him, the sexual message of fairy stories is particularly important. Thus he considers that 'for a child, the greatest riddle is what sex consists of; that is the secret of adults which he wishes to discover'.[9] Throughout his book, he makes explicit the shallowly buried sexual component of most of the popular fairy stories.

As an example, and in contrast to *The Secret Garden*, let us look at his interpretation of 'Jack and the Beanstalk'. If *The Secret Garden* was about a young innocent's discovery in a protected space of her path to inner healing and sexual maturity, 'Jack and the Beanstalk' is an early lesson about the difficult relationship between fantasy and reality in matters of sex.

The story begins when the good cow, Milky-White, stops yielding milk. Jack is sent off to market and makes an apparently foolish transaction – selling the cow for some 'magic' beans (magic again: a warning that unconscious forces are at work). Mother rejects the transaction ('what are we to live on?'), throws the beans out of the window, beats Jack and sends him to bed without supper. Overnight (the time of dreams and fantasy) the beans sprout outside the window so that the house is still dark in the morning. Jack boldly climbs up the beanstalk, into a secret world and into a castle. There he charms a giant's wife into providing food for him but when the giant returns, himself demanding food (like many a father coming in from work at mealtimes) and threatening to eat Jack if he finds him (*fee fi fo fum*), Jack has to be hidden by the giantess in the oven, and she lies to her husband to protect him. Once the giant has fallen into a drunken sleep, Jack steals one of the giant's treasures – a hen which lays golden eggs – and scampers back down the beanstalk.

These events recur, and this time Jack is nearly caught when the talking harp he is stealing summons the giant to its aid. But with the giant in hot pursuit Jack hares down the beanstalk and hews it down with an axe. The beanstalk shrivels and the giant falls to his death. Jack therefore gets to keep the treasures, but access to the castle in the sky is now gone. He discovers that the treasures stolen from the giant actually once belonged to his father, who had been killed by the giant.[10]

Bettelheim interprets this story as being about a child developing his sexuality, passing from the 'oral' phase, in which the child is all mouth, to the 'genital' phase, in which the child first becomes aware of its genitals. The cow, Milky-White, represents the breast from which the weaned child is expelled; the beanstalk is clearly a phallic symbol representing the child's emerging discovery of his or her sexual organs. (Bettelheim suggests that it can symbolise clitoris as much as penis.) 'As in infancy the mother's breast was symbol of all the child wanted of life, and seemed to receive from her, so now his body, including his genitals, will do all that for the child, or so he wishes to believe. This is equally true for boys and girls; that is why the story appeals as much to girls.'[11] In other words, the developing child expelled from the infantile paradise of security and absolute contentment at the mother's breast discovers that 'the unending supply of love and nutriment proves to be an irrealistic fantasy'.[12]

But this fantasy is replaced by another – 'the beanstalk has replaced Milky White. On this beanstalk the child will climb into the sky to achieve a higher existence' as 'the phallic phase replaces the oral one'. Thus Jack dreams of taking revenge upon his mother by selling the cow, replacing a mother figure with a few magic beans, and using these magic beans (surprisingly they are not mushrooms) to enter a fantasy castle in the sky where he can seduce another version of his mother thinly disguised as a giantess – to a child, grown-ups often appear like giants – and thus steal her from his horrid father. (As a Freudian, Bettelheim considers that the prime difficulty a child must face is the sorting out of his or her difficult relationship with his two parents: attraction to the parent of the opposite sex and jealousy of the same-sex parent.)

This level of fantasy endures until it gets too dangerous – the giant, the monster father the child has created, threatens, like Frankenstein's monster, to get out of control and destroy him, and the child feels himself to be in real danger. In any case, reality begins to impinge: if the real father is killed, who will support him and the family? And so, as if waking from a dream, the child quickly brings the fantasy to an end with a satisfying conclusion – he kills off the awful fantasy father, leaving him free to have a proper relationship with his mother in the real world, without the necessity of escapist fantasy, and with his father, about whom he now discovers some facts.

Whether or not one agrees with his analysis of the story, one can accept with Bettelheim that the castle in the sky, like the secret garden, is a necessary part of every child's life. The boy or girl, constantly threatened by the difficulties and dangers of his developing body, needs not only to escape but also to imagine how things might be otherwise: the fantasy world is the source of most of life's good ideas, symbolised by the hen and the harp, which, after all, Jack gets to keep provided that he can distinguish between fact and fantasy.

Indeed, there is what might be styled a feminist interpretation of 'Jack and the Beanstalk' which actually out-Bettelheims Bettelheim. Contemporary thinking, based on Freud, distinguishes the phallus from the penis. The former is the erect penis with all its macho associations; the latter refers neutrally to the anatomical organ possessed by males. The chopping down of the phallic beanstalk at the end of the story can be interpreted as representing the developing male's gradual understanding that a genuine relationship with a woman depends not on macho sexual prowess, often based on fantasies of penetrating the forbidden realms of the woman's body with tool or phallus, but on a full, personal relationship rooted in reality in which the penis is simply a penis – a source of mutual pleasure and not of domination. In the end, the phallus must be demythologised and become a penis if a man is to have real relationships. (Similarly for a woman, clitoral stimulation cannot provide ultimate satisfaction.)

Bettelheim rates the educational content of fairy stories very highly. Subliminally, he claims, they have an important role to play in teaching children about the most difficult things in life. Looking at his interpretation of other fairy stories – 'Red Riding Hood' (seduction), 'Beauty and the Beast' (fear of sex),

33

'Snow White' (parental jealousy), 'Sleeping Beauty' (arrested sexual development) – one cannot reasonably claim that children need to be protected from difficult or unpleasant things. Fairy stories make a realistic and unpatronising assessment of the difficulties, dangers and perplexities of being a child. Contrary to the ideas of the Victorian middle classes, childhood is neither a protected nor a sex-free zone.

The spirituality of children

We are now approaching our goal of understanding how children's sexual development and spiritual development are bound up – both in the mind of adults and possibly, too, in reality. But first we must fill in the other half of the equation and move from the sexual to the spiritual development of children, again beginning in the Victorian world. The writings of the seventeenth-century English poet Thomas Traherne (1637–74) are a paradigm of a vision of childhood innocence. The Victorians may have 'invented' childhood in the sense familiar today, but the raw materials had been around for several hundred years.

Traherne imagines a child's-eye view of the world which is full of wonder, uncorrupted by adult ways of thinking, and where everything is new to the child as he looks at things for the first time. It is often said that Wordsworth was the first to write about childhood in England in a modern sense – children are innocent creatures who arrive 'trailing clouds of glory'. Traherne, however, shows that adult fantasies about children's perception of the world predate Wordsworth. His *Centuries of Meditations*, for example, dating from the 1660s, is probably the first convincing depiction of childhood experience in English literature. It is interesting that the work was lost for two hundred years until its manuscript turned up in a London market in 1896; in other words, it was not until the late Victorian interest in childhood was well under way that his value was recognised.

Here is an extract, one particularly well known for having been gloriously set to music by the English pastoral composer Gerald Finzi in his *Dies Natalis* for baritone and string orchestra. In it Traherne imagines himself as a child, seeing the world for the first time. I quote at length as it is a superb description (better than anything in Wordsworth) of an adult view of the innocence and wonder of childhood.

Will you see the infancy of this sublime and celestial greatness? I was a stranger, which at my entrance into the world was saluted and surrounded with innumerable joys; my knowledge was Divine.

I was entertained like an Angel with the works of God in their splendour and glory. Heaven and Earth did sing my Creator's praises, and could not make more melody to Adam than to me. Certainly Adam in Paradise had not more sweet and curious apprehensions of the world than I. All appeared new and strange at first, inexpressibly rare and delightful and beautiful. All things were spotless and pure and glorious.

The corn was orient and immortal wheat, which never should be reaped nor was ever sown. I thought it had stood from everlasting to everlasting. The green trees, when I saw them first, transported and ravished me, their sweetness and unusual beauty made my heart to leap, and almost mad with ecstasy, they were such strange and wonderful things. O what venerable creatures did the agèd seem! Immortal cherubims! And the young men glittering and sparkling angels, and maids, strange seraphic pieces of life and beauty! I knew not that they were born or should die; but all things abided eternally. I knew not that there were sins or complaints or laws. I dreamed not of poverties, contentions or vices. All tears and quarrels were hidden from mine eyes. I saw all in the peace of Eden. Everything was at rest, free and immortal.[13]

As a child, the poet is like an angel, 'sublime and celestial'. There is no sense of time nor therefore of decay. The corn is always growing (orient), never reaped, never sown. Everything 'abided eternal', was timeless and without conflict. Everything was at rest, 'free and immortal'.

This is a highly sophisticated piece of writing despite its apparent innocence. The way Traherne conveys the timelessness of Paradise, the absence of change, of time, of movement and conflict, makes this a quite superb description of what has since become a standard way of talking about the innocence of childhood, echoed in ten thousand bad poems.

Anyone who knows anything about children can attest that it is pure fantasy. Children themselves – except possibly in those early weeks at the breast – are in constant change; certainly by the time they are able to conceptualise about corn and trees and to distinguish between old men and maids, they are well beyond any possible paradisial relationship with the mother or with the apparently topsy-turvy world. It is adults who need children to be occupants of a timeless, sacred space. Children themselves (largely) cannot wait to grow up and to be able to play with adult toys and enjoy adult freedoms. ('The difference between men and boys – is the price of their toys,' as the old adage wisely puts it.)

And yet again, even if pure fantasy in terms of a child's development, this passage clearly rings true on a different level, a particularly sophisticated one. The literature of childhood comprises some of the finest and most deeply religious passages ever written, some writers aspiring, as in the Traherne piece, to a near-mystical state of simplicity and intensity. Because they evoke a quasi-religious experience, they have come to play a particular role in our present secular society, even if they apparently correspond only dimly to the actual experience of childhood.

From our point of view, what is also interesting is that Traherne is still able in the seventeenth century to see the experience of wonder as an explicitly religious experience and to use conventional religious language to express it: 'Certainly Adam in Paradise . . .', 'Heaven and earth did sing my creator's praises', 'I saw all in the peace of Eden.' But by the nineteenth century, the climate has changed – Traherne's artful unselfconsciousness (rare enough in his own time) is gone and lush sentimentality has set in.

This sacred space which religious writers first evoked and which

Romantic poets and Victorian agnostics then projected on to childhood is still a powerful area of human experience. Even today, one can read the yearnings of a poet like the nineteenth-century French dandy Charles Baudelaire, who probably lived as close to hell as anyone, for the innocent land of his childhood and know exactly what he means.

> Mais le vert paradis des amours enfantines,
> Les Courses, les chansons, les baisers, les bouquets,
> Les violons vibrant derrière les collines,
> Avec les brocs de vin, le soir, dans les bosquets,
> – Mais le vert paradis des amours enfantines,
>
> L'innocent paradis, plein de plaisirs furtifs,
> Est-il déjà plus loin que l'Inde et que la Chine?[14]

(But the green paradise of childhood romances, of running races and songs, of kisses and posies, of violins' vibrato behind the hills, and of pitchers of wine in the evenings in the woods, that innocent paradise, full of secret pleasures – is it really now further away than India or China?)

And one can still be powerfully affected by Edwardian literature even if one can no longer share its world or stomach its sentimentality. Let us explore why.

'Wherever they go and whatever happens to them on the way, in that enchanted place on the top of the Forest a little boy and his Bear will always be playing.' So A.A. Milne ends *The House at Pooh Corner* with a picture of Christopher Robin and Winnie the Pooh playing together for all eternity. Few adults can read this passage to a child at bedtime without tears. As an example of the hugely sentimental it takes some beating. And yet, despite its sentimentality, there is something genuine here.

Whether it be called Arcadia, or Paradise, the Secret Garden or a sacred space, the child in the adult guards something precious and perfectly real. Most adults to whom children's stories are important would accept that the Arcadia of which they tell is much more real than any purely imaginary place could be. Is this pursuit of the world of childhood just an attempt to resurrect their own happy or protected childhood, an attempt to escape from the rigours of grown-up life into infantilism? Or is there something more going on? Some psychologists argue that indeed this is the case, and that the world of childhood is being used as a signpost to a very real sacred space inside the reader.

A great deal has been written about this phenomenon of internal sacred space, much of it reductionist or sentimental. However, there is a particularly sympathetic line of analysis which sees adults' reactions to childhood stories not in terms of particularly early and probably repressed memories, as a Freudian might, nor simply as general examples of cultural paradigms (in Jungian terms), but rather identifies them with a particular moment in the life of a very young baby. This moment, it is claimed, is the source not only of later recollections of childhood paradise but also of almost all cultural activity.

The theory goes that certain important memories become built into the structure of a child's being. Naturally, one cannot possibly remember how it felt to be a baby – a baby can have no concepts, no coat hangers on which to peg experiences. But because they are 'inbuilt' these memories can be triggered by a painting or music or a story that leads one back to very early childhood. In particular, they are connected to the first moment of one's self-conscious awareness, that half-dreadful, half-exhilarating moment when, albeit in a very primitive way, a very young baby first becomes aware that he or she may be separate from his or her mother – the moment when the breast becomes a separate object from the child.

Thus the crucial 'memory' is of the *potential* space that may or may not exist between the child and his or her carer. It is remembered ever afterwards as being the space that may or may not furnish the baby with his or her own identity. Reaching back into this space is supportive – it brings back the experience of union with the carer – and also creative – it suggests the possibility of independent and separate existence; but it is also threatening, dangerous even, for it carries with it the threat of the annihilation of the ego, an 'interruption in going on being'. The baby does not necessarily know that it can survive on its own, away from its carer. This potential space is 'the hypothetical area that exists (but cannot exist) between the baby and the object (mother or part of mother) during the phase of the repudiation of the object as not me, that is at the end of being merged in with the object'.[15]

The particular school of psychoanalysis that champions this theory, which goes by the unpromising name of 'object relations' theory, is unlike that of Freud in that it has the advantage of being able to provide a whole theory of culture. It is described, for example, by Peter Fuller in his *Art and Psychoanalysis*, where he argues that many great works of art, whether paintings, music or children's literature, are in a sense representing (making present) that early experience of potential space – the sacred space from the realms of early childhood which to an adult seems almost 'hallowed' (in other words set apart, mythological, not properly remembered but very important). Fuller goes on to argue that this experience of potential space is the basis of religious experience.

(It seems to me that this whole theory is itself a myth; evidence of a month old baby's experience is inevitably almost impossible to interpret, and also increasing importance is now attributed to what are apparently memories of the womb from before birth, which clearly antedate those of breast or bottle. The 'sacred space' is being pushed backwards in time. Nonetheless, the important point ultimately is that the experience of this sacred place exists, regardless of the particular signposts that are used to point to it.)

But the interesting point about Fuller's description of object relations theory is that he claims that until the formulation of this psychological theory, the best available description of this experience was that supplied by *theology*. Fuller states that 'Rycroft [a pioneer in the field] has, for example, drawn attention to the way in which certain theological concepts were prior to developments in object relations theory, the most adequate accounts of certain kinds of experience for which non-theological explanations are now possible.'[16] In other words, this is another example of a secular description of Paradise which also not only links the adult experience of Paradise with the early experiences of children but also admits to the importance of religion and theology (until their decline) in providing access to and understanding of sacred space.

Looking now at the key aspect of Carpenter's book in the light of object relations theory, we observe a hugely interesting phenomenon. Carpenter claims that all his authors were disillusioned with contemporary Christian teaching. Even though Dodgson was ordained deacon, he was never priested; Kingsley ended up a canon of Westminster but had by then put his children's stories behind him; while the later writers – A.A. Milne, Barrie, Kenneth Grahame – were firm agnostics. In trying to create a new secular sacred space – their Arcadia – they were searching for a substitute for the paradise of Eden and the various possibilities contained within Christian teaching which had previously provided the best opportunities for encounter with sacred space. Now those possibilities have been analysed in turn in the various psychological interpretations, such as object relations theory, which have tried to provide a more 'scientific' theology of the 'sacred' place of mystery and magic by analysing it in the secular terms of childhood development.

If this is the case, when today we are caught up in familiar childhood tales we are returning not to humanity's first (mythical) childhood when God created Adam and Eve and the world was young, nor to a Golden Age of childhood, the product of writers escaping the jaded world of late Victoriana, but to that sacred space which contains the reader as he or she was once safely cuddled on a parent's lap to be fed or to hear a story, just as the walls of the rose garden contained the growing Mary Lennox. This sacred space is real and important, and at the origin of many of the most profound human expectations and yearnings.

Sex and spirituality

The other thing we learn about, cuddled in a parent's lap, is sex. Later we shall look briefly at Freud's theories of sexual development, which are now largely disregarded. But one does not have to go all the way with Freud to accept his proposition that the primary sense, as far as sexual development is concerned, is touch. 'We shall therefore not be surprised to find that very definite erotogenic effects are to be ascribed to certain kinds of general stimulation of the skin,' as Freud puts it in his famous essay on infantile sexuality.[17] It is perhaps more amusing than disturbing to note that when he comes to list 'the sources of infantile sexuality' in this section of the essay he mentions a whole list of possibilities – thermal stimulation, the mechanical excitations of railway journeys and swinging, the muscular activity of romping, intense experiences such as fear or stress, intellectual work – but nowhere does being cuddled by parent or nanny appear.

But, *pace* Freud, there can be no doubt but that we learn this basic instinct as children cuddled up to a parent; and the delights of sexual intercourse are, in one sense, merely that primitive joy of physical contact writ large. (Of course, there is a great deal more to be said, but this is surely its origin.) So once again, if the object relations theorists are right about the origins of religious experience being found at the breast, and if Freud is right about the origins of sexuality being found in simple bodily contact, then one may suggest that a child's earliest somatic experiences are the basis both of religion and of sex later in life. Sexuality and spirituality both crystallise out of the same cauldron of possibilities.

There is here an important pattern which will recur in almost every chapter of this book. As the crisis of faith deepened over the last two hundred years, so in every important area of life secular substitutes for religion (sport, art, dance, fashion and so on) emerged based almost always on bodily experiences. And since sex (in our society at least) is the most extreme and mysterious form of bodily experience, almost always we will find that sex steps in where religion leaves off. We will also find that the notion of sacred space recurs frequently in the context of sex and the religious aspirations that people have of it.

Children themselves are acutely aware of sacred space, not because, as for adults, it is a particular space marked off from normal life, but because their whole life is spent in desacralising their world. In their book on childhood games, *Children's Games in Street and Playground*, Iona and Peter Opie spend several hundred pages describing in great detail the whole variety of games that children play, which they believe they have invented but which actually are probably as old and universal as the hills. At the end of the book the Opies have to admit that 'the peaks of a child's experience are not visits to a cinema, or even family outings to the sea, but occasions when he escapes into places that are disused and overgrown and silent. To a child there is more joy in a rubbish tip than in a flowering rockery.'[18]

This has the ring of truth. To learn what is real, children need constantly to test the limits, to enter fringe areas where the boundaries between reality and fantasy are blurred, where danger may lurk, where hyenas may jump out of elephant skulls at them. In this sense, children are not yet sure enough of the parameters of this world to know what is magic and what is not – and for them, it is a matter of huge importance. Adults know the sun will inevitably rise tomorrow; children aren't so sure, and worry about it as a consequence of their behaviour. Children desperately need to be able to test whether the world is under control, especially at those times in their life which just precede dramatic physical or emotional development; hence, for example, the dramatic rise in interest in Christianity of twelve- and thirteen-year-old boys, who very often go through a 'starry-eyed' religious phase.

But for adults, for whom the world is if anything both disenchanted and too secure, sacred space is a luxury, albeit a precious one, whose allure is perhaps best represented by Milne's 'Vespers'. Although on the surface an irreverent and sentimental poem, and despite the ironic threat 'whisper who dares' and the lack of attention by the child himself ('what was the other I meant to say?'), it still takes the adult reader back to the exposed and yet cosseted world of childhood; to the child who, despite the fears and terrors of his world is still confident enough of the ultimate security of the world, symbolised in the care and attention of his nanny, to be able to mess around during prayer time. (An insecure child, genuinely anxious about the sun's rising, would say prayers with eyes firmly closed and without deviation.) For adults, buffeted by the storms of life, and for whom such confidence in a sacred space of divinely provided security is at best doubtful and at worst impossible, 'droops on the little blond head' can often lead to tears. It is sentimental, certainly, but it is also a brief glimpse of the world of *The Secret Garden*, a barely decipherable pointer to the sacred space guarded by the internal child.

Conclusion: the end of Eden

We have examined the extraordinary childhood Arcadia created by the Victorians and Edwardians, an alternative world inhabited by curiously innocent, idealised creatures shielded from the adults' world of sex, money and politics. Adults used this very upper-middle-class paradise to express their own need for a sacred space, a need that grew more insistent as their faith in conventional religious teaching diminished, and as their own middle-class world began to be eroded by the side-effects of the industrial revolution and the first attempts by workers and employees to accrue the fruits of their labours for themselves. We have examined the demise of the paradise garden as a religious symbol as conventional Christianity decreased in influence, and found support for the view that it was diverted into a more general 'spirituality' – the sacred space of childhood – not only in Carpenter's work on children's novels but also in contemporary psychoanalytic literature. The sense of Paradise, of sacred space, is identified by Peter Fuller, for example, with the 'potential space' that occurs between a child and its carer in the early months of life. And it is the same sacred space that is engendered by contemplating great works of art.

We have shown too how the twentieth century has recovered a more realistic notion of the development of children, and especially their sexual development, thanks partly to a completely different ethos in children's entertainment which is much less protective. The world of childhood can only with difficulty now be used as a protected space, and is therefore unsuitable as a screen on which to project religious fantasies. Today, as children enter the garden of sex, they are not closeted behind walls but following a well-trodden path. The rediscovery of children's sexuality has certainly supplanted any religious interpretation of childhood. The myth of the child, however, is being replaced by an even more dangerous myth, that of the happy nuclear family that achieves happiness not in the sacred space of cathedrals, nor in childhood Arcadia, but only in the great space of large shopping malls. To this we shall return in Chapter 3.

2

Poaching the Gamekeeper
Sex and Nature

In this chapter, we turn from the sacred groves of childhood to another arena into which the religious imagination has projected divine power: that of nature in the raw.

At the very beginning of the nineteenth century, when established religion was beginning to lose its hold, the Romantic poets found in the sublimity of raw nature a substitute for the religious experience they were largely unable to find in church.[1]

The classic example is Wordsworth's 'Lines Composed a Few Miles above Tintern Abbey', which have become the Apostles' Creed of the whole Romantic school, and which, despite their being so hackneyed, I cannot bear not to quote:

> *. . . And I have felt*
> *A presence that disturbs me with the joy*
> *Of elevated thoughts; a sense sublime*
> *Of something far more deeply interfused,*
> *Whose dwelling is the light of setting suns,*
> *And the round ocean and the living air,*
> *And the blue sky, and in the mind of man.*

Wordsworth finds this mysterious presence in nature and in the *mind* of man. A hundred and twenty years later, Freud would show that the romantic yearnings of poets chasing the sublime are generally so closely linked to displaced sexuality that it is often difficult to tell them apart. Whether or not Freud is right, his analysis has certainly caught on, and so today the natural completion of the spirituality that had Wordsworth for its prophet lies in finding religious experience not so much in craggy hills or in the mind of man as in the human *body* – and especially in sex.

Those outdoor elements that took the Romantic poets to the thresholds of human experience – to Swiss glaciers, clouds of remote lakeside daffodils – are now available indoors to all and sundry. Today, rather than sit in bank holiday traffic queues for hours to visit Wordsworth's cottage, we seek the sublime at home. We make our pilgrimage to the shrine of the human body with Alex Comfort as our Baedeker, and a Tibetan Buddhist teacher of sexual healing as our mountain guide.

However, a new generation of pioneers emerged after those Romantic poets who 'discovered' nature as a religious force; they have developed the Romantic vision of nature a stage further. As we shall see, it seems that the very technology which made God redundant has now estranged us from nature as well.

But help is at hand. If we are to believe pioneers of the spirituality of sex such as D.H. Lawrence, sex offers us not only religious experience, but also redemption and healing. Through this religion of sex, our alienation from the earth can be overcome, and we can be reunited with Mother Nature. The body has now changed roles: from being, as it was for hundreds of years, the agent of sin, the corruptible flesh that brings about our temptation and downfall, it is now the means of our redemption – as befits an affluent society. Thus whereas the Victorians and Edwardians considered that it was sex which excluded us from the paradise of childhood, when it comes to nature sex provides the means of our return. In this chapter, we examine what has, I will argue, become the sexual orthodoxy of the twentieth century.

Naturally, this mythology of sex is, as we shall see, quite bogus, but it is nonetheless a fascinating example of our need to create another world (this time, the world of nature from which we are alienated).

Ours is not the first age to be concerned about the relationship between sex, the body and religious experience. To some extent, it has always been a problem for really affluent societies. Before we approach the situation today, and consider the seminal role of D.H. Lawrence's novels in capturing (or perhaps creating) the mythology of our age, I want first to look at another civilisation, quite different from our own, which had similar concerns: that of ancient Athens, where we find curious antecedents to our twentieth-century situation.

After that, and in order to understand the sexual repression that has dominated thinking in the West for 1500 years, we turn to that crucial moment in history when the mediaeval world view began to give ground before the Enlightenment view of the world which has today swept the board. This turning point yields useful information about the relationship between nature and sex and secularisation. We shall look particularly at the treatment of witches in the seventeenth century, and how the figure of the Devil has, in the West, combined at different times the images of raw nature and raw sex. We end the chapter with some contemporary evidence of how deeply rooted the connection between nature, redemption and sex is in our own very secular age.

Greek antecedents

Euripides, one of the three great writers of ancient Greek tragedy, wrote *The Bacchae* at the end of his life in approximately 408 BC, just as the Golden Age of classical Greece was drawing to a close. Despite its being nearly two and a half thousand years old, it has an extraordinarily modern feel; it could almost be the script of a contemporary horror film.

The play is set in the mythological past. At the start of the

47

play, Dionysus, the god of wine and nature, appears disguised as a man. He is furious. His mother, Semele, a human being, had been seduced by Zeus, the chief god, and he had been conceived as a result. However, Zeus's wife (and the goddess of marriage), Hera, had jealously killed Semele with a thunderbolt and as an infant he had had to be incubated sewn up in his father's thigh. But, he tells the audience, people no longer believe this. Semele's sisters are saying that this was a story invented by their father Cadmus, the founder of Thebes (the town where the play is set), as a convenient excuse to protect his daughter and explain away an unwanted pregnancy – the old story: a virgin birth invented to see a girl out of trouble.

Dionysus explains to the audience that he is bent on revenge for this lack of faith, and has now driven all his mother's sisters out of Thebes and up into the mountains, where they are now celebrating Bacchic orgies (Bacchus is another name for Dionysus), wearing the dress of Maenads (literally, ravers), namely fawn skin and thyrsus (a pole wreathed in ivy and vine leaves with a pine cone on top).

A messenger describes their lifestyle. On the one hand, they are living close to nature; even milk and wine bubble from the ground. But there is a wild side to their behaviour: when in a frenzy, they are capable of tearing cattle apart with their bare hands and kidnapping children from the surrounding villages.

The intolerant King of Thebes (and nephew of Semele) is Pentheus, a no-nonsense character who has only contempt for the women who are making Thebes the laughing-stock of Greece. He meets Dionysus, who is disguised as an effeminate Dionysian worshipper, and will have no truck with him; he has this *'thelumorphon xenon'*, this 'effeminate stranger', thrown into jail.

None deterred, Dionysus easily breaks out of prison. ('Our Lord hath risen/To shatter the massive walls of his prison,' as James Morgan Pryse puts it in his 1925 translation – one of a long line of interpreters to try to find Christian overtones in this most heathen of Greek tragedies.)[2] Dionysus finds Pentheus again and, in the course of a long conversation, whips him into a seething rage. Slowly and fiendishly he tempts Pentheus to follow the promptings of his repressed prurient desires, and to act out his sexual hang-ups and latent infantilism which, to a contemporary audience, have clearly been evident in Pentheus's character since the beginning of the play.

Dionysus cleverly gets Pentheus to admit that he would actually rather like to spy on the women, on what he is sure are their sexual activities. 'Pentheus is the dark puritan,' says C.H. Dodds in his commentary on the play, 'whose passion is compounded of horror and unconscious desire and it is this which leads to his ruin.'[3]

And so Pentheus allows himself to be disguised as a Bacchic reveller, and is led through the streets of Thebes 'torn between dignity and lust' (Dodds). The great tyrant and man of iron, ostensibly disguised as a woman in order to spy undiscovered upon the Bacchae, is exposed as a Peeping Tom who is immensely enjoying his new transvestite self, mad with ecstasy as the parts of himself he has been keeping repressed for so long come out.

And come out they do. Pentheus threatens to lift up the whole of Mount Cithaeron single-handed, and Dionysus mockingly dissuades him: 'No, or you'll destroy the grottoes of the nymphs.'

The stage goes quiet. The chorus sing and dance in honour of Dionysus. Then a messenger arrives to describe the bloody dénouement. Pentheus arrived on the scene and Dionysus lifted him to the top of a pine tree the better to spy upon his prey. But he is spotted by the women, who go into a frenzy and, thinking he is some sacrificial animal (like the cattle they have recently despatched) go after him. First they must get him down from the tree where he is perched, and so in a terrifying gesture of emasculation they rip the tree from the ground; then Pentheus is torn to pieces by his own mother, who fails to recognise him despite his screams for mercy, while the other Maenads play ball with his limbs.

The penultimate scene of the play is a grandiose *coup de théâtre* in which Agave, Pentheus's mother, still under the influence of Dionysiac ecstasy, comes on stage, cradling in her arms what she thinks is the head of the sacrificial beast she and her sisters have just dismembered in honour of Dionysus. Slowly, as the madness subsides, she begins, to her horror, to identify the trophy that she is proudly showing off. It is the head of her son whom she has just murdered.

The Bacchae explored, two and a half thousand years ago, what is now, I maintain, the dominant model of sexuality and sexual repression in the West. Sex – libido – is humanity's most direct link with nature. It is pagan, uncontrollable, amoral, an arational, animal energy constantly at war with the 'civilising' forces of order and society which try constantly to build barriers against it but never succeed.[4] We will examine these presuppositions critically later, but there is another point of interest here in the link between sex and religion. Through the gods and goddesses, through, for example, Dionysus and Aphrodite, Greek religion was able to find a positive place for sex, nature and the body, a link Euripides cleverly exploits. Pentheus, in order to keep Dionysus at bay, has to repress his religious instincts by denying that he is a god – a standard way of dealing with that which is threatening, by rationalising it away. In the play, however, Euripides demonstrates that sex is a god and those who deny his divinity are destroyed.

Christianity, by contrast, adopts the opposite approach. It has never, until recently, been able to incorporate sex, nature and the body into its general way of seeing things. Of course, there are some remarkable exceptions to this, which will crop up in succeeding chapters. But for traditional Christianity, the body is likely to be sinful and sex to be diabolical, and better avoided for the sake of heavenly rewards.

From Dionysus to the Devil

The final scene of The Bacchae is a mess. A vital chunk of text is missing, and we are left only with later summaries and a few lines that give complicated mythological details of the banishment of the surviving protagonists by Dionysus, revealed in his true colours as a god. One detail is of interest. Cadmus, Agave and Semele's father, is to be punished by being turned into a dragon and, with his wife Harmonia (turned into a snake), is to drive an ox-cart at the head of barbarian hordes and sack many cities, until finally he is translated alive to the land of the blessed. It looks as if Euripides is in some sense predicting the end of the road for civilisation.

Perhaps, like Freud in *Civilisation and its Discontents*, Euripides believed that civilised society, of necessity forced into repression, carried within itself the seeds of its own destruction. Certainly, his pessimism accords with the contemporary state of Athens, which lay prostrate and humiliated at the end of a disastrous war with its chief rival Sparta and, ravaged by plague, was never again to recover its former glory.

However, his gloom was ill-founded. The Golden Age of Athens, certainly, was past, but even at this point there was a small warrior state near the west coast of mainland Italy which was just beginning to flex its muscles – and the Roman Empire was about to begin where the Greeks had left off.

It was only with the demise of the Roman Empire, just under a thousand years after *The Bacchae* was written, that Euripides' prophecy of barbarian hordes invading the civilised world would begin to be fulfilled. By this time, however, there was another institution in place ready to carry the torch of 'civilisation' through the dark ages that were to ensue: one that combined the practical, administrative apparatus of Rome with an other-worldly spiritual-ity which enabled the darkness of the present historical world to be safely eclipsed by the bright beams of a world beyond, and which also (along with the more civilised Muslim world) preserved the legacy of Greece and Rome in cold storage.

During what was to be a four- or five-hundred-year process of mourning for the vanished classical civilisation, it was this 'other' world beyond the present world which became all that the manifestly unsatisfactory present world (where life was short, nasty and brutish) was not. The Christian Church (for such it was) took care to devalue the things that might attract people to invest too heavily in the earthly world – and particularly sex. In a broken society concerned above all with survival, attention to sex in all except its most basic reproductive aspect was probably too great a luxury anyway. It was perhaps inevitable that the deprivations of the present world should be balanced by the satisfactions of an afterlife beyond. And by a further inevitable logic of compensation, it was also assumed that the more one suffered in this life, the more glorious would be one's state in the next.

This repression of natural instincts and drives over such a long period is probably best understood as a sort of corporate psychic depression, the blocking-off of vitality that follows trauma. Inevitably, it threw up various strange side-effects; for example, a pathological fear of death and judgment, as well as the luxuriant growth of rank superstition and the creation of a supernatural realm, an invisible world that was highly potent and immensely sinister, invested with all the powers which enforced ignorance, passivity and poverty can stimulate the imagination into predicating upon natural phenomena.

The Church found many countervailing remedies against this invisible world, some at the level of superstition, others of high theology; from indulgences that guaranteed one an easier judgment after death to the rituals connected with holy water, genuflecting and making the sign of the cross, devotion to the Blessed Sacrament, special prayers, penances and pilgrimages, and chantry priests who could be endowed by those who could afford them to pray for one's soul after death. Even going on crusade could be a form of penance. Meanwhile the present world was in the grip of the Devil, and so was the body. The only unclothed bodies on general display were those of Adam and Eve in Church art: 'and look what happened to them,' the unwritten caption always concluded.

In its quest for the hearts and minds of ordinary people, the Church adopted a particularly effective strategy. In the ancient world, the old pagan deities such as Dionysus had been morally ambivalent. When, at the end of *The Bacchae*, Dionysus metes out cruel and partly undeserved punishment upon the various characters, none of them complain of unfairness. Even at this late date, the gods were not seen as fair or unfair, just or unjust in a Christian sense, but rather as the symbols of fate. Life was like that. They represented the amoral forces and coincidences to which human beings are subject. (Thus, because they had moral sense, human beings were superior to the gods.)

The Christian faith, however, threw a moral perspective over the amoral universe – and the old amoral pagan divinities were hijacked in its cause. God, the creator, was fundamentally just and in control; and so Dionysus was given horns and hooves and turned into the Devil, the very personification of all malice and wickedness. Thus what had been a complex, ambivalent figure was transformed into a much simpler, evil one who could then be both acknowledged and repressed. Inevitably, this had repercussions, particularly on women.

Once Dionysus – the earth god, god of wine and of nature – found himself a metaphysically evil figure, the object of utter and unqualified hatred and blame for the world's ills, it was only natural that the fear of him should extend to encompass other more vulnerable members of society, especially those who might be considered less rational or closer to the raw forces of nature he represented – notably women. Yet thanks to the perverse laws that operate on human affections, there is nothing more attractive than that which is universally feared and hated. The more the Devil was repressed, the stronger his powers became; the more repressive the Church grew about sexuality, the more the Devil began to be identified with forbidden, secret yet alluring sexual powers, with women his accomplices. And so the story of Pentheus was to be many times re-enacted, but now instead of women disappearing up hills as Bacchic revellers, they were to be accused of attending witches' Sabbaths and to be burnt as heretics.

In the early centuries of the Middle Ages this strategy of repression may have been a necessity for survival – the other, heavenly world had to be the real one, as the present world was simply too awful. However, when the moral and economic situation improved, the Church failed to moderate its repressive stance. By the sixteenth century, for example, the feudal ages were well and truly over. The Protestant Reformation in northern Europe saw the final break-up of the monolithic ecclesiastical empire which the Christian Church had underpinned, and the formation of nation-states across Europe as the life blood of money and ideas began to flow back through the cramped limbs of Europe. Yet even after the Reformation, attitudes to women, nature and sex did not change correspondingly. If anything, the position of women became worse, for two reasons.

Firstly, although traditional Catholic practice had emphasised the importance of worship in church, the home, too, was important, and there were domestic religious rituals associated with it. These lay largely in the charge of women, and gave them a certain status. After the Reformation, almost all religious practices had to take place in the (male-dominated) church, with the female member of the holy family, the Blessed Virgin Mary, demoted from Queen of Heaven to Jesus's earthly mother. (As Mary Daly amusingly and tendentiously puts it, 'The real direction of religious rapism is towards absolute elimination of all vestiges of real female presence. Just as catholicism was an important stage in the refinement of phallocentric myth, protestantism represents a more advanced stage of "purification". Having eliminated Mary, the ghost of the Goddess, it sets up a unisex model, whose sex is male.')[5]

Secondly, the new Reformation churches of North Europe were able to banish such 'superstitious' mediaeval practices as obtaining indulgences (to calm the fear of death and judgment) or making the sign of the cross (to ward off spells), which were deeply offensive to the emerging middle classes. But it was just these popular remedies which had previously made the Church attractive to ordinary people. Now, they had no effective antidote to spells, nor any way to placate unknown powers. Yet neither, and this is crucial, was the Church able or willing to write off the invisible world of magic and powers which gave these 'superstitious' practices their *raison d'être*. After all, a Church's very credibility lies in access to an invisible world. The only difference now, after the Reformation, was that the stranglehold upon this invisible world by the apparatus of the Catholic Church was broken; it was open to anyone who could read the Bible.

Naturally, this excluded most of the population, and indeed, despite (or perhaps because of) the hierarchical and authoritarian nature of the Roman Church, it has always been more accessible to ordinary people than the Protestant Churches – which have often remained bourgeois enclaves for the educated – thanks to its unofficial willingness to countenance those popular aspects of piety which to educated people have always been the height of irrational distaste!

If women had been vulnerable in the Middle Ages, worse was to come. By stripping away the protective veil of ritual and magical practice which had protected the mediaeval lay person from evil and witchcraft, 'the Protestant Reformation had the unintended consequence of exposing women more profoundly to witchcraft accusations', as Bryan Turner explains in his book *The Body and Society*.[6] By banning the apotropaic devices that kept at bay the assaults of the Devil, 'the paradoxical result was that from the middle of the sixteenth century evil in the shape of witches appeared to be everywhere' – and women especially were held to be the Devil's principal accomplices. The Puritans were even more repressive than the mediaeval Church. Their high moralism, energy and discipline, their encouragement of industrious hard work and dislike of extravagance, their repressive attitude to the softer side of life, inevitably engendered a shadow side which surfaced in hellfire sermons and the hanging of witches.

Between 1563 and 1727, according to Turner, about 80 per cent of witchcraft suspects in North Europe were women. The ultimate accusation against the witches, which underlay all the others, was that of sexual intercourse with the Devil. Perhaps to some small extent this is understandable (even if not forgivable). The power of the naked female body over the body of the male, both in the imagination and in reality, must have seemed, in an age when anything over which a man had no control was ascribed to the effects of external influences, the work of the very Devil!

The invisible world at vanishing point

'Our opposites are always robed in sexual sin,' claims the American playwright Arthur Miller in an excursus to his play about witchcraft in seventeenth-century New England, *The Crucible*.[7] He was actually referring to the communists who (despite all the evidence to the contrary) were assumed at the height of the Cold War when he was writing the play (1952) to be highly lascivious. 'At the time of writing,' he continued, 'only England has held back before the temptations of contemporary Diabolism.' Although his play is on one level a morality play about the McCarthyite witch-hunts for communists which plagued America in the 1950s, like all great literature it has much deeper ramifications.

The play is set in the highly repressed and repressive 'dark Puritan' society of a New England that could still remember the first religious pioneers who came over from Europe. A group of girls is alleged to have been spotted dancing naked in the forest and they are accused of witchcraft. The girls' only escape lies in accepting the accusations, and then, as proof of their repentance, implicating several other members of the village in witchcraft. (They were selected, Miller implies, on the basis of independent historical evidence, for belonging to one or other faction within the village or for other ulterior motives.) 'Sex, sin and the Devil were early linked, and so they continued to be in Salem, and are today,' Miller adds. 'It is from this unconscious conviction that demonology gains its attractive sensuality.'[8]

The play is based on fact – the girls' trials took place in 1692 and there is a great deal of extant documentation. Studies of the evidence presented at these and other trials reveals a consistent picture of suspected witchcraft which has little to do with black magic and a great deal to do with entirely natural human jealousies and motivations. In his book *Witchcraft, Magic and Religion in Seventeenth-Century Massachusetts*, Richard Weismann concludes that the majority of witchcraft suspects were very similar to those who accused them: 'To describe collectively the accused witches of pre-Salem Massachusetts is to catalogue the dimensions of social and political disaffiliation in the New England town.'[9] Many were women in dire poverty dependent upon charity who almost certainly peddled homoeopathic drugs and spells to eke out their pittance; the men tended to be labourers or those on the fringes of society. But above all, the underlying precondition of an accusation of witchcraft would probably be 'not a disagreement over the disposition of land or property but rather with a relationship that had deteriorated to a point beyond reconciliation'.[10] 'The formal accusation constituted merely the final dissolution of an already untenable relationship.'[11]

Added to which, often it was the person accused of being a witch who was the injured party rather than the accuser. 'The bulk of the accusations had their common point of reference in the misconduct of the *accuser* and the anticipation of justifiable anger from the witch. The accuser operated not only in defiance of the supposed retaliatory power of witchcraft but in clear violation of traditional village morality. That the accuser-victim was aware of his misconduct is highly probable since it is on this basis that he established the link between his misfortune and the witch.'[12]

Having someone to blame when things go wrong is a natural if sinister necessity for those for whom life is a constant battle to scrape a living, and psychological sophistication a luxury for the leisured. In this case, the unfortunate victims were those already vulnerable, upon whose heads a whole series of accusations approved by both Church and state could be thrown. It was much easier to transfer one's own sense of guilt on to another person, positing a secret and irrational link between one's feelings of guilt and the person one blames for them, than to deal with them oneself. (But then so much of life, among those powerless over their own destiny, generally seems to be the result of secret and irrational links.)

Even at the time, the better-off, and those not forced to share in the living conditions of the poor, even when they lived in the country, might be sniffy about witches. Weismann quotes an English clergyman of the time, John Gaule:

Every poore and peevish olde Creature (such is their ignorance and uncharitableness) cannot but fall under their [the villagers'] suspicion, nay their infamous exprobations; every Accident (more than ordinary) every disease whereof they neither understand the Cause, nor are acquainted with the Symptoms must be suspected for witchcraft. His Cow or his Hog, cannot be strangely taken, but straight it must bee reckoned and rumored for bewitcht.[13]

However, the Salem witch trials were actually the last gasp of the official countenance of witchcraft by the state. From now on, the rational views of a John Gaule were to win the day, although popular belief in witchcraft was to continue well into the eighteenth century. Arthur Miller comments in his postlude to *The Crucible* that twenty years after the last execution, the government awarded compensation to the victims' families, but even so, 'certain farms which had belonged to the victims were left to ruin, and for more than a century no-one would buy them or live on them'. Nonetheless, the world of witches had effectively died. 'To all intents and purposes, the power of theocracy in Massachusetts was broken,' Miller ends.[14] Weismann puts it more wittily: 'The invisible world [was] at the vanishing point.'[15] 'The loss of witchcraft as an actionable offence divested contemporary theories of supernatural causation of their last remaining claim to legal authority. With the decline of witchcraft prosecutions, questions about the availability of the invisible world ceased to be a matter of practical concern for the state.'[16]

The reason is clear. We are observing one of those privileged moments in history, the moment when one world view is yielding to another. It was indeed an extraordinary stage in the history of humanity when the existence of an invisible world of supernatural agents and beings was being generally doubted for the first time since ancient Rome. Like the adult who switches on the light in a frightened child's bedroom to show that there is nothing there, the civilised world suddenly said farewell to the other world of ghoulies and ghosties and long-leggety beasties and things that go bump in the night, the other world that had so often been used as compensation for having no power over one's own life or destiny.

Miller cleverly identifies this by turning his play into a secular tragedy. His hero, Proctor, is an agnostic falsely accused of witchcraft by a girl with whom he had once, in a moment of weakness, made love. Proctor steadfastly refuses to confess to being a witch by implicating others in token of his 'repentance', despite being given every opportunity to do so, and he dies a martyr's death. But he is a martyr not for the Christian faith but for its opposite: for truth and integrity in the face of unenlightened persecution by ostensibly Christian clergy. In this he is the opposite of Pentheus, someone else who dies for denying the power of religion. Proctor is the 'enlightenment martyr'[17] that Pentheus is not; he increasingly draws the audience's sympathy as the integrity of his character emerges, despite all the scheming and contrivance of his outwardly Christian neighbours, intent on breaking him. In *The Crucible* it is religion which is shown to be repressive and a sham, and which is exposed and humiliated so that its power is broken. In *The Bacchae*, by contrast, it is Pentheus who is exposed, a martyr to his own weakness, and who however much we admire him at first, is finally humiliated. (In passing, it is interesting to note that the despairing and cynical *Bacchae* was probably Euripides' last play; *The Crucible*, with its glorifying of human integrity, is a young man's play, one of Miller's first.)

In his book, Weismann clearly demonstrates that the Church, even though it distinguished between magic and religion, could not afford to regard witchcraft as of no account, since witchcraft was based on the same premise of an invisible world as the Christianity of the time. 'The category of witchcraft entered the public domain in seventeenth-century New England through two clearly separable channels. On the one hand, *a popular belief in folk magic* made the malefic power of witchcraft a practical and immediate concern of the colonial villager. On the other hand, the profound theological investment in the existence of a *superordinate invisible world* provided witchcraft with its epistemological foundations.'[18]

And so, inevitably, as belief in this 'superordinate invisible world' declined, witchcraft would inevitably drag down established 'other-worldly' religions such as Christianity with it. The process of secularisation will from this moment proceed apace. From now on, the martyr to human rights will replace the Christian martyr – suffering for one's fellow human beings without hope of reward in heaven is clearly the higher virtue – and when society is ready, the martyr for freedom of sexual expression will claim his or her place among these secular martyrs. The Church was too heavily invested in the 'two worlds' view of life to be able to satisfy the religious needs of the people. The Devil, too, loses his forbidden attractiveness as sexual repression disappears and the present world no longer needs to be devalued for the sake of a higher world beyond. So where will people turn for religious experience? As I suggested at the beginning of this chapter – back to nature. The Devil, in a splendid historical reversal, yields his place back to Dionysus.

Repression springs eternal

Weismann concludes, 'That the Puritan should take magic and not science as the more serious challenge may strike the reader as a colossal historical miscalculation.'[19] Seventeenth-century Puritan ministers, clergy and theologians were quick to act on accusations of witchcraft. And yet they were unable to perceive that, at this very time, the foundations were being laid of a discipline that would attack the roots of the Church much more effectively than ever the Devil and his disciples did.

Ironically, it is possibly thanks to the Puritans that science in its modern sense became possible. Only once there was a clear demarcation between matter and spirit, between the realm of God and the realm of human beings, with no 'superstitious nonsense' to contaminate the one with the other, could proper scientific experimentation take place.

It is debatable which of the two developments came first and is more important, the rise in living standards thanks to the development of technology, or the plugging of gaps in knowledge thanks to scientific research. But the result of both of these is that humanity rapidly became far less prone to the powers of the unknown. Raised living standards and technological developments have given people access to freedom and power previously unimaginable.

But these have had a price – namely what appears to be an

ever-increasing alienation from nature. The Romantic poets were at the forefront of the process of putting this sense of loss into words. At first nature was wild and exciting – Wordsworth rediscovered the powers of Dionysus above the abbey ruins. But the next generation was not so sure. Nature was rapidly disappearing before the encroaching industrial revolution. For example, the remarkable Ebenezer Elliott (1781–1849), an early Victorian industrialist who ran one of the largest copper smelting factories in Sheffield and was also consumed with guilt for what the industrial revolution was doing to ordinary people, wrote this extraordinary and little-known hymn, its first verse memorable for its use in the musical *Godspell*.

> *When wilt thou save the people*
> *O God of mercy when?*
> *The people, Lord, the people,*
> *Not thrones and crowns but men!*
> *Flowers of thy heart, O God are they;*
> *Let them not pass, like weeds, away –*
> *Their heritage a sunless day.*
> *God save the people.*
>
> *Shall crime bring crime for ever,*
> *Strength aiding still the strong?*
> *Is it thy will, O Father,*
> *That man shall toil for wrong?*
> *'No,' say thy mountains; 'No,' thy skies,*
> *Man's clouded sun shall brightly rise,*
> *And songs be heard instead of sighs.*
> *God save the people.*

For Elliott, unpolluted nature and democracy go together, a combination that has given rise today to the environmental movement, that great secular religion of human redemption which seeks to overcome humanity's alienation from nature, whose fuel is provided by this very sense of guilt, the sense that we ourselves are responsible for our estrangement from nature.

The idea is expressed with particular pathos at the end of the last century and in the early years of this one by poets such as Hopkins:

> *Generations have trod, have trod, have trod;*
> *And all is seared with trade; bleared, smeared with toil;*
> *And wears man's smudge and shares man's smell: the soil*
> *Is bare now, nor can foot feel, being shod.*[20]

However, important as ecological concerns may be to the community, it was the individual's alienation from nature which became particularly significant. The great high priest of individual alienation from nature has to be D.H. Lawrence.

Lawrence's *Women in Love*, for example, regarded by some as his finest novel (though derided by others), is a caustic indictment of technological development. His hero, Gerald Crich, another Pentheus figure, is a successful mine-owner, a man of steel, a pioneer industrialist who has streamlined the management of his mine so that it runs like 'the perfect, inhuman machine'. 'It was this inhuman principle in the mechanism he wanted to construct that inspired Gerald with an almost religious exaltation. There were two opposites, his will and the resistant Matter of the earth. And between these he could establish the very expression of his will, a great and perfect machine.'[21] Gerald is the company's 'high priest'[22] whom his men come to admire even though 'the joy went out of their lives'. Lawrence gives us a dreadful description of Gerald riding a horse as it shies away from a colliery steam train on its way to the mine; he will not let the horse run away despite its terror, and man and horse are locked in combat, the latter with blood streaming from its flanks where Gerald has dug in his spurs.

> A sharpened look came on Gerald's face. He bit himself down on the mare like a keen edge biting home, and *forced* her round [to face the train]. She roared as she breathed, her nostrils were two wide, hot holes, her mouth was apart, her eyes frenzied. It was a repulsive sight.[23]

Edwardian man has nature at his mercy.[24]

Gerald, however, falls in love with Gudrun, a *femme fatale*, and the two battle for dominance through the second half of the novel. Gudrun proves far stronger than Gerald's red Arab mare, and at the end it is Gerald who is defeated. Gudrun sets up a situation in which Gerald becomes desperately jealous of another man whom she lets him imagine she favours; at the climax of the book, in winter up in the Swiss mountains, Gerald attacks Loerke, the man Gudrun is using to provoke him, half throttles Gudrun and then goes off into the barren snow to commit suicide by exposure.

Lawrence spends a great deal of time attacking the effects of materialism and industrialisation. For him, Gerald is typical of the hollow man of industry whom he despised, will-bound and alienated from his roots and from his psyche, from nature and from women.

On the other hand Lawrence portrays approvingly the environment from which human beings are now alienated. He sets up the world of nature with its rhythms and seasons as a sort of paradise from which industrialised England is alienated. He can then posit the manner of our redemption: sexual intercourse. Industrial man is alienated from nature ('nor can foot feel, being shod'), but, since sex and nature have, as we have seen, always been so closely linked for three thousand years, it is through sex that we regain access to the natural world from which we are estranged. Sex brings dark, natural yet mystical forces into play.

Of course, Lawrence's view of sex is a great deal more complicated and variegated than is generally believed. But it cannot be a coincidence that *Lady Chatterley's Lover* is Lawrence's best-known (though arguably worst) novel, and the very novel in which Lawrence states his view of redemption through sex most succinctly. For this reason it was banned until the 1960s, when its publishers risked prosecution under the Obscene Publications Act to put it on sale. The ensuing court case gained the book wide publicity and enshrined its message as the dominant myth of the century. Even churchmen subscribed to it. John Robinson, Bishop of Woolwich, later to be famous for his book *Honest to God*, spoke for the defence and scandalised the trial by saying that, for

Lawrence, sex was an act of holy communion – that Lawrence was trying 'to portray the sex relationship as something essentially sacred'.[25]

Sexual intercourse in the cramped conditions of a gamekeeper's cottage may not be in practice ideal (unless there are Laura Ashley sheets and Badedas for afterwards, as in the adverts), but it has become for many the archetypal expression of the ideal of sex: sex as pagan enjoyment. More than that: sex as entry to the earthy world of nature from which we are banished by technological exploitation. The gamekeeper in *Lady Chatterley's Lover* is a sort of high priest, not a high priest of the machine, like Gerald in *Women in Love*, but a Dionysian figure who initiates Lady Chatterley into the primitive rites of sex and brings about her restitution into nature and her maturity as a woman. Lawrence describes them making love (from the woman's perspective):

It came with a strange slow thrust of peace, the dark thrust of peace and a ponderous, primordial tenderness such as made the world in the beginning ... she dared to let go everything, all herself, and be gone in the flood. And it seemed she was like the sea, nothing but dark waves rising and heaving, heaving with a great swell, so that slowly her whole darkness was in motion, and she was ocean rolling its dark, dumb mass ... She was gone, she was not, and she was born: a woman. And now she touched him, and it was the sons of god with the daughters of men. How was it possible, this beauty here where she had previously only been repelled? She crept nearer to him ... And out of his utter, incomprehensible stillness, she felt again the slow, momentous, surging rise of the phallus again, the other power. And her heart melted out with a kind of awe.[26]

Note the religious language Lawrence uses to describe the woman's experience: 'primordial tenderness', her merging with nature expressed in a mystical, 'oceanic' feeling, 'the sons of god with the daughters of men'; above all, the man's erect penis is 'the *other* power' which creates 'a kind of awe.' Mellors, the gamekeeper, is described in demonic language.

Lawrence has surely given expression here to the dominant myth of our time: restoration with nature via sex. Oversimplifying the argument somewhat, one might suggest that while once one might have gone to the confessional to find assurance of forgiveness from God, contemporary preachers, the journalists and advertisers, tell us that good sex is required to overcome one's alienation from nature and each other. Sexual repression is the great enemy. This is the perfect illustration of the general thesis of this book: that with the rise of secularisation in the nineteenth century, people diverted their religious energies from the now barely credible ecclesiastical religions such as Christianity to the new, privatised and diversified spirituality of sex.

For example, let us take a random selection of four consecutive advertisements from a randomly chosen newspaper colour supplement[27] to illustrate the point. Advertisements generally work by depicting a 'fallen' state and then offering 'redemption' from it through the purchase of their product. The more universal or profound the fallen state, the better the advertisement succeeds. Thus advertisements, by definition almost, have to capture the prevailing *mythology* of the people to whom they hope to speak; their way of seeing things, their hopes and aspirations for themselves. The more subliminal and general the adverts' associations, the better. Thus they are extremely useful in charting the dominant mythology of their readers.

The first advertisement shows a naked man supporting on his shoulders a vast bowl of water. The caption reads: 'Treat your body like a temple: use our water filters.' The symptoms suggested by the advertisement are alienation from one's body and from nature because of industrialised water processing and general water pollution; the cure: 'naturally' filtered water; the mythological overtones: a highly sexual picture of a muscular man (with overtones of the giant, Atlas, who held up the sky on his shoulders) representing the redeemed body of one who uses this make of water purifier.

The second is an advert for a car, where the silhouette of an erect, nearly bald, muscular male with bare torso stands in for the letter 'L' in the car's name; the caption: 'The small car with substance.'

Again, a highly sexual, Dionysus-like male gives the artificial and mechanical small car advertised (and you, the potential driver) the aura of having organic (and orgasmic) Dionysian powers.

The third entitled 'Strong hair starts where hair starts – at the roots' shows a large head with virile black hair and eyebrows against a barren field surrounded by arid mountains and covered with rocks and boulders. The only patch of colour in the field is the remarkably phallic shape of a green shampoo bottle apparently growing out of the desert. In other words, the image of nature sprouting in the harsh wilderness (a classic image of redemption, of alienation overcome, if ever there was one) is annexed to a brand of shampoo that claims to produce rugged hair. Again, the phallic bottle leaves no doubt about the role sex plays in the whole business of regeneration.

Finally, 'The last, truly civilised place on Earth' is a more traditional portrayal of a man and woman hand in hand in a deserted tropical paradise. The advertisement plays with notions of Paradise and civilisation, nature and technology; it is ironic, it implies, that the so-called civilised world is uninhabitable (because of technology), while a primitive island paradise is vastly civilised (because it is close to nature). It is quite clear where the couple, a sort of Adam and Eve pair, are heading, and the role that sex will play in their overcoming their alienation from nature caused by living in the industrialised, workaday world.

However, if redemption through sex and reunion with nature and the body are indeed the dominant myths of our age, the difference between our time and that of *The Bacchae* is that our exile from nature is self-imposed. We have no pressing need to fear nature or the body, or to ostracise ourselves from them. The parameters of sex have been thoroughly explored in novels, plays and films, by social scientists, anthropologists and opinion pollsters, its reefs and shoals charted, its highways mapped.[28]

Adequate scientific knowledge enables us to understand nature better, and co-operate better with natural forces and 'laws' than ever before. Vastly improved living conditions and access to resources for most people in the twentieth century mean that they have greatly increased their power over their own destiny;

we are much less trapped by the 'secret and irrational links' that plagued our ancestors. Life is by no means perfect – but access to power, knowledge and wealth are at present in general terms more widespread than ever before.

Admittedly Gerald Crich's ruthless subordination of the body to the will can still be regularly found – for example, in some of our more traditional hospitals, where the body is treated solely as a malfunctioning machine, and a minor operation is rather like taking the car to be serviced. But thanks to scientific knowledge and the development of applied science, we are generally closer to nature than ever before.

And so, on one level, as so often with popular mythology, the whole image of redemption with nature, of alienation overcome through sexual intercourse, is a nonsense. It is one thing to seek to break a strong taboo imposed by some external authority, overpoweringly attracted by the terrifyingly forbidden sexuality of the other. It is quite another to act this out at second hand, in fancy dress, as it were.

One might conclude by suggesting that it is part of human nature to feel alienated, and that if we can invent some fictitious world on to which we can project our dis-ease, we do not hesitate to do so. Alienation – whether from the body, from women, from flesh, from nature, God, Dionysus or sex – is, it seems, a simple fact of human nature, as is the desire for redemption, for readmittance to whichever world it is from which we are estranged or which we have repressed. But, in our present world, it is above all sexuality which plays the vital dual role of both keeping before our eyes and imaginations the hints of this other world, this 'beyond', while also providing access to it in a way that is often a parody of religion, but sometimes, as we shall see in subsequent chapters, a genuine extension of it.

3

Into the Ring
Sex and Marriage

Every religion must have its temple or place of worship. The spirituality of sex is no exception. Contrary to rumour, the real temple of love today is not to be found in brothel or club, in back alley or grand hotel, but at home. Similarly, every religion has its institutional framework: and the institution that currently guards and regulates the spirituality of sex is that of marriage and the family.

In keeping with the secularised and democratic nature of this spirituality, its sacred places are privatised and domesticated, its activities carefully mapped and safely regulated. The experiences of communion with dark and untamed nature described in the previous chapter are always likely to be a minority interest; most people are probably less interested in individual ecstatic experience of the sublime and more interested in satisfying their religious instincts in relationships with each other following well-defined channels. And so most people pursue their religious experience neither in church nor in nature, but in marriage or some substitute for marriage of which sex is the defining key.

In this chapter we shall see how in marriage sex and religion come together as nowhere else in the life of the ordinary person. Thanks to the process of secularisation explored in the previous chapters, and at the same crucial period, the late Victorian and Edwardian era (although continuing a process that had begun with the Puritans in the seventeenth century), marriage became endowed with quasi-mystical qualities. The family gradually replaced the church, and the Englishman's home is now not only his castle but also his temple, while marriage has become its sacred rite with sex as its sacrament, its defining bond. Those who break this sacred bond of sexual fidelity threaten the whole edifice.

However, the nuclear family is not well suited to take on such quasi-religious connotations, as we shall see. No real marriage can actually live up to such lofty expectations under the pressures of ordinary life, whether job insecurity or the instant and hourly hysteria of a demanding toddler, and so these castles in the air sooner or later collapse, causing people to fear for the future of marriage as a whole. But, as we shall see at the end of the chapter, there is perhaps a true spirituality of marriage – based on reality, not fantasy, and still with sex as its sacrament – which may survive.

The Puritans have had a bad press. History is written by the victors, and naturally the restoration of the monarchy in 1660, in England at least, caused Puritans ever since to be generally mocked and regarded as killjoys. The roots of our contemporary attitude to marriage, however, lie, strangely enough, in the Puritan era. Contrary to received opinion, 'the Puritans were not puritanical about sex'.[1] Rollo May, for example, suggests that

> One has only to look carefully at the New England churches built by the Puritans and in the Puritan heritage to see the great refinement and dignity of form which surely implies a passionate attitude toward life. They had the dignity of controlled passion, which may have made possible an actual living with passion in contrast to our present pattern of expressing and dispersing all passion.[2]

It was only natural, for people bitterly opposed to the Roman church which devalued sex and matrimony, to wish to revalue it. It was largely the Puritans who evolved the notion of companionate marriage which is today's standard ideal. (For example, Thomas Bacon talks of marriage as 'that most joyful garden of pleasure'.) It was no coincidence that this took place at the beginning of the modern era. Many Puritans were prototypical business people at a time when capitalism first began to emerge, when the rise of the nation-state and the trade-led surplus economy entailed that (putting it crudely) people began to have time on their hands for 'relationships' rather than the business of subsistence.

However, the joys of marriage were, for the Puritans, still firmly ensconced within the religious framework of deep and pious Christian belief. It was with the crisis of faith of the late nineteenth century that marriage began to be truly secularised.

The process of marriage becoming a substitute for religion and church has been well documented. Lawrence Lerner, for example, in his book *Love & Marriage*, quotes the famous letter from Leslie Stephen to his future wife Julia in 1877: 'I feel for you something which I can only call reverence as well as love. You see, I have not got any Saints and you must not be angry if I put you in the place where my Saints ought to be.'[3] For Lerner, this is proof of 'the ability of married love, because of its religious aura, to fill the gap left by the retreating sea of faith.'[4] He adds, 'corresponding to that poetic rashness there is a human rashness in the situation: it is an enormous burden to lay on a frail human relationship . . . One can see modern divorce looming, the divorce that follows too much trust, too high an expectation – the displacement of religious feeling into *sexual* love.'[5] Similarly, G.K. Chesterton commented rather piously, 'This was the first generation that ever asked its children to worship the hearth without the altar.'[6]

As another example, there is the poem to which Lerner refers, Matthew Arnold's 'Dover Beach', which is a picture of the sea of faith going out like the tide.

> *The sea of faith*
> *Was once, too, at the full and round earth's shore*
> *Lay like the folds of a bright girdle furl'd;*
> *But now I only hear*
> *Its melancholy, long, withdrawing roar . . .*

As Don Cupitt puts it in his book of the same name, the poem 'expressed the sense, common in his [Arnold's] time, that the ancient supernatural world of gods and spirits which had surrounded mankind since the first dawn of consciousness was at last inexorably slipping away'.[7] (Although I do not think that any respectable Victorian Christian would have recognised his religious world as being that of 'gods and spirits'!) But 'Dover Beach' is a love poem, something that Cupitt ignores. The moral is that the sea of faith may be going out, but at least we can be faithful to each other:

> *Ah, love, let us be true*
> *To one another!*

The faithful love of two people is a substitute for the religion that has let the poet down. Once again, the world of religious belief is replaced by human love; more than that, human fidelity must take the place of God's vanished unchangeability.

For the contemporary reader, this process is perhaps most influentially portrayed in D.H. Lawrence's *The Rainbow*, where the secularising process attains its completion. So we shall look again at D.H. Lawrence, not this time as the great high priest of the sacralisation of sex, but as the prophet of the secularisation of religion into marriage.

Lawrence's *The Rainbow* is a pioneering fictional study of married life across several generations. In 1868, Tom, a Nottingham farmer whose family have farmed the land for generations, marries Lydia, a half-German, half-Polish refugee, the widowed daughter of an aristocrat, who already has a daughter, Anna, by her first husband, a dashing revolutionary who burnt himself out in a futile struggle against the Russians for a lost Poland. The two could hardly be more different: the strong yeoman farmer and the dark, passionate mid-European. Anna is a strange little girl, who clings precariously to her mother, fiercely jealous and self-contained, old for her years.

After the birth of Tom and Lydia's first child together, their relationship goes through a difficult patch. Their physical attraction for each other, the spark that once enlivened their relationship – and which, Lawrence implies, is the only thing that unites them, for they have no common ground of understanding at all – is nearly quenched by the growing distance between them and Lydia's absorption in children and home. Finally Lydia, who is six years older than Tom, takes the initiative and confronts him. When he complains that he cannot get close to her, she accuses him of no longer trying to reach out to her. 'Paul used to come to me and take me like a man does; you only leave me alone or take me like your cattle, so that you can forget me again.'[8]

As a result of this row, their relationship is healed, their sexual passion rekindled. They still do not understand much about each other, but at the most profound level their marriage is complete. This is summarised by a passage later in the book, where Lydia, in old age, talks to Ursula, her granddaughter: 'She loved both her husbands – the other [Tom] she had out of fulfilment, because he was good and had given her being ... he had served her honourably and become her man, one with her.'[9] Sexual union was, for Lawrence, the essence of marriage.

Lawrence symbolises the new strength of their marriage by showing its effect on their child, Anna. Whereas before Anna had been nervous and clinging, once her parents have sorted out their sexual relationship she becomes a normal child, able to play freely. She loses her sense of strain. But what is most interesting is the image Lawrence uses to describe this.

As a boy from a devout nonconformist background, Lawrence would have imbibed the Authorised Version of the Bible with his mother's milk. The biblical references and vocabulary of the first chapters of *The Rainbow* have often been noted. Of the explanatory footnotes in the Penguin edition, nearly a quarter in the early chapters are elucidations of biblical references. In this case, Lawrence uses a particular image from the very beginning of the Bible, one that is today rather obscure, but no doubt very familiar to his first readers.

When the writers of the first chapter of the Bible describe the creation of the world, heavily influenced by the mythology prevalent in ancient Babylon where the first chapter of Genesis was probably written, they used water as the symbol of primaeval chaos, much as today we might use space. 'The waters' were hostile to life, the lair of monsters. (The much older chapter 2 presents a completely different water symbolism – here it is life-giving and fertile.)

Before he can do anything else, God has to deal with the waters of chaos, which otherwise would make creation impossible, and so he creates a sort of bubble in the middle of the water, in which life can take place. The upper wall of the bubble is called a firmament (in Hebrew *rqiah*, 'spread out'), which acts like an arch holding up the span of the heavens. Without this arch, life could not have taken place, and indeed when in chapter 4 God decides to destroy all that he has made, he simply removes the firmament and all is blotted out – except for Noah in his ark, which somehow rides out the flood, more like a submarine than a conventional boat.

After the flood, God promises never to bring down a similar catastrophe and puts his rainbow in the sky as a reminder of the covenant. This is both the title of Lawrence's book and the key symbol of its ending: Ursula, Lydia's granddaughter, recovers from a breakdown in a ghastly mining town and, seeing a rainbow in the clouds, takes it for a sign of hope. Also, Anna's husband, Tom, is drowned in a flood: water symbolism runs through the novel.

Beneath the arch her parents make, the young Anna refinds her lost childhood. 'She was no longer called upon to uphold with her childish might the broken end of the arch. Her father and her mother now met to the span of the heavens and she, the child, was free to play in the space beneath, between.'[10]

This is a magnificent image from one of the first novels in the English language to describe an early modern view of marriage: husband and wife strong in their separate identity, mutually incomprehensible, but solidly linked by the sacrament of sexuality that binds the two contraries together, who like God create the protected space in which their children may play, holding up the sky, a sacred canopy under which their children will be safe. It is what Lerner calls 'phallic marriage'. This has become the basis for the modern conservative ideal of marriage, where the two parents, like God, create a sacred space safe from chaos for their family to thrive in. But it is a secularised vision of holy matrimony – God has been replaced by parents.

Whatever his own views on religion (*The Rainbow* describes Ursula slowly losing her religious faith at puberty, presumably modelled on his own experience), Lawrence creates a distinctive blend of secular and religious images; no doubt he himself would have been well aware of the religious background and resonance of his every word and image. But the vast majority of people whose views of marriage have been directly or indirectly influenced by Lawrence will be entirely unaware of this level of interpretation, and only eighty years later (the novel was written in 1914) respond to his work without perceiving its religious basis.

Three further consequences of the secularising of our institutions and of the ensuing sacralisation of marriage are prefigured in the work of Lawrence. As long ago as 1977, in his book *Facing Up to Modernity*, the sociologist Peter Berger remarked on the increasing privatisation of life as institutions have become devalued:

> This *privatisation* of identity has its ideological dimension and its psychological difficulties. If the 'real me' is to be located in the private sphere, then the activities of that sphere must be legitimated as decisive occasions of self-discovery. This legitimation is provided by interpreting *sexuality and its solemnisation in the family* as precisely the crucial test for the discovery (definition) of identity.[11]

In similar vein, Anthony Giddens suggests that 'sexuality has become imprisoned within a search for selfhood which sexual activity can only momentarily fulfil'.[12] Not only is the importance of the family the result of its being a substitute for the church, it is also about validating one's own sense of self-identity, something that is, by any standards, a religious function.

Secondly, Niklas Luhmann argues in *Love as Passion* that 'the transition from traditional societies to modern society can be conceived of as the transition from a primarily *stratified* form of differentiation of the social system to one which is primarily *functional*'.[13] In other words, the question is not what status does marriage give, but rather what does marriage do, what function does it serve? Whereas once simply getting married was justification in itself for both men and women in different ways – it had been sanctified and ordained by God on high, and that was enough – today functional questions are being asked about marriage. Institutions are expensive to maintain in terms of money, time, energy and the suffering of those who for one reason or another cannot enter them, and many of what were once our most cherished have been found out to be not worth the investment. From being an institution made in heaven, it has to prove itself of some earthly use.

Thirdly, in an age when it was believed that God worked through society as much as, if not more than, through individual lives, the necessity of baptising so universal a human institution as marriage was clearly desirable, another attempt by the Church to regulate the wilderness of human behaviour. Today, however, faith in institutions has suffered a breakdown, and it is the individual family that has become the little church.

The first signs of this development can be seen in the popularity of Holy Family pictures from the time of the Reformation, their popularity growing with the advance of capitalist society and the decline in importance of the central institution of the Church. These pictures ('icons' of 'Christian family life') can be seen as giving religious sanction to the secular family: Jesus himself was a member of a nuclear family, they seemed to say, and thus he sanctified 'family life'. From now on, the Englishman's home is his temple with, in high Victorian times, his wife 'the angel in the house' (a phrase from a poem beloved of the Victorians by Coventry Patmore, referred to in *The Rainbow*); her angelic task is to decontaminate her man from the world of selfish passions in which he is forced to earn a living!

This also ties in with other recent developments in society. Instead of the large units comprising several generations of the traditional extended family, securely located in one part of the country, linked to a particular place of worship, family units became small and mobile. Since traditional religious practices were often firmly rooted in a particular geographical location, the family church for example, they tended to break down under the new circumstances. By divinising marriage, by contrast, the household gods became eminently portable and, as with the children of Israel in the wilderness, the family's spiritual tent of meeting could move with them wherever they went.

Thus younger generations, who had been to college or moved to another part of the country altogether, where they had no links to community or place of worship and therefore no public support or local expectations from people who knew them well before their marriage, tended to invest heavily in the bond of sexual fidelity – an entirely portable and personal way of defining a continuing relationship between two people – rather than in a local or family community.

The Church has responded to this change in emphasis by transferring its emphasis from the divine institution of marriage to the individual. It set out to show that individual marriage could be the focus of divine presence. The old Anglican *Book of Common Prayer* (1662) gave as the first reason for marriage the procreation of children, and the second its efficacy as 'a remedy against sin, and to avoid fornication; that such persons as have not the gift of continency might marry and keep themselves undefiled . . .' (While most people would agree about the importance of children to marriage, the idea of marriage as a means of controlling 'men's carnal lusts and appetites' – i.e. better marry than burn in hell – is rather quaint. Many women today, to judge from letters in women's magazines, wish their husbands were a little more carnally lustful, especially when they reach forty!)

By contrast, the new Anglican service book (ASB 1980) suggests that the purposes of marriage are firstly 'that husband and wife may comfort and help each other', and secondly, 'that with delight and tenderness they may know each other in love, and through the joy of their bodily union may strengthen the union of their hearts and lives.' (Having children comes a poor third.)

However, this presents a problem. As long as the aim of marriage was the procreation of children and the avoidance of lust, objectively measurable criteria, it could be shown that marriage in general and in particular was blessed by God regardless of a couple's feelings: children and fidelity were the criteria of a successful marriage. But once the Church saw couples' feelings for each other as the locus of God's presence, the sacrament of marriage became rather precarious: for if the relationship itself appeared to have died, then God would presumably approve the transfer of affections to someone else with whom one might have fallen in love – a problem whose magnitude we shall shortly explore.

The wedding service

A sure sign of the religious, transcendental expectations we have of marriage even today is the amazing ritual we regularly attend when a couple get married, whether in church or registry office.

Getting married is still regarded as a highly significant, once-in-a-lifetime event, involving putting on a fancy-dress show of amazing extravagance with a well-worn routine and well-defined cast (best man, chief bridesmaid, etc.) dressed in improbable clothes. It does not seem a very serious or authentic thing to do. Yet even in economically straitened times, expenditure on a white wedding as a proportion of salary shows the extraordinary importance still given to the marriage ceremony today.

The symbolic nature of the wedding service itself – the fairytale elements of white veil and bridesmaid, page and groom – sheds light upon the quasi-religious expectations of marriage. For a sociologist, the traditional wedding service is a *rite of passage*, a transition from one state of life to another. It marks the public setting up of a new household, and thereby gives the couple status within the community. For a certain percentage of couples, this still holds good. But for many more, weddings are the culmination of a relationship, the crowning of a vision that has proved itself stable. In many inner-city churches, for example, a new tradition has developed whereby the children of the couple being married are bridesmaids and pages: the visible fruits of their nuptial success. Rather than being a rite of passage or change, the wedding ritual is becoming an expression of stability. But there must therefore be more to it than this.

I suspect that it has to do with the hope that the wedding ritual will reveal an element of magic. The marriage ceremony is, in a curious way, designed to express our yearnings for the transcendent, for a glimpse of some other world. For example, the white fancy dress may be inappropriate and anachronistic, but it is one way in which an attempt can be made to signal the transcendent possibilities of the day. On this special day, the spark may occur which gives access to the other world – and the photographers and the video recorders, tape recorders and guests with flash cameras are willing witnesses to the moment, should it happen.

Nevertheless, the success of a film such as *Four Weddings and a Funeral*, the most commercially successful British film made to date, is due to the fact that it neatly and affectionately parodies our expectations and hopes for transcendence in this ritual by pointing up its feet of clay. The funeral service featured in the film, in contrast to the fripperies of the weddings, is down-to-earth, unpretentious and genuinely moving. But the weddings point up the absurd gulf between the unlimited expectations and the very this-worldly reality, as in the inappropriate substitute wedding rings and dreadful folk singers that grace its opening scene.

Another extraordinary aspect of the wedding ritual is the extravagant nature of the vows the couple make to each other: nothing less than unconditional, lifelong fidelity no matter what. Given that a third of marriages end in divorce, this seems somewhat unrealistic. For so many couples, the icing sugar paradise quickly dissolves into rows and the temptations of adultery. But to the student of religion, whenever the unconditional or the very excessive (out of proportion) make an appearance, it is probably realistic to see religious elements at work – and indeed in this case one is not disappointed.

The lifetime vow (especially of sexual fidelity) is a courageous statement of love that is certainly religious in character in that it goes beyond all the odds. As Roger Scruton puts it, 'love seeks not a promise of affection but a *vow* of loyalty'.[14]

This is something that even sociologists may pick up. Diana Leonard, in her book *Sex and Generation: A Study of Courtship and Weddings*, based on her research into several score weddings in and around Swansea, suggests that although weddings are at base simply a form of contract, they take on ritual form. 'Rituals say things which are difficult to think.'

> Forming a new family unit is very different from making other forms of contract. A major, mystical union is affected. The experience is dramatised with magic, myth and religion ... Stress is laid on expressive and symbolic actions rather than legally prescribed technical aspects.[15]

In other words, there is still the hope of discovering a secular flash of transcendence at the charged moment of human life when a couple are voluntarily submitting to the marital yoke, entering a relationship defined almost exclusively by sex. Outside marriage, one may sleep with whoever one likes and is able to seduce. After marriage, the one thing that can certainly kill it is sexual infidelity. The wedding service is one of the few potentially sacred moments in a society that has largely forgotten what the sacred is about.

The sky on their shoulders

Inevitably, the sacred appears rarely. The quasi-religious expectations of marriage are as potentially harmful as any of the other mythologies we consider in this book. Taking the sky upon one shoulders to create a protected space for one's family may require superhuman strength.

Generally the first thing to crack is sexual fidelity. Sexual infidelity by one of the partners is the betrayal of the symbolic bond which, according to Lawrence's myth of phallic marriage, should be the cement that holds the marriage together. (A far cry from the previous era and a Victorian mother's advice to her daughter: 'After your marriage, dear, unpleasant things will happen to you; but take no notice of them. I never did.'[16])

The Victorian era, with its high moral standards, was able to buttress the difficulties of marriage with a scaffolding of public blame and private licence (at least for men), not to mention the easy availability of prostitutes to supply anything lacking in a marriage. There was an implicit acceptance of a necessary hypocrisy. But this no longer applies. Today a degree of openness unimaginable before is demanded in marriage.

With the buttressing gone, the strains upon a frail human relationship are too much for an individual couple to bear. Who better than Lawrence in *The Rainbow* to describe the appalling strains of the early years of married life on a very young married couple, even when they have a sympathetic family to support them. On Anna and Will's honeymoon (according to Lerner 'the first honeymoon in English literature'), the newlyweds are shut up in their house on holiday, divorced from the world's rhythms, and away from all their familiar props and supports. It is as if they are in a Noah's Ark – 'they were the only inhabitants of the visible earth, and the rest was under the flood'.[17] The loss of fixed boundaries affects them both, and their honeymoon is a series of rows and reconciliations.

Lawrence records their struggle for dominance over each other (the chapter is entitled 'Anna Victrix', Anna victorious), their desire to wound each other where it hurts most, their mocking of each other's most cherished illusions, the onset of black, bitter hatred and their terrible feelings of being trapped – all as the other side of the coin from passionate, physical and highly sexual love. It is sex that is the symbol and sacrament of their reconciliations. (In Lawrence, Lerner suggests, 'hate is an allotropic state of love'.)

This has become the pattern of contemporary marriage aspirations as recorded in almost every film Hollywood has produced for thirty years (with *Love Story* still probably its finest example). As Lerner puts it, 'we are all Lawrentians now'.[18] Anna and Will stay together. The heroine of *Love Story* dies, faithful unto death. In real life, however, many couples split up, their marriages collapsing under the weight of their pseudo-religious expectations, their sex life not strong enough to work miracles.

Affairs

If marriage has become a sort of domestic religion substitute, there is an even more secluded sacred grove, with, again, pseudo-religious expectations: the world of affairs. To have an affair risks the ruination of one's marriage.

An affair is defined simply by sex (and so, therefore, must be marriage). A non-sexual liaison, which may be far more draining to the marriage, is not popularly considered so dangerous. Many studies of affairs have been carried out: almost all agree that the discovery of an affair (which, by definition, must involve a married person) by the other partner – especially if involuntary – is probably the greatest possible jolt to a marriage.

According to Janet Reibstein and Martin Richards, in their book on affairs, *Sexual Arrangements*, men generally have a great desire to confess their relationships to their wives – especially when they have just ended. After all, your wife is the one person to whom normally you tell everything, and you have just endured a major bereavement. Apparently men often fail to realise how shattering the effect of their confession will be.

Any public figure – politician, member of the Royal Family or clergy – discovered in an affair will be wildly censured. Surveys reveal that 70 per cent of the population disapprove of affairs. But there is a strange contradiction here. Recent research shows that 60 per cent of married men and 40 per cent of women will probably have had affairs at some time in their married lives (and the figures, especially for women, are growing). In other words, a significant proportion of the population are being thoroughly hypocritical in their condemnation of public people's affairs. Rather as in Victorian times, we have dual standards; we expect our politicians and public figures to obey a set of standards we do not apply to ourselves as individuals.

Why? Clearly, an affair would have no point if it were licit – it would lose much of its dangerous excitement (always a ready fuel for sexual passion). Marriage is needed to make sense of affairs, just as non-believers often feel that the survival of the Church is important and have great respect for a hard-line Pope.

Human nature is such that no one can give themselves to an institution without enormous cost. Like weeds breaking through concrete, the power of the ego for self-assertion cannot ultimately be repressed. The greater the importance we give to marriage in public, the greater the pressure to escape from marriage in private. The affair gives access to a highly secret world apparently defined solely by sex.

In fact, affairs have a whole variety of purposes, contrary to popular expectation; not all are connected with inadequacies in the marriages of the partners. Reibstein and Richards report a whole range of needs which affairs take care of. Some people find a level of openness simply not possible with their spouse. There is too the excitement of the chase and the thrill of doing something sexually illicit. Thus one woman did not enjoy sex so much with her friend as with her husband, except that she found it exciting to think of herself as an adulterer. Precisely because sex has been given the ultimate defining role in marriage, it is sex which causes its breakdown.

Thus an affair is an even more secret world alongside what is already a very private world. And if marriage is already a religion substitute, then affairs are even more so. Everyone needs access to a secret world, to break out from the confines of institutionalised existence – and the demanding role sex has to play in marriage means that sex outside marriage becomes inevitable, it seems, for half the population. In this sense, the reawakening described in *Sexual Arrangements* by many people who had had affairs is almost religious, akin to a rebirth. People claim to feel themselves coming alive after years of emotional stultification. They claim it triggers access to darker, remoter regions where they feel more alive. However, the price of such an emotional shot in the arm is often disastrous. Few can control their emotions when they are suddenly given full rein, and almost inevitably one partner will crack. And there is always the danger of affairs developing into obsession (as films from *Last Tango in Paris* to *Fatal Attraction* explore).

Sometimes, *Sexual Arrangements* reports, there can be beneficial repercussions for dormant marriages – the emotional high may carry over into the marital relationship. Many more times, it leads to destruction as the desire to go public overrides the desire to keep the marriage going. Even so, affairs – where 'it's all prime time'[19] – often don't stand the transition to marriage. 'My wife doesn't understand me' cannot work when you are married to your mistress! Similarly, women who have affairs because it is the one way 'I have something that's only for me'[20] find, if they marry their lover, that they have to share all over again.

Idolatrous expectations

In conclusion, therefore, one might say that weddings used to be a rite of passage in a stratified and relatively rigid society but today their symbolic importance is even greater. For marriage is not less but more highly valued today. While the diminishing number of people getting married and the increasing prevalence of divorce might at first appear as an argument that marriage has either been hopelessly devalued or is now on the way out altogether, many writers contend that the opposite is the case. For example, Peter Berger, in *Facing Up to Modernity*, argues that 'typically individuals in our society do not divorce because marriage has become unimportant to them, but because it has become so important that they have no tolerance for the less than completely successful marital arrangements they have contracted with the particular individual in question'.[21] Janet Reibstein argues in *Sexual Arrangements* that contrary to popular belief, 'monogamy is held to be a more important basis for marriage than at any other time in the last century'.[22]

Throughout the century, as external pressures to marry and the internal constraints on marriage have declined, so the institution has grown in power. In the fifties, if a man lapsed, his wife was generally advised (for example, in the problem pages of women's magazines) to ignore it, and wait for him to come back. Today, such advice would be unthinkable. Either the man must return at once (and even then, forgiveness cannot be taken for granted) or else he must leave at once and the marriage is at an end.

Small wonder, then, that many lack the possibly foolhardy courage to commit themselves to such a risky course and refrain from marriage, living in one or a series of *de facto* relationships, hedged about with all sorts of legal documentation if children are involved (although getting married is generally a cheaper way of protecting one's children than agreements forged by lawyers). The crisis of marriage is, like the crisis of the family, the subject of endless debate on television and in the press. With the divorce rate in Britain running at 160,000 a year, the second highest in Europe, with three out of ten marriages ending in divorce, one in two second or subsequent marriages failing, and with the average length of a marriage being nine years (and falling),[23] surely, it is argued, marriage will soon be dead and buried.

In a society dominated by, say, a strong Church or strong moral expectations which define secure roles for married couples and families, however uncomfortable, marriage may be relatively stable. But where 'society' does not care particularly whether a couple stay together or not, the self-imposed strain on a couple trying to stay faithful to each other when things between them have become impossible reaches positively heroic proportions.

In marriage, counsellors report, one must accept the fact that one's partner will periodically change into a demon, particularly at the classic times of stress – during the first year, on the arrival of the first children, when the children leave home – and that quite regularly love will appear to have died. Accepting that there is nothing that can be done except to hold on and wait for things to change (all the time hoping that your partner has the same tenacity) is immensely difficult. As Reibstein and Richards comment, people are not good at accepting lapses of intimacy during marriage.

Traditional Christianity had plenty of ammunition to help people cope with such acute psychological suffering (healing symbolic rituals, the sacraments, confession, absolution, the possibility of displacing one's anger away from one's spouse on to a personal devil). The heroic, individualistic religion of sex provides little such support. It is all very well to wish for *absolute* and total acceptance by your God; the desire for absolute acceptance by another human being (who will even pardon your sexual lapses) is mirrored in the fierceness of disappointment when things go wrong and the acrimony with which divorce settlements are very often pursued, with even the children being used as a weapon against the other partner.

Of course, this has nothing to do with marriage as such; it is a problem faced by all who live together under any circumstances, and not to get married for fear of divorce is simply shooting the messenger! The chances of unmarried couples splitting up are three times higher.

The Church might rather smugly conclude that here, as elsewhere, idolatry is shattered upon the rocks of reality. Putting another human being in the place of God is bound to lead to disaster. And yet (as the Anglican theologian Adrian Thatcher points out in his book *Liberating Sex*) the marriage service is the only place where Christians are permitted to worship anything other than God, for the partners must worship each other.[24] ('With this ring I thee wed, and with my body I thee worship.') Worshipping your partner is at the heart of the particularly Christian intuition about the strength and fullness of the married state.

There is another aspect of our expectations of marriage not so far examined. Some writers, such as Jeffrey Weeks, claim that the whole 'traditional' wedding is a middle-class invention, and that today we are simply reverting to a pre-Victorian era, when the working class had a different sexual morality.[25] Usually, they could not afford to get married, nor would they have seen it as corresponding to their status. But in the highly status-conscious Victorian era, a church wedding and a family were status-symbols for Victorian man, so that the upwardly mobile element of Victorian society, who traditionally might not have had a formal marriage, became attracted by the respectability offered by a church wedding. Thus marriage became nearly universal as more and more people sought for themselves (and had the money to afford) a classy white wedding.

Roger Scruton puts it more icily: 'the rest of mankind pillages the wardrobe of aristocratic disguises – so as to be a real lady or a real gentleman if only once'.[26] The aristocracy play, freed from the taint of utility. We, at moments when we need to be 'purposeful without purpose', imitate them. He applies this to courtship, but it could equally well apply to weddings.

The result of this process is, as Diana Leonard reports from a sociological perspective, an extraordinary similarity across all classes. 'British weddings today show astonishingly little difference by class: weddings of the élite differ only in detail and scale from the 'proper' weddings of the provincial middle class and working class. This suggests that in regard to marriage at least, Britain is an extremely cohesive society, with shared values and aspirations across the social strata.'[27] Scruton differs: he concludes that 'the disguise has worn thin'.

The future of marriage

So, is marriage to disappear, and sexual relationships become simply a wasteland of impermanent liaisons, as Anthony Giddens suggests?[28] Can there be a genuine spirituality of marriage? The two questions are linked.

First, I suggest, marriage may survive if it is divested of its illusions, stripped of the accretions of bogus spirituality with which, in our yearning for the transcendent, we have endowed it. Like all bogus spiritualities, that of marriage is dangerous and clouds the reality of the matter. One needs particularly clear vision to survive and enjoy marriage. If we go into marriage expecting a mystical rose garden and final salvation, there is not much hope of its surviving. If, however, marriage is stripped of its mystical accretions, so that it no longer has to function as a religion substitute held together by a mystical sexual union, one might be surprised by its genuinely religious quality, which the Puritans first sensed.

Secondly, the contractual basis must be better defined, its terms possibly made more variable and the get-out clauses certainly clarified. It is bad enough to face the terrible sense of bereavement that generally follows divorce without having the extra burden of unspecified moral stigma. At present, according to L.J. Weitzman, 'the marriage contract is unlike most contracts: its provisions are unwritten, its penalties are unspecified, and the terms of the contract are typically unknown to the contracting parties . . . In fact, one wonders how many men and women would agree to the marriage contract if they were given the opportunity to read it and to consider the rights and obligations to which they were committing themselves.'[29]

There is, certainly, a genuine spirituality in marriage which may be glimpsed only when it has been thoroughly demythologised (and then often only in retrospect), and when couples – if that is their intention – get on with the business of sticking to each other through thick and thin for the sake of some ulterior purpose such as creating a stable family. But this sense of spirituality is not something for which one can legislate.

Religion on its own can never shore up an ailing institution, no matter how the pages of the New Testament are scoured for their references to 'Christian family life.' What the Church can do is to show how a committed relationship may open up on to the transcendent, and, more importantly, to help couples deal with the inevitable pain that any committed relationship entails.

In practice, whether marriage survives will probably depend as much upon economic conditions as upon, say, improved sex education in schools. As long as there is pronounced economic polarisation between rich and poor, those excluded from wealth will always, of necessity almost, have fantasies of the perfect marriage, fantasies that will inevitably be disappointed and that will threaten their relationship. Similarly, if, economically, parents become trapped in relationships, marriage will again be seen as a prison, to be escaped from at the first opportunity.

If, however, economic conditions are such that there is enough wealth around to be able to dispense with pain-killing fantasy, and if the contractual basis of marriage is clarified, then the institution is likely to survive – especially if there are sensible expectations of the reality of living with another human being and appropriate structures in place to enable people to deal with their problems as they arise. A recent *Panorama* programme emphasised the importance of the availability of counselling to married couples at times when their marriages are under stress.[30] They interviewed a GP, for example, who refers patients who come to him in the early stages of marriage difficulties to a counsellor he employs in his surgery. The success rate is surprisingly high if couples are seen early. If things are left until separation is on the cards, results are less impressive. Counselling is expensive, but so are the costs of broken marriages. Up until recently, it was the well-off who were most likely to divorce each other. Now, given that there is less compulsion to be married in the first place, it is likely to be the well-off who stay together, as they will be able to afford the counselling that will enable them to grow together.

A more realistic view of marriage will also take the pressure off sex, which can then be enjoyed for its own sake, rather than having to serve as a quasi-mystical glue! Couples are still likely to perceive a religious dimension to their married sexuality, but not a sugary confection that turns to ashes in the mouth. One of the original discoveries of Old Testament theology is the notion that God can be found in a contract. Rather than regarding such matters as of no interest to God, the Jewish authors of the Old Testament saw God as regularly making contracts with his people. The whole Bible is based on contracts (technically 'covenants'). It is perfectly possible, in Jewish theology, to discover the infinite God, to have profound religious experience, within the very finite situation of living out a contract. Such down-to-earth mysticism flies in the face of most people's religious expectations. But this experience is reflected elsewhere in the Western tradition.

For two similar examples of the spirituality of marriage, one might consider a pair of contrasting poems. The first, 'Im Abendrot' ('In the Dusk'), by Joseph von Eichendorff (especially as set to music the year before his death by Richard Strauss, the late Romantic German composer, as one of his 'Four Last Songs') is a beautiful and extremely moving farewell.

> *Wir sind durch Not und Freude*
> *gegangen Hand in Hand;*
> *vom Wandern ruhen wir*
> *nun über stillen Land . . .*

(We have travelled through distress and joy hand in hand; now we can rest from wandering above the silent land.)

The poet compares himself and his wife to two skylarks singing as they fly. The poems ends 'O *weiter, stiller Friede! . . . ist dies etwa der Tod?*' ('O broader, quieter peace: is this really death?') If one needs a religious dimension in marriage, it is surely here: in the vast spaces of human experience that can never be directly glimpsed, only known fully at the time of death, at the end. Here is a genuine transcendence based fully in reality, hinting at how the real opens up into the infinite through time and suffering.

In a remarkable collection published in 1961 the Cornish poet Jack Clemo, a modern Puritan who became both deaf and blind, included a poem 'Intimate Landscape' in which he compares his beloved 'on my nuptial night' to a volcanic landscape running with springs.

> *Here is the holy ground,*
> *earth-womb where springs abound,*
> *some frank for my refreshment, laughing still*
> *if clumsy hand disturb them, others numbed*
> *to poison at an uncouth touch. I thrill*
> *sensing these waters yet unplumbed . . .*[31]

In describing the unplumbed waters that lie beneath the landscape that is his beloved, Clemo hints at a spirituality of marriage that begins with the mystery, the unplumbed depths of the other. Misreading the signs may lead to disaster: barrenness, aridity, 'kiln-rafters darkening on my nuptial night's despair', and in his usual pessimistic manner, Clemo ends on this note. But the poem begins with the richness and satisfaction of glimpsing the boundless and unpredictable vitality of the other, her springs 'frank for my refreshment'. Marriage, he seems to suggest, becomes mystical when it is based on getting to know the mystery of the reality of another person.

In both these love-poems, the poet describes the reality of the beloved, no sugar-candy fantasy. Reality itself is erotic – quite erotic enough not to need spurious fantasy – a theme that will be further developed in the last chapter. Reality is also spiritual. Acceptance of the real leads to genuine transcendence. God can be found in a marriage contract.

Jeffrey Weeks, at the end of his article, 'An Unfinished Revolution: Sexuality in the Twentieth Century', concludes that, in the light of 'the tempest of AIDS', it is vitally necessary for proper sex education to take place. 'Our moral system must move closer to what we actually do and are, rather than what inherited tradition says we should do and are.'[32] The same argument could be used about marriage. The price of prurient hypocrisy today is not only unwanted babies and fatal illness but broken families and the danger of the next generation being brought up in a 'wasteland of impermanent liaisons'. It is vital we get this right.

4

Feasting on Flesh
The Shock of the Nude

In this chapter, we take a short break from the argument, and preview some of the themes that will crop up in the second half of the book: notably the sexuality of men and women and the role of art and possibly pornography in 'justifying the body'.

Sex, the subject of so many taboos, is uniquely placed to be an unofficial court jester to our society. Although it is in the world of sex and reproduction that many people find their sense of stability and meaning (for example, assuring us that, through having children, we are part of the 'great circle of life', as the Disney film *The Lion King* rather piously puts it) it still contains the seeds of that sense of blasphemy or shock which can provoke religious disclosure. For Georges Bataille, author of *L'Érotisme*, sexuality and spirituality are very closely linked, for just this reason.

The whole erotic enterprise has, as its basis, the destruction of the state of self-sufficiency which is the normal condition of those who take part in it. The decisive action is taking off your clothes. Nakedness is the opposite of self-sufficiency, that is, of the state of being self-contained. It is a state of communication, which reveals our yearning for a possible extension of our being beyond our self-containment. Our bodies are opened up to this extension by those secret activities which give us a sense of obscenity. Obscenity signifies that disturbance which upsets those bodily states appropriate to self-control, to the possession of permanent and active individuality.[1]

For Bataille, this is the essence of spirituality. In sex, we remove our certain certainties with our clothing and are exposed to a state of being that is out of our control: a state so disturbing we tend to characterise it as obscene if anyone else is looking on. In the presence of someone we love (and on this contrast hangs the main point of this chapter) nakedness is exciting and arousing; but without the redeeming presence of our lover to mould it into desire, our naked state is at best ridiculous, at worst obscene. The bare matter of our animality – all those smells and body fluids stripped of clothes and culture – is the most appalling turn-off. In a sense, this is what gives sex its particular thrill, perhaps especially for the male (insofar as one can generalise between the sexes) – that one is dicing with dissolution and death, like someone walking along a precipice; one's independence, one's very being, as Bataille correctly points out, is excitingly threatened.

Perhaps, again, for the male particularly, sex pushes at the foundations of his separate existence; sex is about body fluids, about the unclean, about things that remind one of the death that one spends one's life seeking to avoid. Julia Kristeva argues that unclean things such as menstrual blood have traditionally required purification rites because they threaten the structure of society, they imply death.[2] In sex, one deliberately exposes oneself to the unclean and therefore to death.

Anthony Giddens puts it differently: 'The extension of internally referential systems shields the individual from disturbing questions raised by the existential parameters of human life, but it leaves those questions unanswered. Sexuality gains its compelling quality, together with its sense of excitement and danger, from the fact that it puts us into contact with these lost fields of experience.'[3] Or Georges Bataille again: 'L'érotisme est, dans la conscience de *l'homme, ce qui met en lui l'être en question.*'[4] ('Sexuality is, in the human mind, that which threatens our very being.') Camille Paglia describes how, in intercourse, men make the journey to non-being and back – like Orpheus descending to Hades.[5]

Thus the excitement of sex can be compared to combat with a gorgon – a battle with the unconscious monster that may consume one and will certainly remind one of death and dissolution. This dicing with existential death certainly adds to the excitement of sex even if these fears are rarely expressed directly. More than being just the expression of a biological need, the scratching of a prurient itch (so that sex, to read some people, such as Desmond Morris, might simply be rather a complicated version of blowing one's nose), sex is a struggle with the abyss, with that from which one may emerge with the reason torn.

James Park, a popular writer on psychotherapy, comments in his book *Sons, Mothers and Other Lovers*:

> What does a man look for in his partner? If it were simply a person who did not provoke his fears, all men would seek out someone who was compliant, weak, pathetic. Male desire, though, is usually more complex than that. A man wants to experience the spark of battle together with the comfort of safety. He seeks a woman who will make him feel afraid and then enable him to prevail, who will challenge him and let herself be conquered, provoke him and then surrender'.[6]

Thus for most men, who are not explorers, racing drivers or mountaineers, the woman is popularly seen as a prime source of adventure. In a society that has so few avenues of adventure left, sex is virtually the only way to the 'other', to having the foundations of one's existence shaken. (The appalling things this is responsible for in men's attitudes to women are something we shall examine in Chapter 7.)

But if sex is a quasi-religious activity for a male (insofar as one can differentiate) it has also been argued that for women sex is equally a religious matter, but for different reasons.

When it comes to the body, there is always a terrible gap between myth and reality. The human body is never perfect. Not even top models, those endowed with stunning natural beauty, report having an easy time of it; in fact, in their case, the business of keeping their bodies in good shape is nearly a full-time occupation. The gap between what we expect of our bodies and the way they actually look is always vast – requiring constant penance: exercise, dieting, saving up for expensive coiffure and clothes . . .

But more than that, centuries of mistrust of the body have left us doubtful about the acceptability of our bodies in what is actually a religious sense: the body is impure, smelly, hairy, lumpy and animal. The gap between actual and potential is so vast that some sort of religious justification is necessary to make our bodies acceptable. As Roger Scruton puts it, 'we yearn to *justify* the human body, to give grounds for our feeling that this is God's image'.[7]

Suffice to say here that this need to justify the body is exposed time and again through articles and books on health, diet and beauty, in fashion columns, advice columns and gossip columns, and it is what underlies those terrible plagues, bulimia, anorexia, self-abuse, and the ultimate malaise of our time, stress – the bodily correlate of good or bad lifestyle, the straightforward modern equivalent of 'sin'.

If the body needs redeeming, how is this achieved? Apart from the ritual purgation of dieting, cosmetics, depilation, manicure, herbal infusions, pedicure, waxing, tanning and toning, the real justification, the real vindication of the body, especially the female body, is in sex. It is sexual intercourse, above all, which redeems the body, which justifies it, which proves that the body is acceptable, especially as one grows older. Similarly with the consequences of sex: many women report that they enjoy sex more after having had children, an experience that somehow 'justified' their bodies, despite the physical damage it caused.

There are, of course, other ways of 'redeeming the body', of justifying it; two, in particular, have quasi-religious attributes. The first is fashion, the second art.

Maybe it is true that for men bodies – and especially women's bodies – are secretly a *memento mori*: a reminder that they are embodied and will therefore one day die. The female body changes physically quickly and dramatically, and is thus a terrifying reminder of mortality to the male who, according to stereotype, does not like to think about bodies anyway. In which case, if the great structures once elevated by the religions to protect us against death (immortality, eternal life, nirvana) now no longer have much credibility (or 'faith'), if now there are no guarantees of immortality, one can always take refuge in *style*. To gaze upon the bare bones of our mortality is too terrible a thing for most human beings – except for saints and ascetics – and so images of women and men must be filtered through the medium of style.

Style is a way of making the body erotic without drawing too much attention to its corruptibility. And if this is so for men, how much more so when it comes to the extraordinary variety of outfits and even body shapes and sizes to which women have to submit. A recent interview with a fashionable woman designer, for example, whose clothes are of the sort that might actually be worn away from the catwalk, elicited the following remark: 'Real women want comfortable clothes which will flatter them. More than that, they want to hide their bodies instead of showing them off – and to hide the fact that they are hiding.'[8]

And even the naked body changes according to fashion. As Anne Hollander puts it in her book on fashion, *Seeing through Clothes*, 'all nudes in art since modern fashion began are wearing the ghosts of their absent clothes'.[9] Even Rembrandt's most famous nude, *Bathsheba Reading the Letter from King David*, we are told, has her waistline 'at the proper raised level fashionable at the time.'

Which brings us on to the second strategy that justifies the body against death and decay. The arts, and especially visual art, provide not only a humanistic grammar of the body but also a quasi-religious way of redeeming it.

For example, one might take one of Rembrandt's greatest paintings, the painting of Bathsheba of 1654 just referred to. *Bathsheba Reading the Letter from King David* in the Louvre is the curmudgeonly old artist's tribute to his mistress of many years. It shows a mature woman sitting on a bank; next to her is spread, on one side, a pleated blouse, on the other some rich gold brocade, probably her dress. She holds a letter, presumably that from King David, who has spotted her bathing, and now summons her to his bed, despite her being already married to Uriah the Hittite (a mercenary soldier in David's employ). The woman is beautiful but not idealised.

It is probable that the model, who recurs in many pictures of this period, was Hendrickje Stoffels, who served as nanny to Rembrandt's son Titus and as housekeeper, model and eventually mistress to Rembrandt himself after the death of his wife Saskia in 1642. If Rembrandt's model here was Hendrickje, she may well have been pregnant when this picture was painted; their daughter, Cornelia, was born in October 1654.

Rembrandt never married Hendrickje, perhaps because of a clause in Saskia's will that entitled him to the interest on her estate only as long as he remained a widower. (The estate itself was to go to Titus on his coming of age.) It seems likely that this was because Rembrandt was profligate with money.

The painting itself is square, and the life-size nude figure occupies about a third of the total surface. The light, from above on the left, falls flat upon Bathsheba's upper torso, picking out especially her breasts and left shoulder; her lower legs are cut across by the shadow of a maid who is drying her mistress's toes. The rest of the painting is in darkness. Bathsheba's expression is one of resignation, of tired surrender to the inevitable; there is a contrast between the weariness and introspection of the face – her unseeing eyes pondering what will be – and the radiance and richness of the flesh, its tactile surface positively glowing in the light.

In contrast to other works, for example a contemporary *Bathsheba* by Willem Drost, probably inspired by Rembrandt, where Bathsheba is made to look like a successful and compliant courtesan, or *Bathsheba at the Fountain* by Rubens of *c.* 1635, where a seductive Bathsheba looks positively delighted at having hooked the royal gaze, Rembrandt here paints his subject as a tragic heroine. It is as if he has given her foresight of what will follow: her becoming pregnant by David, her husband Uriah's murder, the prophet Nathan's famous entrapment of David into self-condemnation ('Thou art the man'), the death of their child as punishment despite David's entreaties, and the eventual birth to Bathsheba of Solomon, who will become Israel's greatest king (rather than any of his better-qualified half-brothers).

Rembrandt himself would have been well acquainted with babies dying (Saskia's first three children died in infancy, Saskia herself dying nine months after the birth of Titus, her only surviving child), and also with religious denunciation: Hendrickje was excommunicated by the Reformed Church after having confessed to whoring (living in sin) with Rembrandt.

In this magnificent painting, it is almost as if Bathsheba regrets her fleshliness, her voluptuous torso which has roused another man's lust and brought her into peril. The intimate gesture of the almost invisible older woman washing her feet adds quiet pathos; Bathsheba will have to submit to more than having her feet washed before the day is done. As Tim Hilton pointed out in his review of a recent Rembrandt exhibition in London, the picture is certainly about death.

A couple of years ago, a television programme on breast cancer used this great painting as its mascot. Although it was a matter of some irritation that one of the greatest of all nudes should be flashed up on our screens before and after each commercial break, what the programme had to say was interesting. On Bathsheba's left breast there is a dark shadow, and the edge of the breast is curiously swollen. Experts on the programme interpreted these as symptoms of breast cancer, dutifully painted by Rembrandt with his dispassionate eye for detail and his concern not to idealise his subject-matter. It is difficult to establish whether or not this is true. Hendrickje did not die until 1663, nine years later, which would presumably have been a long time for a cancer sufferer at this period without access to the drugs and medical treatment that are available today to treat the disease.

However, the theory adds yet another layer of mythology to the picture, if the fate of his model is so publicly exposed: beauty and death stand in awful conjunction. The letter she is reading might in this case almost be the equivalent of the letter from the Doctor informing the patient of the diagnosis and prognosis – another reason for her to regret her fleshliness and for the awful sense of sadness in the picture: the contrast between the unidealised fleshliness of her body which harbours the intimate presence of death and the presence of a real human being – so much personality, richness, vitality hanging by a thread.

Bathsheba's vulnerability is heightened by the rich clothing lying around her, coverings that cannot afford her any escape. The dramatic use of light and shade for which Rembrandt is famous give his work, especially in a picture like this, a positively existentialist flavour: surrounded by darkness, Bathsheba endures the agony and the ecstasy, the glory and the terror of the lone embodied human being facing a decision that has in effect already been made and resignedly accepting its consequences. (One wonders if the locket she wears around her neck contains Uriah's picture.)

Rembrandt fills his paintings with an entirely human quality of understanding; the biblical stories are interpreted in the light of human experience. The vitality of the first bourgeois society in Europe pervades his work; one can sense the rise of the middle classes with spare cash available for pictures and prints, creating that great luxury of the middle classes, an art market, on the fringes of which a really great painter could scrape a living without having to pander too closely to the whims of his patrons.

This picture, however, is the complete opposite of commercial erotica. It is a portrait of the reality of a particular person whom, in his way, we presume the artist loved – and it roots the viewer in the reality of his or her own embodiment. Naturally, all art falsifies, exploits its objects; but the best art returns from imagination to reality. In this picture, flesh is invested with value in a sense that is profoundly religious. Despite the presence of death, the picture is affirming; it affirms the richness, the intimate, tragic and glorious strength of the naked body of someone who is loved. In this sense, it is *sacramental*: it reveals the presence of the extraordinary in the very ordinary and real. Our own bodies, too, take on divinity as we contemplate this picture, despite our sense of their unworthiness, the sense of shame that absorbs us when we are confronted by our own nakedness, thanks to which we can never believe that our own bodies can ever really be made in the image of God.

How do women, in particular, feel when confronted by a

Rembrandt nude? Margaret Miles, an American theologian and art historian, claims that male patrons of the arts have inevitably corrupted female nakedness, so that it can never entail innocence (as here). Looking at similar paintings of *Susanna and the Elders* (including one by Rembrandt), she concludes, 'it was impossible to paint a naked female body in such a way that it symbolised innocence ... The possibility of seeing Susanna's nakedness as innocence was blocked by repeatedly reiterated and reinforced associations of female nakedness with Eve and original sin ... In the visual mode, Susanna's nakedness inevitably contradicted her virtue.'[10]

And yet women I have interviewed remark that this picture of Bathsheba does, in some sense, make them feel good about themselves, justified in some way, even innocent. It has an effect opposite to that transmitted by a pornographic or advertising image. Paintings such as Rembrandt's seem to represent, somehow, an answer to their deepest yearnings: that someone will love them for ever, even when their body lets 'them' down – even when, during moments such as breast-feeding or pregnancy, they are immersed in their bodies, 'all body' – an absolute guarantee that their bodies are rich with meaning, lovable as they are.

In this sense, the best erotica is actually sacramental; it reveals the profound value of matter, of flesh, based not on fantasy but on the reality of real bodies containing vast realms of richness and connections. For another example of art redeeming the body, a secular icon of a 'spiritual' truth, one might consider the French painter Matisse's famous *La Danse*.

Here, a circle of five naked and stylised figures join hands in a ring while whirling round in an outdoor dance. There is none of the heaviness of Rembrandt's flesh here; rather there is sheer exuberance. Matisse's vision of innocence is caught by the child-like unsophistication of both the picture and the naked dancers (the style imitates the subject). In fact, the hands are not quite joined: we are invited to join in too.

The example of Matisse shows that even in the twentieth century there are a few who can combine nakedness and innocence, for whom the image of Paradise is the sacred place of Baudelaire's *amours enfantines*, children's frolics, as glimpsed in Chapter 1. For Matisse, Paradise is a place where you can take your clothes off. And in his *Luxe, Calme et Volupté* (inspired by a Baudelaire poem), Paradise is a place where you can simply bask or dance naked in the pointillist glory of a Mediterranean sun. Although this is a very different sort of paradise from the fleshly paradise of Bathsheba, it, too, is rooted in the reality of the child cuddled in its parents' arms. To refer back to a theme first adumbrated in Chapter 1, psychologists are quick to point out the connection between the adult paradise of Adam and Eve naked and unashamed and the world of children.

Freud finds dreams of nakedness almost universal among adults, and in *The Interpretation of Dreams* assumes that this is actually a throwback to childish desires to exhibit oneself.

> We can observe how undressing has an almost intoxicating effect on many children, even in their later years, instead of making them feel ashamed. They laugh and jump about and slap themselves, while their mother reproves them and says 'Ugh! Shocking! You mustn't ever do that!' Children frequently manifest a desire to exhibit. One can scarcely pass through a country village in our part of the world without meeting some child of two or three who lifts up his little shirt in front of one – in one's honour perhaps.[11]

And yet there is a great deal more to these dreams of nakedness.

Clothes are particularly associated with the restraints and inhibitions of society, and the fantasy of being able to take off one's clothes without having to adopt a sexual persona, unselfconsciously like a child, is gloriously liberating for some adults, a fantasy that Matisse captures beautifully, as does Charles Kingsley in *The Water Babies*, when Tom pulls off his clothes and enters the waters of rebirth.

In art, the deathly face of the body, its corruptibility, becomes acceptable; in art, the strange, lumpy and uncontrollable body can be readmitted to Paradise. It may be that it is women who particularly sense that their adult and no longer innocent bodies need redeeming, although these gender distinctions are increasingly doubtful. If so, it may be that men find the naked body equally sacramental, but in quite a different sense. Why do men spend so much time and energy on erotica, even the page-three photographs in tabloid newspapers? Why are men such easy prey for advertisements featuring scantily clad women?

Rembrandt's painting of Bathsheba works on a sophisticated level, but there is a sense in which the erotic calendar in the garage or the barber's shop, featuring month after month of well-endowed women, has the same relationship to Rembrandt as a popular trashy religious artefact from a souvenir shop at Lourdes has to the mystical experience of St Bernadette.

Both are abhorrent in devaluing a profound and sacred mystery, but both are here to stay, and just as the Church railed hopelessly against popular religious abuses, so feminists rail against the abuse of women in pin-ups and calendars and striptease. If religion was the opiate of the people in the Middle Ages, sex serves that function today, certainly as far as males are concerned. There is no doubt that, for the male, the hormones released in erotic fantasy are an analgesic. Perhaps, therefore, it is inevitable that those for whom life is particularly painful (those in difficult, dangerous or unpleasant employment, for example) should have most recourse to such remedies.

Even on a more sophisticated level, many men report that there is a sense in which the very contemplation of a picture of a naked woman is actually sustaining in an almost nutritional sense. Men graze on such pictures. These pictures of naked women are, perhaps in a diminished sense, sacramental: they are the bearers of a richness of meaning such that they provide a symbolic nourishment.

Much has been written about the male gaze, and about how it can terrorise or imprison women. More recently, under the influence particularly of lesbian writers and photographers such as Della Grace, women, it seems, are discovering their own gaze, and the delights of looking at both men and women. (No doubt if men were less inhibited by fear of homosexuality, they too would enjoy gazing at pictures of both sexes.) Pornography can be exploitative and demeaning, but occasionally contemplation of the naked body can be sacramental insofar as it puts one in touch with the mystery of life.

But just as, notably in the Middle Ages, sacraments can be abused, religious experiences used for propaganda, so the vision of sex as a sacrament can easily lead to disaster. The male tendency to escape relationships by retreating from people and making tools of them always runs the risk of abusing a sacramental action – of trading it, making money out of it, going after extreme and excessive forms. Religious experience is double-edged, and can easily (as the Church has always warned) become destructive.

It is possible to be more specific about the link between sex and religion in this area. For example, Roger Scruton, in his book *Sexual Desire*, views this philosophically. He notes the difference between the 'animal' experience of simple copulation ('penis entering vagina') and the richly human one of 'making love' ('man uniting with woman'). The 'pleasurable exercise of copulation is *moralised* by the concept of gender'.[12] (By 'moralised' he understands being 'given meaning', being raised from the animal level to the richly human one.) As he explains, sex is 'an object of that intentional understanding whereby we *make sense of our world*'.[13] Since religion is the ultimate means of making sense of the world, sex, at its most profound, is, I would claim, therefore religious. It is that which makes us, as Scruton puts it beautifully, 'see the human body as so peculiarly luminous among the objects of our experience'.[14]

This is a parallel with a particularly intense problem that arises at the time of death of someone who is loved. Today, it appears that fewer people believe in a heavenly realm or afterlife. But if one cannot say that the soul has left the body, or that the real person has left the husk behind,[15] one is left with the bare mystery of the flesh which one moment is charged with life – recognisably a person – the next dead and decaying. Without a spirit world (and even orthodox Christianity has never been very keen on an immediate passage to a saccharine heaven, preferring to defer resurrection to Judgment Day), the body becomes even more sacred. Those who cannot believe in another world of the spirits of the dead may be especially sensitive to the sacredness of the human body. If the human body *is* the human person, and if the human person is the subject of love, then the human body is the locus of the most highly valued aspect of our lives. In a non-dualistic world, therefore, the body becomes in a sense divine.

Bathsheba, displaying her flesh to the viewer, is thus both sacramental and profoundly moral; she has shed her clothes, her court persona, as she prepares for what may be death (her husband's, if not her own). In the face of such a reality (and the tender detail of the servant drying her toes with a small but hugely important gesture of tenderness, of concern for her mistress's body, adds bitter poignancy) the glorious depiction of the physicality of her self enhances her nudity. Her body is particularly luminous because it reveals our own unconscious investment in sex as a way of making sense of the world, of flesh and of death. In the absence of a belief in an objective and transcendent God, thrilling existential fears push at our foundations. But a picture such as this reassures us that, despite all the evidence to the contrary, we are not mere animals in rut; we can invest with meaning, we can justify, the precarious human business of making love.

The last hundred years have sensitised us extraordinarily to the suffering of the human body – our own and others' – and even those of animals. We have invested huge resources in the curing of bodily suffering, and in the artificial perfecting of its blemishes. Everywhere you go, large advertisements draped with florid images of mechanically touched-up bodies look down on you. These are the icons of our body worship.

But wherever you have a religious icon, as the old masters knew well, you will generally find its opposite. You cannot paint Paradise without Hell. The one pole demands the other, and the more the human body becomes the locus of the sacred, the greater must be the repressed desire to subvert it – to commit acts of blasphemy.

From this point of view, pornographic pictures are perhaps counter-icons, presenting the destructive side of humanity. Pornography represents the blasphemous desires that all human beings experience at nightmare moments – to desecrate the sacred, to tear down the temple of the body, to mutilate, pierce and thrust, to drown, diminish, stab.

It turns out that some women enjoy pornography. For example, Sallie Tisdale, a well-known American women's writer, wrote an article for *Harper's* in February 1992 confessing that she enjoyed pornography. The result was howls of protest from conservative feminists ('their insults were graphic and vile'[16]) and later a sensible and enjoyable book, *Talk Dirty to Me: An Intimate Philosophy of Sex*, in which she reflects on her experience: 'There was clearly something much deeper than a political disagreement going on.'[17]

Some pornography is appalling, especially for the way it injures its models. Other pornography is enjoyable and liberating, and educational both for men and women: it makes it clear that it is perfectly in place, for example, for women to enjoy sex, and that men should help them. Nancy Friday, in her bestselling series of sexual fantasies submitted by male and female readers (the first, *My Secret Garden*, was first published in 1973, and is still in print), reveals how much both men and (particularly) women enjoy sexual fantasy.

Another example of the positive value of pornography is Valerie Kelly's *How to Write Erotica: Turn Your Fantasies into a Fortune*. Ms Kelly, in this admirable guide, combines extreme cynicism with a certain evangelical zeal. For an example of the former, she has a list of five hundred 'sensual words' ('a list of the sexiest words in the English language'); 'the sexiest letter is "S", which is not surprising since sensual, sexy and sensitivity all begin with S. Stories with S-words are sure to be successful.'[18] (One might mention svelte, smoulder, stiffen, submit, starlight and straddle, not to mention squirt and spiritual.)

She also provides a splendid glossary of sexual terms. For example, I suspect few readers will know what a 'fluffer' is – 'a person who stays off stage and "fluffs up" the actor's cock between scenes. Usually a female, she gives the actor a blow job to help him keep his erection for the next scene.'[19] Or what about 'Auto-fellatio: kissing one's own penis. Ron Jeremy, the porn star, is the only one I know who can do it'?[20] Or her advice on paperback cover copy:

There's a really easy job that brings in a bit of pocket money on a regular basis: paperback blurbs. Since adult publishing houses re-cover, or put new covers on, books they have already published, someone has to write the new cover blurbs. Your job is to create new cover copy making this little erotic novel even more exciting than it was the first time around. You skim the book, write a short paragraph on it without giving away its plot line, and send it off into the reading public again under its new banner. Publishing houses own thousands of these little novels and you can tell by reading them just how long they've been circulating. The heroine may be wearing a miniskirt and platform heels and the man sporting a new crew-cut. But, heck, a buck's a buck, right?[21]

Her advice on getting material is invaluable. If your imagination falls short, you can always start with your own experiences – or those of your friends, who usually, she explains, will love being asked about their own experiences in the name of research.[22] However, Ms Kelly also has a crusading instinct.

As a writer of 'adult' material, it is your responsibility to free erotic literature from the heavy burden of its bad reputation – which some of our early magazine pornography surely deserved – and to develop a new language, a new form, which will enlighten the reader and celebrate the joys of sex ... a force that drives us out of control at times and yet brings us as much ecstasy as any other earthly thing. As a writer, you can relay these impressions and sensations to others. You can illuminate this dark and murky corner and exalt its wonders.[23]

Writers such as Sallie Tisdale, Nancy Friday and those schooled by Valerie Kelly are rapidly demystifying the world of erotica. No one need feel hypocritical about the enjoyment of erotica, they suggest, just so long as no one gets hurt.

Insofar as the campaign against pornography is an expression of the genteel niceties of certain groups of society – a campaign for good taste – then it needs to be gently and humorously exploded.

In Chapter 9, we shall enter the very different arena of those who are maimed or exploited in the nightmare world of sexual exploitation.

As so often in this book, what has until recently been a religion substitute (the dark, secret world of sex which, because it was so rigidly suppressed, became highly charged with the curious electricity that results when sex and religion come together) is, thanks to writers such as Ms Kelly, becoming illuminated, its wonders exalted in a very straightforward way.

5

Unfrocking the Priest
Sex and Religion

Old traditions die hard. Once upon a time, in an unpredictable and disease-ridden world where life was short and economic conditions uncertain, war episodic and destructive, unknown maleficent powers ubiquitous and human life dispensable, religion was naturally a necessity. The assurance of Paradise beyond, of ultimate justice for all (kings, emperors and popes included), of some purchase over the malign powers, and some antidote to bodily suffering – all these are no mere luxury for people in straitened circumstances.

In a relatively affluent world, religion continues to flourish and to play a major role in society, despite the gloomy prognoses of its critics, even if it is no longer the universal institution it once was. Its role has now changed to match prevailing economic conditions. Salvation is generally of this world as much as of the next ('eternal life', for example, tends no longer to refer to a life after death but to an enhanced 'quality of life' in this world).

Religious teaching tends, too, to concentrate more upon the level of individual and inner thoughts and feelings than outward observances. Rather than rejecting these inner voices as mere epiphenomena, like the ticking of a clock, religious teachers increasingly encourage people to take their internal dialogue seriously. Perhaps this is because, despite the traffic outside, the external world is actually quieter today, with fewer alarums clashing from the reeling spires to drown out these inner rumblings. Religious spirituality has become a principal lubricant to ease the workings of the labouring psyche.

Personal and spiritual development are therefore growth areas in religion. In a fragmented and extrovert age, religion offers an inner journey, a means of exploring the 'inner' or 'true' self – a way of discovering inner peace. Similarly, Protestant Churches at least now tend to offer an individualistic and portable salvation, no longer dependent on the ancient, fixed communities of faith. Previously, salvation came through membership of a universal community – the Church – outside of which there was no certain hope. Today, the fastest growth is in house churches and small, dedicated groups.

Such a development of religion from the outer and corporate to the inner and personal is probably inevitable if it is going to survive, and at the end of this chapter we shall return to how this has affected the Church's understanding of sex. However, what is interesting to us at this stage is not so much what the religions are themselves doing to make themselves more marketable, but the perceptions people have of them. If, as I am arguing, sex is the new spirituality, it would be highly likely that people project on to the established religions an interest in sex which they themselves might well not recognise. If sex is spirituality, then secular people might well expect the 'official' purveyors of spirituality (for example, the Churches) to have a particular expertise in – or, at least, interesting things to say about – sex. And this is what we shall find. An extreme interest in anything to do with the Church and sex by those outside, something that often takes those inside by surprise, is an indication of how the importance of sex in people's imaginative and inner lives has caused it to leach into their understanding of religion too.

On the face of it, the whole business might appear ludicrous. The Church has rarely taken much interest in sex – rather the opposite. Families, certainly, have always been important to established religion and the procreation of children, but the idea of sex as a legitimate approach to God, a valid avenue of transcendence, is of very recent origin in the West. Such things might have been spoken of discreetly, a confidential matter for discussion between Christian and spiritual director, but the relationship between Church and human body has in the past been far too ambivalent for the Church ever properly to celebrate the body's self-expression in sexual ecstasy. But for those outside the Church, for whom there is a constant need to find sex everywhere, the thrill of discovering sex at work even in this unlikely area is unbeatable. After all, the combination of sex and religion has always been exciting and dangerous.

There are two areas in particular where this thrill may be detected. The first is in people's fantasies about the clergy, especially (but not exclusively) celibate priests. The second is the growth of interest in oriental religions, perhaps because institutional Christianity is still too hopelessly familiar from Sunday School, school assemblies, weddings and funerals, and too tied up with sexual repression, to be much of a vehicle to the beyond for ordinary Westerners. A variety of authors and makers of videos are currently combing oriental religions (which have in many cases been much less hidebound about sex) with a view to discovering sex secrets. At its best, this may be a search for true spiritual ecstasy. At its worst, it is simply the fantastic hope that religion can improve one's sex life.

Sex and the clergy

On 25 September, 1994, the Bishop elect of Durham, the Right Reverend Michael Turnbull, hit the headlines in the *News of the World* shortly before his enthronement. His predecessor, David Jenkins, had been a highly controversial figure, often quoted as denying key elements of the Christian faith, such as the Virgin Birth. The historic York Minster, one of northern Christianity's most ancient and revered public buildings, had been struck by lightning at the time of his consecration as bishop – a clear sign of displeasure by an interventionist and miracle-working God upon a bishop intent upon upgrading His image. And so the translation of Bishop Jenkins's successor from Rochester diocese was awaited with a certain media interest – especially as the see of Durham is by tradition given to an intellectual heavyweight.

When the scandal broke, it emerged that twenty-six years previously, in 1968, the respectable Bishop Turnbull had pleaded guilty to an act of gross indecency with a Yorkshire farmer in a public convenience. At the time, he had been chaplain to the Archbishop of York (in other words, a man tipped for the fast stream from his early days, correctly as it turned out).

The press were delighted – especially since Turnbull was said to take a hard line on homosexuality.[1] Turnbull and the Establishment gritted their teeth and persevered. A few weeks later, the noise had died down and he was duly enthroned as Bishop of Durham.

There were a number of factors behind the attentions of the press. The appointment was of high profile; also, the man had been chosen by the Archbishop of Canterbury to head the highly important commission charged with making recommendations about the future structure of the Church of England following the loss of a quarter of its assets thanks to ill-advised investments in the property market by the Church Commissioners. Secondly, homosexuality was in the air. People were predicting that it would be the next big controversy to hit the Church, once the battles over the ordination of women to the priesthood had died down. But more importantly, any story about sex and the clergy sells like hot cakes. Almost every day, it seems, clergy feature in the tabloid press because of sexual sins.

What, then, is the basis for this extraordinary interest in the clergy and sex? One would have thought that after four hundred years of married priests in this country, people would have had ample time to realise that clergy are ordinary human beings with ordinary human interests and failings.

Clearly, the interest is partly linked to the fact that the priest is one who preaches morality, a parent figure who bids people uphold certain standards, and so it is always amusing to watch the discomfiture of a moral guardian of the community, someone who has the power to make one feel guilty or uncomfortable, when he or she slips, given that most people dislike hypocrisy and any authority that is not earned. The child in us is always ready to enjoy the sight of someone hoist by their own petard, or of the media shaking the pillars of the Establishment. But there is more to the matter than just this. Other pillars of the establishment – accountants or bank managers, for example – rarely suffer such extremes of publicity. Whenever a clergyman is involved in anything to do with sex, the media are on to it at once with an alacrity that suggests something more than merely a desire to expose hypocrisy. My suggestion is that at the root of this interest in the clergy is a powerful fantasy that clergy have heightened sexual powers.

This whiff of heightened sexual powers is in part a hangover from mediaeval times. Precisely because the Church has always denied or repressed sex, the celibate priest especially has always been seen as sexually highly charged, and the married priest suffers by association. (Even today, in many parishes, a single male curate is known to teenage girls in the choir as 'the forbidden fruit',[2] while so great are the fantasies of some women concerning priests that most clergy have a story of how a parishioner actually contrived a situation whereby they had to be physically touched or even manhandled by their priest.) Not only Christian clergy, but priests of religions the world over find that they are sexually powerful figures, with a hold over their congregations that can all too easily be used or abused.

For example, in 1995, the Reverend Chris Brain was disciplined by his diocese for sexual impropriety. Brain was the mastermind behind a whole new style of Christian liturgy which adapted the atmosphere of the rave to Christian worship. His liturgies took place in a sports centre outside Sheffield at 9 p.m. on Sunday evenings and became known as 'The Nine o'Clock Service.' He built up a large community of highly dedicated young people, who would spend hours shifting tons of expensive video and sound equipment in preparation for the service, which used a great deal of technology, from video loops to dry ice, to create its effect – a charged atmosphere that was very attractive to young people. His congregation, largely in their teens and twenties, had a missionary zeal. They believed that they were 'going to change the Church . . . and the country'.

A film of a service shown on television showed leather clad girls dancing in cages in a highly sexual routine as part of the liturgy. However, in common with the rave ethos, sex as such was not particularly important, although it was earnestly discussed. Brain 'would talk about how we were discovering a post-modern definition of sexuality in the church', as one participant put it, although she added, 'Again, it's language covering up what was going on – one bloke getting his rocks off with forty women.'[3]

And indeed, this was the problem. Many of the female participants found Brain a powerfully attractive figure, and allowed themselves to be taken advantage of. That he was married made him seem safe, initially, when he was counselling them to 'explore sexual healing, sexual ethics, how we could be physically and erotically intimate without being lustful, genital or unfaithful to our marriage partners' – something they later bitterly regretted, especially when they began to discover that others were involved as well.

There is a sense in which the Church has always used sex for its own purposes. (The Devil has rarely had the best tunes for long.) The traditional Anglo-Catholic liturgy, for example, with its combination of restraint and display, of men (mainly) performing a powerful rite of profound emotional significance in an impersonal manner, is for many people immensely exciting, sexually. Many evangelical or Baptist Churches which attract young people use sex consciously or unconsciously, but generally in safely controlled circumstances, and in the context of strict teaching on sexual morality (for example, attention to permissible degrees of petting) which in a less charged context would appear absurd. (One interpretation of St Paul's warning women in Corinth to wear veils in church 'for fear of the angels' sees this as a reference not to supernatural beings but to the church leaders!) But in Sheffield, without proper restraints in place, the sexual element ran out of control.

Perhaps the best symbol of the Nine o'Clock Service congregation's fantasies about their priest was the cassock they bought for his ordination. Unable to find a conventional cassock to suit him, they clubbed together and bought the cassock that Jeremy Irons wore in the film *The Mission*, in which he played a heroic Jesuit priest in Latin America fighting the corruption of the established Church. Hollywood has always known of and played on the sexual attractiveness of single clergy. Here, by clothing their priest in the cassock worn by an attractive and sexually charged priest in a popular film played by a handsome male actor, the congregation of the Nine o'Clock Service symbolised the general confusion about sex and religion in the minds and bodies of young people. In their search for a brave new post-modern Christian sexuality, they ended up buying a Hollywood fantasy as old as celluloid, and thus laid themselves open to all manner of sexual abuse.

For another example of popular fantasies about sex and the clergy, we might contrast two popular Australian film productions which also exemplify the two popular stereotypes of the priest – the married, naïve Anglican priest who is sexually maladroit in contrast to the celibate Roman Catholic priest. (It will be a bad day for the film industry if ever the Church of Rome permits its clergy to marry.) *The Thornbirds* featured Richard Chamberlain as an Australian Roman Catholic priest from the outback who discards his vows for a brief fling with a local girl who has a baby by him, and many years later dies in her arms. The extremely sensual and handsome priest provided a sentimental love story with enough suppressed sexual passion to sustain a whole seven-part television series which nearly achieved the highest ratings of anything that season.

By contrast, another film set in Australia, *Sirens* (1994), featured the English actor Hugh Grant as an English clergyman sent out to Australia with his young wife in the 1930s. This film is about his wife's sexual awakening, brought about by her associating with some uninhibited artist's models who help her to discover her body, something her husband is conspicuously unable to achieve. Here is the contrast in popular perception between celibate and married clergy: the one is highly sexual, the latter almost not at all. Even so there is always sex in the air. Again, religion is pressed into service to serve the interests of sex.

It is fantasies such as these which exploit what is at root a genuine relationship between sex and religion. It is almost as if there is an archetype of the sexual priest which the press and Hollywood need to project on to real clergy, leading to frustration when they (inevitably) fail. Possibly, even if the clergy do not have such heightened powers, tabloid treatment of priests represents the general desire that even the staid clergy of the Church of England *should* exhibit some flash of sexual otherness, of the transcendent unknown.

In all this, there is nothing new. In *Montaillou*, his portrait of a French mediaeval village drawn from records deposited with the Inquisition in the fourteenth century, Emmanuel le Roy Ladurie gives us some splendid examples of mediaeval priests who used their position to attract women. For example, Béatrice de Planisoles (a member of the lesser nobility of Ariège in the Pyrenees) has two priest lovers (in between her two husbands). To one of them she says: 'You priests and priors and abbots and bishops and archbishops and cardinals, you are the worst! You commit the sin of the flesh more: and you desire women more than other men do.' And she had reason to know what she was talking about.[4]

Grazide Rives enjoyed her affair with the priest Pierre Clergue and continued (with her husband's knowledge) after they were married. 'And my husband knew about it and was consenting. Sometimes he would ask me, "Has the priest done it with you?" And I would answer "Yes." And my husband would say "As far as the priest is concerned all right! But don't you go having other men."' 'With Pierre Clergue,' she continued, 'I liked it and so it could not displease God. It was not a sin.'[5] The Fournier register which Ladurie quotes from tells of over a dozen authenticated mistresses of Pierre Clergue, but the list is certainly incomplete.[6]

The shepherds in Montaillou saw priests as a sort of equestrian class, who finally bestrode anyone they fancied.[7] Admittedly all this sexual misconduct was committed by heretical priests who were later to be put on trial, and might not have been typical of the orthodox Catholic Church of the day – although it might have. Georges Duby, in his study of the development of marriage in mediaeval France, describes how the Cathar heresy found particular support from 'priests living in concubinage who refused to be forced into celibacy'.[8] There can be little doubt that this chance discovery of what happened in a small French backwater in the early fourteenth century cannot be completely untypical of elsewhere.

We are now in a better position to understand the interest that the popular press have in clergy. Precisely because sex is the religion of the age, the tie-up between sex and official, established religion is almost unbeatable for interest and excitement. Priests have always been sexual figures – even in the Middle Ages. Since priests are also thought to have access to an other world, put the two together and the result is a highly charged cocktail which can stimulate the most jaded appetite.

The lure of the East . . .

In the last analysis Christianity is for most people probably too familiar to bear the weight of such exalted expectations. While one may fantasise about Christian clergy having an advanced knowledge of sexual secrets, or dress them up in fantastical mystico-sexual vestments, sooner or later mundane reality is likely to intrude.

Other people's religions are more liberating because less is known about them, and so more can safely be projected on to them. They can provide all that one longs for in a religion – an escape to the transcendent, a pathway to the unknown – but is prevented by over-familiarity with one's own roots and culture from finding at home. Like the mistress who provided the excitement lacking in many a Victorian marriage, the great Victorian affair with the Orient generated a *frisson* of excitement that persists today. For if oriental religions are closer to the transcendent than the materialistic West, they must also in an age that equates sex and religion have secret access to sexual ecstasy.

The Orient has long been associated with the sensual and erotic. As the Palestinian scholar Edward Said shows in his book *Orientalism*, a ground-breaking attempt to demythologise 'Western conceptions of the Orient', the association dates back at least to the eighteenth century. He tells the story of how, in the Western imagination, the Orient, the 'harems, princesses, princes, slaves, veils, dancing girls and boys, sherbet, ointments',[9] became directly linked to sex. He cites the example of the French novelist Flaubert.

> Woven through all of Flaubert's Oriental experiences, exciting or disappointing, is an almost uniform association between the Orient and sex. In making this association Flaubert was neither the first nor the most exaggerated instance of a remarkably persistent motif in Western attitudes to the Orient ... the Orient seems still to suggest not only fecundity but sexual promise (and threat), untiring sensuality, unlimited desire, deep generative energies.[10]

What is particularly interesting from our point of view is that Said links the West's obsession with the sensual Orient, where every imaginable shade of sexual experience is to be had ('sensuality, promise, terror, sublimity, idyllic pleasure, intense energy'[11]), with, again, the demise of Christianity.

> My thesis is that the essential aspects of modern Orientalist theory and praxis ... can be understood not as a sudden access of objective knowledge about the Orient, but as a set of structures inherited from the past ... which were in turn naturalised, modernised and laicised *substitutes for Christian supernaturalism*.[12]

In other words, 'modern Orientalism derives from *secularising elements* in eighteenth-century European culture'.[13] Even when Orientalism became a respectable academic discipline, it retained 'a reconstructed religious impulse, a naturalised supernaturalism'.[14]

Once more we find a direct link between secularisation and sex. The demise of what Said calls 'Christian supernaturalism' and the progress of secularisation in the West lead to the projection of all that the West has rejected on to a recipient associated particularly with sex. The Orient (in Western imagination) becomes all that the West no longer is: non-material, religious, sensuous, lax and undisciplined. This same attitude persists even today, although it does not equate with any particular Asian location. The current economic boom in the so-called tiger economies of the Pacific Rim shows that the Orient is no less materialistic than the West, and the mystique of oriental sex has now been ruthlessly commercialised in the grotesque sex tourism prevalent in several parts of the Orient, enabling wealthy whites to indulge their stereotypical oriental fantasies at the expense of what appears to be virtually a slave population of girls desperate to escape from grinding poverty.

As Said points out, many of the great explorers, such as Richard Burton, who translated the *Arabian Nights* and the *Kama Sutra*, were fascinated by sex.

> ... the Orient was a place where one could look for sexual experience unobtainable in Europe. Virtually no European writer who wrote on or travelled to the Orient in the period after 1800 exempted himself or herself from this quest: Flaubert, Nerval, 'Dirty Dick' Burton ... Gide, Conrad, Maugham ... What they looked for often – correctly, I think – was a different type of sexuality.[15]

Inevitably, whatever it was that sexual pioneers may have found in the Orient, it rapidly degenerated into falsehood and stereotype.

Nevertheless, the myth is still powerful today. When we are not projecting innocence on to children, chthonic passion on to nature or sanctity on to marriage, we are finding sensual spirituality in the East. For example, Neal's Yard in Covent Garden, London (a fashionable resort for the trendily creative, a self-styled 'travel agent for inner journeys') offers a 'taster' in *Ancient and Modern Secrets of Sexuality with Misha and Zek Halu* ('Misha and Zek studied techniques of sexual transformation with Tibetan and Chinese masters') which will 'enable you to step beyond the usual limits of sexual experience.'

Or you can purchase videos about techniques of oriental sex. For example, a video called *The Love Plan: Sex from the Heart* has its presenter Adam Cole claiming that despite the 'sexual revolution' there is still something missing in contemporary Western attitudes to sex; it is a 'roller-coaster to nowhere', it has 'left a vacuum'. This vacuum, however, is being filled, he claims, by Tantric and Taoist ideas which are surfacing in the West. Thanks to them, we now realise that 'sex is something to celebrate, to hold sacred. Union with your partner means to experience the unity of all things.'[16]

The film recommends turning your bedroom into a temple for lovers by creating an altar filled with things you value – a collection of photos, candles, joss sticks. In sex, apparently, we experience 'the Dance of creation'; through sexual intercourse, we are 'at the leading edge of the energy of creation'.

In other words, the secular West is once again looking over its shoulder to a mystical realm that it locates firmly in the East. The Eastern masters, the Tantrist writers – these can be your guides to enlightenment through sex. You too can experience the mysteries of the Orient – and, thanks to your video player, in your own front room (no need to experience the hardships of the overland route to India to achieve enlightenment).

There is, admittedly, an element of truth in the claim that some Eastern religions were not afraid to employ sex as a means to finding God in ways that the Christian tradition has always shunned (though whether what a Buddhist means by 'God' is in any sense related to what a Westerner might mean by that word is a moot point). In Tibetan Buddhism, for example, there is a great deal to do with sex as an avenue of mysticism, a source of spirituality. David Snellgrove, in his book *Indo-Tibetan Buddhism*, quotes from a particular set of instructions from a late tantric initiation rite:

The master gives the right hand of the Wisdom-maiden into the left hand of his pupil addressing him thus: 'You must take her; the Buddha declares her suitable in excellence. Experience the Holy Bliss.'

Then the Wisdom-maiden speaks.

'Boy! Can you eat my faeces and urine, blood and semen and human flesh? Such is the vow with women. Can you suck the lotus of my pudenda? Speak, boy, how is it?'

The novice replies:

'O Goddess! How shall I not? I can eat blood and semen and all. I will always perform this vow with women, and your pudenda too I shall suck.'

The girl replies:

'My open lotus is the resort of all bliss, hurrah! You who take possession of her, use the lotus as should be!' Then the pupil kisses the lotus and unites in her embrace.[17]

However, in this rite, coitus is not consummated:

As the boddhicitta descends, he [the initiate] should hold it as instructed, and the knowledge that he experiences is the consecration of the Knowledge of Wisdom ... He unites in embrace, performs coitus, and as the great bliss descends to the place of knowledge, he reverses it upwards to the level of non-cognition, holding it there.

In other words, enlightenment has nothing to do with perfecting one's orgasm and a great deal to do with control and abstinence. The perfected yogin uses passion to learn the secret of the *absence* of passion. Bliss is part of a whole metaphysical system (tantra) to do with controlling the passions of which it is difficult to take any one element in isolation.

And in any case, it is hotly disputed as to whether this tantric rite was actually performed. Apparently present-day lamas consider that texts such as these are purely symbolic, and were never intended actually to be enacted, while Western scholars consider it more likely that they were put into practice. But the point is that this world of Tibetan Buddhism is light-years away from the cultural world and structures of thought of the West. For example,

> Every *tantra* ['means of gaining enlightenment', 'set of spells'] has its presiding divinity with his or her particular entourage arranged on a mandala. There are a great variety, but the same function: a means of integration of the religious practitioner with the chosen divinity.[18]

It is in passages like this that one has the sense of looking into another world, not only because Tibetan Buddhism is so far removed from Western ways of thinking, but also because, like so much ancient spiritual writing on sex, both Eastern and Western, it is based on incorrect biology. As Geoffrey Parrinder explains in his book *Sex in the World's Religions*,

> Ancient Western notions were based upon Greek philosophy and medicine, which had no knowledge of the process of conception, and it was thought that the embryo was made from a mixture of semen and menstrual blood. Until the sixteenth century, male semen was thought to be 'almost human'.[19]

This was not only a Western misapprehension. In China, it was believed that male semen was strictly limited. Thus, 'every emission of semen was thought to diminish a man's Yang, which could only be compensated for by the man's gaining an equivalent amount of Yin' (vaginal secretion, considered to be unlimited and absorbed by the male during intercourse) from the woman. This, Professor Parrinder implies, made for good sex even if bad biology, but also had the consequence of encouraging *coitus reservatus*:

Ejaculation was often prevented either by mental discipline or physical pressure, and the Yang fortified by the Yin was thought to flow up the spinal column to strengthen the brain and the whole body and personality. A similar belief was held by Indian Yoga, which may have derived it from China

– something also exemplified by the tantric rite described above.

Janie Gustafson finds evidence that a similar philosophy lay behind courtly love in the early Middle Ages:

Prolonged coital union was indeed present in these relationships, but if historians are correct on this matter, it was coitus without orgasm.[20]

while Jack Dominian also traces the influence of incorrect biology upon the Roman Catholic Church's teaching:

The Roman Catholic Church's view on contraception requires that every act of sexual intercourse should allow the unfettered deposition of semen in the vagina with no interference to the procreative potential of sperm and ovum. At this level it is pure biology and must be assessed as such. Such a view is a throwback to the ignorance of sexual physiology when the sperm was considered to be the [sole] agent of fertilisation.[21]

So, he argues, since the ovum is only fertile (i.e. 'potentially procreative') for twenty-four hours a month, clearly nature intended sexual intercourse to be largely non-procreative.

Such views were held even in the last century. The historian Peter Gay recounts a splendid (probably apocryphal) story told of the French novelist Balzac. 'Eager to conserve his resources, Balzac would generally practice coitus reservatus with his mistresses. But once, carried away by the ardor of his sexual partner, he allowed himself to reach orgasm, only to comment afterwards, ruefully: "Well, there goes another book!"'[22]

The pre-modern world is certainly a strange country, and the world of Tibetan Buddhism even stranger. It seems unlikely that there is any sense in which a Westerner can enter this thought-world without years of study and acculturation, nor any guarantee that the same time and energy invested in Western religious traditions might not yield the same results. And yet clearly its strangeness is its attraction, as is the notion that sex can be a vehicle for enlightenment. The extraordinary thing is that perfectly sane, rational and otherwise level-headed people, who have 'seen through' Christianity or Judaism and have problems with belief in God and certainly do not go to church for any but rites of passage, find Oriental spirituality immensely attractive, partly because it is more explicit about sex.

Sexual epiphanies

It is easy to mock other people's beliefs without making any attempt to understand what it is that makes them important. Controlling the emission of semen because it is believed to be the sole agent of generation and therefore sacred may be bad biology but it does say something about the sanctity of life. Similarly, seeing priests as charged sexual beings may be absurd, but let us be a little romantic and try to follow through the symbolic importance of this general yearning in the West for some link between sex and religion, and specifically try to discover the particular associations of priesthood which give rise to erotic fantasy.

Ever since Byron, the archetype of the priest has been generally that of someone who wrestles with the void, one who has encountered the demonic, shadow side of existence. He (and mythologically this priest is always a 'he') is someone who has looked on violence and come to terms with it. He is a person for whom the sugar coating of easy religious experience long ago yielded to an anguished and lonely exploration of the dark and dangerous territory where known ways fail. The mysteries of death, violence and suffering are his speciality, the desert (whether literally or the urban deserts of the back streets) his habitat. His celibacy is thus only a part of a life that has been disciplined, its energy channelled into an encounter with the unknown.

Now add sex to the equation. By viewing such a Romantic figure in a sexual light – by wishing that one's actual flesh-and-blood clergy were a little more like their Romantic archetype – one is giving expression to the desire that there should be more to sex, and therefore to life, than simple orgasmic pleasure. Paul Ricoeur has a splendid phrase: 'sexuality is the flotsam of a submerged Atlantis'. In other words, the whole rich, symbolic culture of myth, folk tale and religion of the pre-modern world has now been drowned out. Even so, people still use sex as a reminder of the once-religious world of the pre-affluent society of peasant culture from which we are now alienated as if from a mediaeval village beneath a reservoir. Curiously, priests are one of the few classes of people in our present society who retain something of the symbolic value of this vanished world. The symbolism of the priest is passing into oblivion almost (but not quite) as fast as that of those other great fairy-tale characters, kings and queens. But even so, priests retain something of that antique resonance of an ancient world. This is another reason why the combination of priests and sex is so powerful. Together, they are the flotsam of a lost world.

This may seem mere sentimental nostalgia, and so in a sense it is. But there is another aspect of sex which is indicated by our fascination with *celibate* clergy. As Ricoeur puts it, there is a sense in which sexuality does not fit in well with the rest of society. 'Eros is not institutional; one offends by reducing it to a contract.'[23] This sense that sex has something of the untamed about it is, as we saw in Chapter 2, an ancient one in civilisation. Sex cannot easily be domesticated or brought to heel. There is ultimately no 'safe sex.' But you can renounce it. The myth of the celibate priest is an archaic reminder that sex is like God – you cannot negotiate with it. It is ultimately all or nothing. Ricoeur continues: '. . . thus by its very essence it must threaten the institution with the demonic – any institution, including marriage.' Priests, of course, are experts at the demonic; they have wrestled long and hard with the demons of the void. Hence it would be natural to associate the myth of the priest with perhaps the only area in most people's lives where they sense themselves to be potentially open to the demonic – that of the enigma of sex, something greater than themselves and potentially able to tear their lives apart. If this is the case, allying it with a figure that is as near to being supernatural as our cramped imaginations will allow is a gesture of yearning that sex, at least, be allowed to keep its mythic dimension in a post-modern world without foundations.

A similar point is made by the doyen of comparative folklore studies, Mircea Eliade, who, in his book *Images and Symbols*, pours scorn on Freud for taking sex too literally.

> In fact the brutality of [Freud's] language arises from a misunderstanding: it is not the sexuality in itself that is annoying, it is the ideology that Freud built upon his 'pure sexuality'. Fascinated by his mission – he believed himself to be the first Awakened One, whereas he was only the last of the Positivists – Freud could not bring himself to see that sexuality has never been 'pure', that everywhere it is a polyvalent function whose primary and perhaps supreme valency is the *cosmological function*: so that to translate a psychic situation into sexual terms is by no means to belittle it; for, except in the modern world, *sexuality has everywhere and always been a hierophany*.[24]

This may seem at first rather dense, but means more or less that, as a result of his studies of comparative folk literature from all over the world, Eliade believed that sex always had the kind of profound, mythological resonance that I have been trying to describe. Sex in folklore is *polyvalent* – has many meanings and can never be pinned down; it is always associated with *hierophany* – with the revealing of the sacred. Always, that is, 'except in the modern world'. But even in the modern world, I would suggest, there is still a residue of more primitive attitudes and expectations about sex. Much of this is pure fantasy and escapism – but there is also a very serious aspect which connects with the essence of our humanity.

Jack Dominian, too, sees a genuine religious dimension in sex.

He too is anxious that since sex today is mainly non-procreative – i.e. not about having children – it is constantly in danger of becoming devalued, of 'falling into insignificance', as Ricoeur puts it, because it is relatively easily available and relatively safe. He is very critical of the Churches (especially of his own Roman Catholic Church) for not trying to counter this by giving a more realistic and biologically accurate value to sex. For example, he suggests that sex is unique in being able to maintain what (for him) is the fundamental unit of society – the man-woman relationship – by enabling a couple to give themselves totally to each other in 'mutual surrender'; sex creates meaning for the couple. (Creating meaning can be a religious function.) Alternatively, he suggests, coitus can give one personal affirmation 'of immense proportion'.[25] This is clearly a religious statement. By 'immense' he is, I suspect, straining towards 'divine'.

Real sex

Finally, to return to our mythological priests, those who alone have access to the white peaks of the old dispensations, they are clearly more fictional than real. Real clergy are much more mundane, distracted by dozens of diverse calls on their time and energy. Today, in practice, clergy are more likely to regard themselves as rather broken people, who, precisely by virtue of their brokenness, are able to bring healing to others. They would see themselves not as lofty mountaineers, but as lowly geologists, used to exploring the scarred surface of the human psyche. However, just as springs of water warmed on the rocks of the earth's core can bubble up through geological faults, and sometimes turn out to have healing properties, so a damaged or broken sexuality in real life can be the fault-line that allows the mystery of life to reveal itself and potentially to bring a sort of healing to those who share it.

There is, too, a perfectly realistic sense in which through sex the boundless can be opened and explored. This has always been known and often used by the Western tradition. For example, the authors of the Hebrew Bible (the Old Testament) were never afraid to use sex to describe their dealings with God. One might take the *Song of Songs*, a series of love-poems:

> *How beautiful you are, how charming,*
> *My love, my delight!*
> *In stature like the palm tree,*
> *its fruit-clusters your breasts.*
> *I have decided, 'I shall climb the palm tree,*
> *I shall seize its clusters of dates!'*
> *May your breasts be clusters of grapes*
> *your breath sweet-scented as apples,*
> *and your palate like sweet wine.*[26]

These poems have been interpreted by pious souls as a love-song between God and the soul; the sixteenth-century Spanish mystic St John of the Cross, for example, wrote a beautiful series of poems paraphrasing the *Song of Songs* explicitly entitled: *Songs of the soul in rapture at having arrived at the height of perfection, which is union with God by the road of spiritual negation*:

> *On a dark night, with the flame of desire burning within me,*
> *I went secretly to my beloved's house.*
>
> *I ran through the darkness, opened my lover's door, and*
>   *climbed the stairs,*
> *Up to his room, my heart ablaze with desire . . .*[27]

However, as Robert Bates comments in his book *Sacred Sex*, it is just as likely that the poems of the *Song of Songs* were a celebration of the divine potential of sexual intercourse. 'It was a celebration of sexual passion, and its place within the canon of Scripture was asserted in the conviction that passion between a man and a woman in love is the supreme divine gift.'[28]

A very different example of the Bible's use of sex can be found in the language of the Old Testament prophets, the equivalent of the newspaper leader-writers or television satirists of their day, who did not hesitate to use sexual relations in order to shock people into an understanding of God's judgment. Some of these passages are among the most vital and vibrant religious literature ever written, as the prophets' vitriolic abuse lambasts their victims.

For example, when the prophet Ezekiel wishes to condemn the government of Judah (modern-day Israel) for flirting with the two superpowers of the day, Egypt and Babylon, he compares Judah to a prostitute called Oholibah. (The prophet assumes the persona of her God.)

> The Babylonians came to her, shared her love-bed and defiled her with their whoring. Once defiled by them, she withdrew her affection from them. Thus she flaunted her whoring, exposing her body, until I withdrew my affection from her ... But she began whoring worse than ever, remembering her girlhood, when she had played the whore in Egypt, when she had been in love with their profligates, big-membered as donkeys, ejaculating as violently as stallions.
>
> You were hankering for the debauchery of your girlhood, when they used to handle your nipples in Egypt and fondle your young breasts. And so, Oholibah, the Lord God says this, 'I shall set all your lovers against you from whom you have withdrawn your affection, and bring them to assault you from all directions: the Babylonians and all the Chaldaeans, the men of Pekod and Shoa and Koa, and all the Assyrians with them, young and desirable ... I shall direct my jealousy against you; they will treat you with fury; they will cut off your nose and ears, and what is left of your family will fall by the sword. They will strip off your garments and rob you of your jewels ... They will treat you with hatred, they will rob you of the entire fruit of your labours and leave you stark naked.'[29]

And in all this, Ezekiel is making a valid political point about Judah not getting ideas above her station and playing power politics with larger nations, the consequences of which she will not be able to control. His language rivals any political satire available today. None of our archbishops ever had the courage to attribute a previous prime minister's infatuation with the people of the United States to their being 'big-membered as donkeys, ejaculating as violently as stallions'.

But it is one thing to use sexual language to make a political point or to express one's love for God; another to use it as a mysticism substitute, a pseudo-spirituality that actually inhibits relationships with real people.

And yet perhaps this is too harsh. It is a well-documented fact of human life that everyone, even the most level-headed, does occasionally, if the moment is propitious or the crisis acute and the concern deep, experience an intuition of another world, of an extension of the human spirit. The Christianity of one's school and childhood may seem altogether too earthbound, too blighted by its dualistic structures, to do justice to such an epiphany (to employ another current buzz-word). And yet, as noted at the beginning of this chapter, the Church is beginning to develop considerable expertise in assisting people to understand their inner life – including, at last, their sex life.

Sex and religion: two strange but related species roaming the same veldt? Or two of the welter of 'lazy universals' with which the human mind, at moments of weakness, tends to assimilate anything that cannot be easily understood?[30] The next chapter may shed further light upon this ancient dilemma.

6

Painted Flesh
Sex and the Fine Art Tradition

Art and sex have always been bedfellows. From the earliest fertility goddesses through to the most luxuriant Victorian oil painting, from Exekias to Etty, from Michelangelo to Picasso, one can sense the charge of human sexuality informing, electrifying the artist's vision and stirring the interest of the viewer – whether it is directly expressed through pictures of the human body, clothed or unclothed, or indirectly through rolling landscapes or still lifes of fruit bursting with vegetable fecundity.

It cannot be denied that one enjoys the majority of painting and sculpture primarily through the eyes, through the embodied sensation of looking, rather than through the brain and intellectual processes. The initial appreciation of a work of art – one's immediate 'gut feeling' about it – is always somatic, something that is ultimately always even if indirectly related to touch, taste and feel. A baby learns about the world of objects by putting them in his or her mouth, and the instinct of sucking objects to get the feel of them never leaves us, even if only in the abstract. In a sense, looking at works of art is a sort of abstract touching (or even sucking). And if the body is important in relating to art, sexuality, that extreme form of being embodied, is never truly absent.

This applies not only to lush and sensual oil painting. Even the driest painting imaginable may have some sort of erotic charge. Take, for example, Piet Mondrian (1872–1944), the Dutch painter whose most famous works are rigid black grids of irregularly parallel horizontal and vertical straight lines, with some of the resulting squares filled in with primary colours. They are synonymous with all that is most restrained, unemotional and intellectual in art. On the surface, there is not a shred of emotion or sexuality in his work. Yet the historian Peter Gay in his book *Art and Act*, shows how Mondrian's grids were the result of powerful sexual repression. He sees Mondrian as dominated by a strict and moral father, and sublimating through his art a sexuality that would otherwise have been intolerable. His grids are an iron mask; behind them hides the great painter's damaged sexuality.

> Had he been anyone else, he would have been just another fussy bachelor, starting affairs he could not consummate, driven back into himself by his awe of female superiority, staring at the provocative nudes that cater to such tastes ... but fortunately for himself and for art he was Mondrian, an artist who could transform his neurosis into painting.[1]

Thus, like the celibate priest who has renounced sex and yet remains a highly sexual figure, Mondrian's works are powerfully charged compositions, sexually.

Even abstract oil paintings without any obvious subject-matter are often clearly sensuous if not actually sensual. As Willem de Kooning (another well-known Dutch painter who, like Mondrian, emigrated to New York) famously commented, oil paint was invented precisely to portray human flesh. His own paintings, even the most abstract, are highly charged and sensual.

I began this chapter by implying a dichotomy between mind and body. In the West there is a long history of pitting mind against body, reason against emotion, art against science. Yet all through the twentieth century voices have been raised to suggest that this distinction is actually largely mythical. For example, as early as 1905, in his second essay on sexuality, Freud comments how thinking can be sexually stimulating:

Finally, it is an unmistakable fact that concentration of the attention upon an intellectual task and intellectual strain in general produce a concomitant sexual excitation in many young people as well as adults. This is no doubt the only justifiable basis for what is in other respects the questionable practice of ascribing nervous disorders to intellectual 'overwork'.[2]

while the American theologian Paula Cooey reports in her book *Religious Imagination and the Body: A Feminist Analysis* that empirical studies by R.B. Zajonc and others have revealed that 'whereas thought does not always accompany feeling, *feeling always accompanies thought*'.[3] In other words, thoughts do not exist neutrally in the mind, but rather all thinking has feelings bound up with it. If this is true, and we do respond even to abstract thoughts somatically, then even the most dry and cerebral art is certainly as much about the body – and therefore eventually sex, the body's richest expression – as the mind. In art, mind and body are more like two ends of a spectrum than completely different entities.

There is a sense, as Camille Paglia points out, in which art and religion in the West have always been bitter enemies. Parallel to the split between mind and body, the antagonism between Apollo and Dionysus, Christian and pagan, cerebral and visual, runs all through European history. She spices up her argument (and gains herself thereby the unrelenting hostility of all conservative feminists) by identifying this split with male and female[4] – a claim we shall evaluate in the last chapters of this book. Perhaps, however, that old enmity between mind and body, as we shall see at the end of this chapter, may soon be laid to rest.

Be that as it may, for the purposes of this chapter I shall take for granted the close association between the visual arts and sexuality, and concentrate rather on the relationship between art and spirituality. In this, I shall concentrate mainly on the visual arts, although the same argument would certainly apply to the other arts – film, drama, literature – and especially to music, the most somatic of all the arts, whose relationship to bodily states such as dance, excitement, sorrow, anger, meditation and passion has been commented on since Socrates. I am aware that this premise is not uncontentious, but it would take a whole book to do proper justice to it. And it is in the arts, *par excellence*, that we find religion, sex and spirituality all heaped together as nowhere else: it is the perfect example of the thesis of this chapter.

As the ecclesiastical channels for religious energy began to silt up in the nineteenth century, so religious fervour was poured instead into the arts. The arts quite clearly became a religion substitute. As early as 1805, Goethe had proclaimed that artists were the new priests. Now, in the second half of the nineteenth century, we find the Victorians increasingly diverting their fast-secularising religious instincts into art – and especially sex in art.

All the usual factors were at play – increasing wealth, education and leisure, not to mention the arrival of the railways, which permitted access to aristocratic country homes for all. The newly affluent bourgeoisie were able to visit the homes and borrow the clothes and habits of the aristocracy, which, along with such practices as getting married in church and having Arcadian children included purchasing 'high' art, that is, art which could provide moral uplift or else which could offer the spice of mild sexual transgression. And a combination of these two, as for example in a rich oil painting of the (naked) *Penitent Magdalene*, was, as artists such as William Etty discovered, unbeatable. Initially, religious or mythological subject matter made sex safe, but it was only a matter of time before the sex came to replace the religion. Thus art rapidly became spirituality. But, ironically, as we shall see in the last part of this chapter, today this sort of high art has been just as effectively secularised and 'democratised' as was religion in the Victorian period.

Art steps in

The history of how art became a religion substitute is long and complicated. It would be impossible to do justice to it in a few paragraphs and so I shall content myself with sketching the merest outline.

During the Middle Ages, art was almost entirely under the control of the establishment. Art was the handmaid of the Church. Paintings were commissioned either by the Church or by a few aristocratic private patrons. A cursory inspection of any collection of mediaeval art reveals large numbers of religious paintings and only a few non-religious subjects. These religious paintings would have been largely intended for *use* in church or convent, for example as altar pieces.

Once the old mediaeval feudal economic system had declined, and as trade and money began to circulate and individual nation-states to crystallise out, especially in Protestant Europe, an art market rapidly emerged, especially in places such as Amsterdam. Paintings came to be within the financial means of the new merchant classes – as exemplified by the endless Dutch 'genre' scenes of everyday life.

Here, religious art was still important, but not for churches. Bare, whitewashed Dutch churches had no need of religious art, and in any case there was an absolute ban on paintings in church in Calvinist Holland ('Let not God's majesty be debased through untimely representation,' said Calvin). Even the idea would have been appalling; religious art was associated with the dark mists of mediaeval Roman Catholicism which the light of science in enlightened Holland was busy piercing and dispelling. Religious art was for the home, and intended to be moralistic, like a good sermon, to inspire its viewers to better living. So that whereas traditional religious art was always related to an environment of worship or liturgy, religious paintings by, for example, Rembrandt would have been commissioned by a religious patron but for display in his home or a secular public building. This in itself was already a clear sign of secularisation – of the privatisation of public religious symbols and the domestication of the great religious themes.

Rembrandt (1606–69) is a good example. He was a deeply religious man who had a great devotion to the Bible and knew it backwards. He painted more religious works than any other type

(850 known religious works as against 500 portraits, the next most common category). However, his religious subject matter never included the dogmatic, mystical or overtly sacramental paintings beloved of the Counter-Reformation artists at work in Catholic Europe. His well-known *Belshazzar's Feast* in the National Gallery, London, is a magnificent picture whose opulence – it is rich with emotion, flesh, fine dresses, drama – was probably intended for a dining room, for the edification of the diners. The Book of Daniel relates how King Belshazzar, King of Babylon, gave a feast for a thousand of his noblemen, his wives and the women who sang for him, and drank from the gold and silver vessels looted from the Jewish temple at Jerusalem. As he did so, the fingers of a hand appeared and began to write on the plaster of the palace wall. The message of doom perplexed the king's consultants, but was at last correctly interpreted by the young Jew, Daniel. Belshazzar died the same night, as Daniel had predicted. Rembrandt's dramatic painting magnificently depicts the crucial scene of fingers writing on the wall. And yet this great religious drama was probably used to illustrate a trivial moral about gluttony: those who gratify their craving for pleasure invite God's wrath (a common theme in Dutch art).

Although Rembrandt was himself deeply religious, and painted religious themes, already the two aspects of secularisation noted above can be seen at work in this picture. The more trivial is the domestication, the making safe, of religious experience by debasing it into moralism. The other, more profound, is the search for personal, human and this-worldly equivalents for religious experience. Rembrandt was particularly interested in subject matter that showed human beings encountering the divine, especially moments of recognition or conviction. In this case, the magnificent Belshazzar is seen at the very moment at which he becomes aware of his fate. The enduring popularity and fascination of Rembrandt's art are undoubtedly due to the depth of his humanity and his appeal to the widest ranges of *human* experience. He is often compared, in this respect, to another great seculariser, his older contemporary, William Shakespeare (1546–1616). (Even Van Gogh makes the comparison.)[5] Rembrandt's attempts to try to understand biblical teaching in human, psychological terms parallel those of his contemporaries such as Descartes who were trying to understand the universe in a purely intellectual way. For Rembrandt, the excitement of this new psychological realism was more important than traditional aesthetic criteria such as harmony or beauty. In this case, Belshazzar is not strikingly handsome by any stretch of the imagination – and the girl behind him is a plain rather than idealised beauty. The writing was on the wall for conventional, other-worldly religious art and belief.

A further stage in the process of secularisation is exemplified by another Dutch painter, Jan Vermeer (1632–75), an artistic genius who was able to transform mundane genre scenes into miracles of intensity. A generation later than Rembrandt, he exhibits none of Rembrandt's passion but rather an extraordinary precision in the painting of texture, colour and form. The effect of the light always so evident in Vermeer's works is to create a lifting of the spirit – especially when the light falls on ordinary objects and gives them a strangely meditative quality. Kenneth Clark, a great admirer of Vermeer, saw in his paintings what he called 'almost a spiritualisation of matter': although, he suggests, Vermeer probably used the technology of the *camera obscura* in order to achieve his perspective and composition, 'yet the scientific approach to experience ends in poetry ... an almost mystical rapture in the perception of light. How else to account for the joy we feel when we look at the pewter jugs and white pots in Vermeer's pictures?'[6] Here we have an almost mystical rapture found in everyday, secular things. Art conveys the spiritual, at least in his eyes.

In the eighteenth century the process of secularisation continued with art achieving an increasingly autonomous status. In England, for example, the Grand Tour of Europe fashionable among the children of the aristocracy brought them into contact with classical European painting, much of which, sacred and secular without distinction, was shipped home to grace their country seats. At the end of the century, a new, quasi-religious element was injected into art, as the light and reason of the eighteenth century became sluggish, and the sublime made its appearance. The 'sublime'

137

(literally sub-limes, 'beneath the threshold') became a technical term in the eighteenth century for a certain genre of painting which dealt with experiences of the transcendent (as opposed to the beautiful). Burke defined it as 'tranquillity tinged with terror', associated with 'greatness of dimensions' as well as a sense of fusion with the environment. Now one might find another experience that had always to date been associated explicitly with religion – that of awe – appropriated by secular art and applied to landscapes, at first of the Alps and later back home in England. And even in reactionary Spain, Goya injected a welcome note of hell into all that eighteenth-century sweetness and light with pictures of the appalling human consequences of war.

It is in the Victorian period, however, that art finally achieves its greatest glories as a secular credo, bought and sold in large quantities in a secular temple. Graham Howes, reader in sociology at Trinity Hall, Cambridge, has done considerable research into the role of fine art during the Victorian period as an indicator of religious attitudes, looking especially at the function of the annual Royal Academy summer exhibition. This immensely prestigious exhibition which attracted (and continues to attract) great crowds of visitors every year was one of the most important sources of sale for contemporary painting and sculpture. Howes has performed a fascinating analysis of the purchasers of pictures of different categories of subject.[7]

There was a strict hierarchy of pictures at the summer exhibition, from 'popular' to 'high': genre scenes and 'scenes domestic' through portraits, landscapes, 'subjects poetic and imaginative' to 'high art, sacred and secular'. Religious art was the highest of all. One remarkable finding is that at the very time when Victorian secularisation was reckoned to have accelerated to its peak, the period from 1865 to 1875, there was a boom in the exhibition and purchase of religious painting at the Royal Academy. In 1841, only six out of the 381 paintings exhibited were of religious subjects, and three were sold. In 1871, twenty-two of the 401 paintings exhibited had religious subjects, and of these twenty were sold. (The figures for other years show a similar trend.)[8]

Howes puts forward a number of suggestions to explain this apparent anomaly, which demonstrate the rapidly changing pattern of religious belief in the Victorian era. For example, the growth of a nostalgic mediaevalism in the architecture of Pugin and the liturgy of the Oxford Movement which spread to parish churches all across the country indicated not just increased tolerance of Roman Catholics (and increased tolerance is always a sign that the cause of the intolerance – in this case, the Church of England – no longer matters) but also a sense that religion was no longer compatible with modern life. The new engravings industry meant that cheap reproductions of religious imagery could now be mass-produced and the break between image and ecclesiastical context was now final. Everyone could have a Rembrandt in their front room. Also, Howes suggests, a more 'scientific' attitude to the life of Jesus meant that religious paintings tended to be better researched, with plenty of local colour and often with copious historical or topographical notes; artists were less concerned with myth and more with verisimilitude. Again, this is a sign of the distinctively religious element being abandoned for a more strictly this-worldly one. Very soon, the *National Geographic* magazine would bring us pictures of the Holy Land and see no need to include the figure of Jesus at all.

Howes also suggests that there was a growing tendency towards mannerism at the end of the century, and the increasingly hysterical character of some religious painting (for example, Solomon's *Beheading of John the Baptist* features Salome as a *femme fatale* screaming for vengeance) was both eye-catching and probably true religious painting's last gasp. Most importantly, however, from our point of view, is the change in the patronage base that he records towards the 'multiplication of middling fortunes in this country'. Art sales followed the new money towards the north of England, where town halls would purchase religious art to articulate their secular social status, while many of the individuals who purchased religious art for themselves 'were religious non-conformists of one hue or another'; for them, these works would have been partly indications of social status but also 'there are hints, from the primary sources, that such paintings may have functioned in providing (in a fashion analogous to the sexual double standards revealed by Steven Marcus in *The Other Victorians*) a private, potent and culturally approved set of religious sensations which the sobriety and sensory deprivation of chapel culture officially denied them'.

Howes draws a graphic picture of a Methodist factory owner from Bradford surreptitiously caressing the feet of a naked and busty *Penitent Magdalene* by William Etty after chapel while sipping an illicit sherry before Sunday lunch.[9] Religious art was deliciously transgressive, partly because religious art was – except the most sober – forbidden, and partly because, in the case of so many Victorian paintings, it was associated with sex. The prohibition against sexual pleasure was symmetrical with the prohibition against religious art.

For the less inhibited, religious art was still a very safe way to enjoy sensuality. Peter Gay, in *The Bourgeois Experience*, demonstrates how what he calls 'the doctrine of distance' permitted the Victorians to enjoy naked bodies if they were mythological or religious in character. 'The doctrine of distance was a mechanism for licensing what was impermissible under ordinary circumstances.'[10] He cites as a classic example Clésinger's *Woman Bitten by a Snake* modelled on the body of Baudelaire's beloved Mme Sabatier whom we will meet again in Chapter 7, where the tiny snake, added as an afterthought (presumably a reference to the episode in Numbers 21 wherein the children of Israel are attacked by serpents in the wilderness), 'was designed to supply the kind of scanty cover that the doctrine of distance required'.[11] Christianity is clearly being assimilated to other mythologies as an excuse for enjoying sensual art without guilt. William Etty (a pious Methodist who converted to Roman Catholicism) justified painting voluptuous nudes by claiming that naked women reflected the glory of God. But it was only a matter of time before people would take the nude and leave the glory, finding all the religion and the glory they needed in art, especially in so sanctified an establishment (in both senses of the word) as the Royal Academy, like the Science Museum a great Victorian cathedral – and both of them hosts in their own peculiar ways to a secular spirituality.

Vincent Van Gogh

But art as religion substitute was not only the province of prospering industrialists, who could transfer their allegiance from religion to art as prosperity overtook them. Those from the poorest backgrounds might also aspire to the same thing – to finding salvation in highly sensual art, or even offering a new, universal, secular salvation to others through their painting.

The best-known example is probably Vincent Van Gogh (1853–90), the artist who died in poverty without selling a single painting, and whose works are now among the most valuable in the world. In fact, contrary to popular opinion, Van Gogh was not a nobody from the backwoods, nor a predestined outcast.[12] He had two uncles who were generals in the Dutch army and a third who attained the highest rank in the navy. Other uncles made good money as reputable art dealers. Family expectations were high. Van Gogh's father was a Calvinist minister in Brabant, a poor, mainly Roman Catholic, part of Holland.

Van Gogh was destined, like his uncles (and younger brother Theo), for the art business. For this purpose he was attached to the family firm of his uncle, Goupil & Co., first in the Hague and then in London. While in London, he fell in love with his landlady's daughter, Ursula Loyer, who turned out to be already engaged to someone else. Thus began a pattern that repeated itself many times throughout his life: passionate love for a woman who would reject him. After this setback in love (though not necessarily because of it) his work declined and he was eventually sacked.

On his arrival in London, Van Gogh would certainly have visited the Royal Academy summer exhibition. At an exhibition in the Barbican Centre, London, in 1992 which focused on Van Gogh in England, the designers reconstructed one wall of a putative Royal Academy summer exhibition of the mid-1870s: an alcove was clothed in deep Victorian red, and hung with two dozen assorted Victorian works of art, all beautifully finished, nicely framed and extremely sentimental. Each of them contained enough material for a full forty-five-minute Victorian sermon. The exhibition was a useful reminder of the role of art in the nineteenth century – and of why twentieth-century art was necessary. It also explains how the young Van Gogh developed what would now be termed appalling taste.

However, the artistic side of Vincent's nature was to lie dormant for many years. He had always been deeply religious. Even when in England, he had preached a now-famous sermon on 5 November, 1876, at Richmond Methodist Church, of which the text survives in a letter to his brother Theo ('The end of this life is what we call death. It is an hour in which words are spoken things are seen and felt that are kept in the secret chambers of the hearts of those who stand by . . .'), while teaching at a private school run by Mr Jones, a Methodist minister in Isleworth. (His failure in the art world had led to his wishing to become a teacher.) Back in Holland for Christmas 1876, he decided to train for the ministry like his father.

His lack of qualifications was a problem, and Van Gogh moved to Amsterdam to study for the university entrance exam to gain entry to theological college. He was not a good academic, and after fifteen months he gave up his studies and entered a Bible college in Brussels (surviving there only three months), accusing the university of being a 'breeding place of Pharisaism' (an epithet he later reserved for art dealers). The story goes that, asked by his teacher 'Is this dative or ablative?', Van Gogh replied, 'I don't really care, sir.'[13] He just wanted to get out and help people.

Finally he had his chance. He was sent to the Borinage, a poor mining area in South Belgium, where he identified with the exploited miners to such an extent, going without food and sleeping rough, that the Belgian Committee for Evangelisation felt that he was no longer a fit person to represent them and did not renew his licence. However, he stayed on for a year, doing practical first aid, caring for the sick and bereaved.

In July 1880, he hit upon a vocation that satisfied his revolutionary instincts, his desire to identify with the poor and downtrodden, and his particular talent: he would become a peasant painter, after the model of his hero Millet. He immediately began to draw miners, and, later, on his return home (April 1881), the peasants who scraped an existence off the infertile plains near Nuenen (near Eindhoven) where his father had now been sent.

In eight years, this rather elderly art student (Van Gogh was now twenty-seven) assimilated with extraordinary speed everything the contemporary art world had to teach him, in both Holland and Paris, in the process producing masterpieces such as *The Potato Eaters*, as unsentimental a picture of peasant life as has been painted. Art historians have often identified this as a secular version of a well-known religious subject: the supper at Emmaus. In February 1888, he left Paris (much to the relief of his brother Theo, with whom he had been lodging) for Arles in southern France where in only a year he painted most of the pictures for which he is now famous. This period ended with the famous 'attack' that led to his rushing at the painter Gauguin, his housemate, with a razor and then cutting off part of his own ear and presenting it to a local prostitute called Rachel. The final few months of his life see him moving from an asylum at St Remy nearby to the one in Auvers, north of Paris, where he ended his life.

In the life of this one artist, we can see reflected the process that was taking place in a less dramatic way across the whole of Europe. Van Gogh was on any count a deeply religious man. His letters give us virtually unparalleled insight into the soul of a warm-hearted, passionate and deeply committed human being, desperate for love, rejected at every turn (often his own doing). One can trace how his early religious longings gradually give way to devotion to paint. He became one of the pioneers of our European secular spirituality, a somatic spirituality of the eyes and the body. And he did this quite consciously.

A brief survey of what Van Gogh says of two of his best-known paintings bears this out. *The Night Café* is a secular depiction of Hell, in which Van Gogh famously uses red and green to paint 'the terrible passions of humanity'.[14] A red room with ghostly yellow floor and lights has a great billiard table in the centre. Around the edge of the room are smaller tables with glasses and five lonely-looking inmates. On the table a phallic billiard cue leads the eye from three balls towards what Van Gogh describes as 'the tender Louis XV green of the counter on which is a pink nosegay';

behind this, there is an opening that presumably leads out to the brothel.

Gauguin also painted a picture of this same *assommoir* while staying with Van Gogh, which makes it quite clear that Van Gogh misrepresented it. His isolated figures are actually the expression of his own feelings, as are the colours he uses. The picture is as good a painting of Hell as any ostensibly religious one.

A completely different picture is that of the *Starry Night*. When Van Gogh eventually rejected God (although not Christ) he was ruthless in his criticism of the Church. 'The religion of the respectable, what a madhouse they have made of the world.'[15] He was suspicious of clergy (he describes the priest at Arles as looking 'like a dangerous rhinoceros' in his surplice[16]) and similarly clergy wives: 'There are no more unbelieving, hard-hearted and worldly people – with some exceptions – than clergymen and especially clergymen's wives'[17] (this after yet another frustration in love). He warmed to Tolstoy's idea of a new, humanist religion: 'There will also be a private and secret revolution in men, from which a new religion will be reborn ... which will have the same effect of consoling, of making life possible, which the Christian religion used to have.'[18] This became his artistic credo, and is an excellent definition of secularisation.

Nevertheless, Van Gogh was fascinated by churches, and at the end of his life the church at Auvers is a frequent (and doom-laden) subject. In *Starry Night*, however, we have a different kind of religion – a substitute for the one that he despised. 'That does not keep me from having a terrible need of – should I say the word – religion. Then I go out at night and paint the stars.'[19] 'I can do without God, but I cannot do without some power which is greater than I – power to create.'[20] Here is the beginning of the process whereby the artist's own expressive power begins to replace God. *Starry Night* has been called 'a secular expression of transcendence', a 'pantheistic rapture'.[21] It is a religious painting, certainly, but there are no religious symbols, no angels. Instead, it preaches a secular spirituality to replace the ecclesiastical one to which he was temperamentally unable to conform – stars instead of angels, snooker players instead of demons – and, most importantly, a spirituality expressed in paint rather than in words, one in which sensuality, the body and therefore sex are always just around the corner.

To anyone even briefly acquainted with Van Gogh's letters, a rich confessional stream of the outpourings of a broken heart, the degree of sexual sublimation in his paintings is quite clear. Desperate for love, Van Gogh directed his erotic energies into his painting. Always rather moral, he rarely drew or painted nudes (with one or two rather wonderful exceptions). Nonetheless, a displaced eroticism is one of the key elements of his art reflected particularly in his use of colour, his energy and vitality. This implicit somatic spirituality – the expression in paint of a man's yearning for the warmth and acceptance of God – would lead to a much more explicit link in the following generations between religion, art and sex.

Hot and holy . . .

We look now at three younger contemporaries of Van Gogh who flourished in the crucial late Victorian/Edwardian period, and who were pioneers in bringing together sex and religion.

The oldest, Edvard Munch (1863–1944), who was heavily influenced by Van Gogh, is the Norwegian artist whose famous *Scream* has become one of the most reproduced icons of our time, especially after being stolen from its gallery in Norway and then being dramatically recovered by English police in 1995. This picture contains prophetically (it dates from 1893) almost all the defining features of twentieth-century art and culture: alienation, depression, neurosis, ugliness, artistic isolation, loneliness – in a word, *angst*. It is the very icon of the tortured soul. The story goes that Munch was walking along a path with two friends when the sun was setting. 'Suddenly the sky turned blood-red . . . I stopped, deathly tired . . . My friends walked on – I stood there, trembling with anxiety, and I felt a great, infinite scream pass through nature.'[22] So this is what he painted. As with Van Gogh, self-expression and autobiography are all-important.

However, angst for Munch was as much sexual as existential. His paintings are obsessed with sex – for example, with powerful women making short work of unwary men. *Sphinx* (1894), a picture of four figures, two light, two in shadow, depicts a rather unconvincing girl with long hair, wearing a pale dress and holding flowers, looking across the sea from the shore; under the trees behind her a more convincingly painted naked woman, legs apart, hands behind her head, invites the viewer's gaze (and more). A woman, in shadow and dressed in black, looks soulfully down; and a man, also in dark clothes, has his eyes closed, almost hidden by the trees. The title alludes both to the riddle of the Sphinx (what goes on four legs in the morning, two legs at midday and three legs in the evening?) and thus to the three ages of man (as Freud pointed out, in terms of sexual innocence and maturity) and also to the use of 'Sphinx' at this time to refer to a *femme fatale* – the woman who allures and then consumes unwary males. (We have already come across Solomon's *John the Baptist*, and there are more to come; indeed, 'no century depicted woman as vampire, as castrator, as killer so consistently, so programmatically and so nakedly as the nineteenth'.[23]) In his analysis of this picture, Peter Gay sees it partly but not entirely as a psychological reaction to the Victorian fear of powerful women which arose from their rapidly approaching emancipation.

> The psychological universe that Munch inhabited was very large … But it was less the time-bound problems of the nineteenth-century bourgeoisie that they [the *femmes fatales*] captured and portrayed, than universal, timeless masculine concerns. What made the age distinctive in this respect was not that it made men fearful of women, but that it permitted them to pour their sexual malaise into their work and to use their art as an expressive vehicle as it had never been used before. The fashion of fatal women in the nineteenth century reveals less the menace of feminism than the contours of liberal culture.[24]

Although Gay does not expressly mention religion at this point, it is clear that he sees art as the focus of what would previously have been seen as religious questions. Like many others, Munch pours his 'sexual malaise' not into religious faith but into his artistic work, even if his women tend to be adolescent caricatures, his painting of them a bizarrely schematic analysis of woman as virgin, whore and mother.

Adolescent is a word that inevitably recurs in reactions to Munch's work. There is in his art an overwhelming sense of adolescent sexuality, rooted in fantasy and misogyny, typical of the prurient theorising about the other sex that goes on among adolescents. One would almost think that he had never known a woman, rather than having indulged in the bed-hopping encouraged by the avant-garde circles he frequented, first in Christiana (now Oslo) in the 1880s – where he was part of the Christiana-Bohème led by the anarchist Hans Jaeger – and then in Berlin in the 1890s, where he was a member of the Bohemian group meeting at a café christened the 'Black Piglet', and where among his international circle of writers and artists there was great speculation about the nature of (idealised) womanhood and the religious and mystical nature of sex. (When, however, Munch introduced a real woman called Dagny Ruels, who obligingly put flesh on their theories by sleeping with each in turn, into the group, it quickly dissolved, riven by petty feuding and sexual jealousy.)

In a sense, the sexual immaturity of Munch and his group is hardly surprising, given the repressive nature of the society against which they were kicking, and how little hard information they had available on such matters. But it is a classic case of a group of fashionable young thinkers escaping from the grasp of religion and the Establishment only to fall into the maw of spurious sexual mysticism.

As well as quasi-mystical eroticism, Munch and his contemporaries were also obsessed by its inevitable concomitants – the occult, neurosis and death. These can be seen at work in one of Munch's best pictures, *Puberty*, a painting of an adolescent girl sitting naked on the edge of her bed, covering herself with her arms, looking vulnerable and alone. The picture is tender and emotionally penetrating; there is a look of teenage defiance in the girl's eyes, even as she feels ashamed of her body. But behind her on the wall is a grotesque dark shadow, its spooky shape probably derived from Munch's interest in the occult, symbolising the approach of sex and death. The origin of the girl is possibly a memory of his sister, Sophie, who died of TB aged fifteen in 1877 when Munch was fourteen, an event that profoundly marked him. Many of his paintings are scenes of the sick child on her deathbed, powerful analyses of the effect of her death upon her family group, broken up by grief.

Munch's influence across Europe, especially through his graphic work, was enormous.

The second member of our trio is the German painter Emil Nolde (1867–1956). Nolde, again, was an expressionist painter, more concerned to express the 'inner truth' of his subjects than to represent them accurately, something (as with Van Gogh) particularly evident in his use of colour. Unlike Van Gogh, Nolde did paint specifically religious themes, albeit from a secular perspective.

His religious works are of particular interest. Ian McKeever, a contemporary British artist and champion of Nolde's work, claims that 'Nolde ... is perhaps the last artist who could take on board the great tradition of religious painting, work with it literally and authentically ... For a painter to now paint such epic religious themes would almost certainly appear a cliché.'[25] Nolde was able do this because, far from being convinced by Christianity, he saw religious themes as being an important part of what it means to be a human being, and like other expressionist painters, he therefore felt free to explore if only for their humanist, secular content. And, as we shall see, this humanist content was particularly related to sex.

For example, Nolde's *Ecstasy* (1929), is an expressionist version of Bernini's *Ecstasy of St Teresa*, originally entitled *Mary's Conception*, a title he abandoned because he thought it might be offensive. We see a naked woman, presumably the blessed Virgin,[26] with a very full body, staring ahead of her with wide eyes and parted lips, kneeling; the shadows of her body are painted in iridescent

148

purple, while above her a male figure holds a cross. The picture is very erotic; ecstasy and orgasm are clearly bound up with each other in Nolde's vision (as in Bernini's). Two worlds collide – the sacred, transcendent world of Jesus and the secular world of a sensual woman. The juxtaposition is fraught with tension.

As the art historian Felicity Lunn puts it, Nolde saw sex, art and religion as sharing a similar intensity.

> Art for Nolde was itself a religion, a vehicle for ecstatic union with one's inner forces ... The abandonment of all rationality to an inner spiritual energy linked – in the ideology and language of the expressionists – art, religion and sex ... Nolde's identification with Christ was due partly to his adolescent sense of insecurity and his growing awareness of his own sexuality. Although the pubescent egoism decreased in later years, Nolde's relationship with the religious paintings was marked throughout his life by a strong element of eroticism.[27] ... For Nolde, sexuality was an important aspect of religious faith for it signified in this connection abandonment of all rationality to an inner spiritual energy.[28]

In an oft-quoted statement, Nolde describes how at the age of fifteen he had had an experience of Christ's crucifixion as he lay upon the earth: 'I turned myself around, dreaming in undefinable thoughts that the whole large round, wonderful earth was my lover.' And later on, in 1909, he wrote: 'I had to be free artistically, not having God before me ... but God in me, hot and holy as the love of Christ.'

Nolde's painting has been rather unflatteringly called 'grunting in paint'. Certainly, his work is at the inarticulate end of the expressionist spectrum, and his wild and inchoate fantasies were to get him into trouble later on, for along with sex and religion, there were other similarly general concepts and symbols that appealed to Nolde, namely race, blood and land, that played into the hands of the National Socialists when they came to power. Nolde was supported by Goebbels, Hitler's minister for culture, until a power struggle between the latter and Alfred Rosenberg (who disliked his work) led to his being included in the great *entartete Kunst* exhibition of 'degenerate' modern art of late 1937, which retrospectively proved his salvation. The temptation to participate in the Nazis' illusory fantasy of race, motherland and nature existing in a mystical relationship was scarcely avoidable once Nolde had replaced religion by a spirituality of lazy universals, much as Munch became obsessed with the occult.

Not all artists interested in art and sex were expressionists. The English sculptor Eric Gill (1882–1940) was a Roman Catholic convert who made sculptures and engravings of a beautiful and measured elegance which still grace many English churches. His *Crucifixion* of 1910, for example, is a world away from the art of Munch or Nolde. (Stone carving is in any case not the best medium for expressionism.) An impassive, smoothly carved, naked Christ figure hangs peacefully on the cross (no nails or wounds visible) with thin legs and tiny genitals. In beautifully incised lettering, on either side of his legs, is written in Latin a quotation from Psalm 147: 'neither delighteth he in any man's legs', while in raised letters there is a quotation from Matthew 19: 'there are eunuchs which have made themselves eunuchs for the sake of the kingdom of heaven. Let he who can receive this receive it.' (Gill was also a very fine typographer.) The texts are presumably intended to be a commentary upon the Christ figure's very unmuscular and sexless legs and genitals.

However, this carving has a pair, entitled *A Roland for an Oliver* (i.e. a tit for tat) also of 1910. A fully frontal naked woman, hands on hips, legs akimbo, her nipples and lips painted and wearing a painted gold necklace, is looking straight ahead of her as if ready to take on any spectator. She also has an engraved text, taken from a controversial poem by Algernon Swinburne, 'Hymn to Proserpine' (in a book dealing with the attraction of *femmes fatales*, a recurring theme, as we have seen, in fin-de-siècle literature and art): 'O pale Galilean, but these thou shalt not take: the laurel, the palm and the paean, the breasts of the nymphs in the brake'. In other words Jesus, who was called 'the pale Galilean' by Julian the apostate (the Roman emperor who tried to turn the clock back against Christianity in favour of pagan religion), is denied the spice of natural life. In his juxtaposition of these two sculptures, the anaemic, sexless Christ with a fecund earth mother (her artistic roots clearly owing something to India), Gill is making a point about Christian sexual renunciation and its opposite, a matter that was to interest him all his life. He maintained to the end that it was possible in this case to have one's cake and eat it, even if the Church taught otherwise.

Compared to Munch's *Sphinx*, Gill's woman, despite the allusion to Swinburne, is certainly no *femme fatale*, but merely powerful and confident in her sexuality. Paradoxically, Gill's woman is much more believable as a portrait of a woman of flesh and blood, despite the extreme stylisation of the carving (the symmetrical body, the circular breasts, the painted decoration, the Hindu influences), than Munch's apparently more realistic portrayal of four recognisable figures which, as noted above, has something quite adolescent about it in its splitting of the female persona. The models were in Gill's case probably his sister Gladys, who served as his role model of the sensual woman in these years, with whom he was to have an incestuous affair later (Gill's intimate relationships with members of his family are now well known), and in Munch's case the 'Mrs Heiberg' of his diaries, in reality Millie Thaulow, the wife of Munch's cousin, with whom he had had a tempestuous affair years earlier.

Nineteenth-century Europe was a society out of touch with the body, and juvenile as the attempts of the expressionists at sexual liberation now appear, it could be argued that they were part of a necessary process of correction – one that Gill too considered important, though in his case he was also concerned with the alienation engendered by the working habits of mass production.

Munch himself never married, and after his breakdown in September 1908 never again painted with the same fervour, ending his days a recluse, surrounded by his pictures. But much as Munch's work may be self-absorbed, unpleasant, even misogynist, it has all the vitality of the rebel. By contrast, Gill's vision of a society of craftsmen seems like romantic mediaevalism compared with the brash self-absorption of Munch's prose and paintings, his work maverick rather than truly revolutionary.

All three of these artists shared an interest in religion and sex. Their religion was by any standards hardly orthodox (even though Gill was a practising Catholic). Perhaps it is not too extreme to suggest that for them religion served to add a touch of spice to their already dominant interest in sex.

The end of art

In any case, their influence has been considerable. Despite their clearly neurotic sexuality they were perhaps the first to give voice to what has now become an orthodoxy, namely that while religion certainly of the ecclesiastical variety, may have become redundant, the arts, partly because of their sexual component, are still able to generate the *frisson* of excitement that comes from glimpsing vast and unknown possibilities, the prospect of those other worlds that were once the unique preserve of religion. Artists are seen by many today as offering a secular salvation, and large institutions and secular structures (the great art galleries, which the French man of letters André Malraux famously called 'the temples of the twentieth century') have been constructed to support and exhibit their work.

There is today a whole industry selling art as spirituality. (That sex is rarely mentioned explicitly is not altogether surprising as it is so obvious.) In 1968, for example, Jean Gimpel, son of a distinguished French art collector and brother of well-known gallery owners, published *The Cult of Art* – its French subtitle, *La naissance d'une religion*, even more explicit. The book quickly became infamous, particularly because of its author's unique inside access to the art world. In it, he claimed simply that art had become over the years a religion substitute in its own right, with the artist a high priest who possesses a special sort of perception and understanding. He poured scorn on what he argued was pure mystification, claiming that the sooner art returned to its useful role of serving society the better.

The book gave voice to the anxieties of a whole generation of art students, concerned about what they felt to be the corruption of the gallery system. Like the mediaeval Church at its worst, they suspected that commercial art galleries exercised a stranglehold on 'their' artists' creativity and prostituted their talents, hyping the works of a few favoured protégés so that they could be sold for fabulous sums of money while ignoring the work of the rest. As a result, the next generation of artists began to make works out of perishable materials – snow, icing sugar, blood, ice, urine – or in remote areas where it would be unseen except perhaps in photographs, to avoid the possibility of its being bought and sold. (The photographs are now very valuable.)

Others, however, were not so cynical. One of the best examples of recent years was the art critic and pugilist Peter Fuller, who died tragically in 1990 in a car accident. His parents were pious Protestant Christians; he early rejected their Christianity for Marxism, but then found a new spirituality in art – particularly in the great, moody and inchoate canvases of the American abstract expressionists, whose work he did much to interpret and popularise. Reading him on the numinous abstract paintings of Mark Rothko or the more lyrical work of Robert Natkin ('Rothko reveals to us the sombrest and blackest of human emotions. He reveals a black hole at the base of consciousness which is beyond even despair'),[29] many students of the 1970s and 1980s, impervious to ecclesiastical religion, were impressed by an avowed materialist writer and critic who was clearly struggling to bridge the gap between the aesthetic and the holy.

Naturally, this applies equally to all the arts. Among the poets, Wallace Stevens famously claimed that 'after one has abandoned a belief in God, poetry is the essence which takes its place as life's redemption'.[30] At this point, the process of secularisation is complete: art has taken over from religion.

That the arts can be a source of redemption is one of those current orthodoxies that needs more space than we have here to examine properly. Suffice it to say here that although there may be an element of truth in this, generally it is reading too much into art to see the particular tingling down the spine produced by, say, a Rothko painting as religious. It over-mythologises both art and the sex with which it is so easily and often associated, and neglects the fact that fine art has been as effectively demythologised over the twentieth century as Christianity. Many claim that fine art is as dead as the Church that it supplanted.

There are a number of reasons for what has been regularly billed as the 'death of art'. The sort of fine art that is exhibited at institutions such as the Royal Academy is clearly a middle-class preserve, despite all the laudable attempts by such institutions to encourage a wide cross-section to visit; and thus with the economic demise of the middle classes fine art is being abandoned by its key constituency. Secondly, the fine art tradition has always, some would claim, been pretentious and hypocritical, never really able to deliver to people's exalted (quasi-religious) expectations of it. Thirdly, technologically, it has been overtaken by photography and devalued by the flooding of the market with mass-reproduced copies of its finest works (*Haywain* chocolate boxes and *Mona Lisa* ashtrays).

Possibly the most serious argument, however, is that fine art has suffered the secularisation we have examined already with regard to religion. Fine art became exalted, after all, not because it is decorative but because it was billed as a way of enabling suffering human beings to transform the passivities of their human condition. Some of the creations of art are among the deepest and richest essays in our understanding of what it means to be a human being, vulnerable to the vagaries of fate, accident and mischance. But it is probably inevitable that, as life becomes more comfortable, so first religion and now the arts are becoming less important.

This is not to say that the arts receive less media hype than before, rather that their 'redemptive' function (if such it be) is less necessary. They are less sacred, more to do with entertainment; less to do with representing the great myths which united a community hemmed in by suffering, more to do with offering a privatised anaesthesia from individual pain. The best symbol of what has happened is the cinema screen. Cinemas now come in multiplexes of twelve, so that they no longer present one great screen where a thousand people can gaze up in united rapture, one great shrine to goddess-like film stars, but rather, just as in the corruptest mediaeval times a cathedral would offer a multitude of private masses each with smaller or larger congregations (or none at all), a series of lesser and greater auditoria focused on small screens showing (mainly) different films at the same time, offering privatised experience.

To put it in another way, it could be argued that the arts, at their most profound, voice the pain of the human condition, whether the everyday pain of ordinary life in the soap opera, or highly stylised and correspondingly more intense pain in grand opera. This voicing makes the pain bearable. Therefore, as pain diminishes (thanks to the discovery of new drugs and the creation of greater wealth) so the world of the creative arts is replaced by the secondary world of *criticism*. If the igneous matter of primary raw experience is no longer available for transformation into art, so the arts institutions turn in on themselves and indulge in self-analysis, like a support group that runs out of new people to support. (Some argue that this secondary world of art criticism quickly gives way to the tertiary world of the dealer, as the products of art, now no longer sacred, are turned into commodities like everything else).

George Steiner, in his book *Real Presences*, makes a link between the decline of religion and the rise of arts criticism. The reason for the lack of great art, he suggests, is that we do not have substantial enough foundations to support its weight. He proposes a quasi-religious solution rather than an economic one: if only we could recover a sense of transcendental certainty, some 'real presence' that would give real and solid foundations to what we say – even though we sense that there are none – then we should really be able to say something profound. He should be so lucky!

Carnal spirituality

Once art has been demythologised and is no longer seen as some bogus religion substitute or as a semi-licit route to sexual stimulation, perhaps it can still be used by a competent artist to lead the viewer to a sort of down-to-earth mysticism. For example, a now well-known work called *Corps étranger* (Stranger Body) by the Lebanese artist Mona Hatoum might point the way.

To view the work, you must shuffle into a large, plain white, vertical tube where there is a flickering light on the floor inside. The flickering light turns out to be a huge round television screen, occupying most of the floor space, which is taking us on a journey: a journey inside the woman artist's body. She has used the techniques of endoscopy and colposcopy to penetrate and explore every orifice in her body, and she has taken us along with her on her journey, revealing the mysteries of her innermost being in glorious technicolor. The reason for the title of the piece becomes clearer. By exposing the bare reality of her own body, peeling away the myths that have blighted women's lives over the centuries, by cunningly making viewers aware of their own bodies (we have to stand in the tube with our backs pressed uncertainly against its wall in the confined space), she makes us aware of how estranged we are from our real bodies, as opposed to our mythological ones. We, all of us, are made not of sugar and spice nor of frogs and snails and puppy dogs' tails, but of this colourful morass of tubes, fluids and organs, this gurgling labyrinth without even a minotaur inside.

And yet, even though Hatoum strips the interior of herself of all the mystery that people (men, certainly) like to attribute to women, the very context in which she shows herself means that she does undoubtedly create a sense of *sacred space*. The human body is seen as sacred not in the old hierarchical, mythological sense, but simply as an unknown place, a strange place of awe and terror. Who needs mythology when the everyday can be so strange – even erotic?

Or, for another example that is more explicit about sex, there is the *Reliquaries* series by the Californian artist Daniel Goldstein. A reliquary was an elaborately decorated display case created in the Middle Ages to contain a relic – generally part of the body of a long-dead saint which was still reckoned to have the supernatural powers, for example of healing, that the saint himself or herself would have had while alive. Goldstein has taken worn-out leather skins from the work-out benches used in gay gymnasia in San Francisco and stretched them out inside viewing cases. The leather is heavily marked by being rubbed by the bodies of macho gay males over many years (many of them now dead of HIV-related illnesses). Along with absorbed body fluids, this has left patterns in the leather many of which bear an uncanny resemblance to those of the Turin shroud.

For Goldstein, these leather skins are deeply religious pieces: the hides of dead animals have undergone a 'mystical transformation' thanks to the almost ritual contact they have endured with the sweat and flesh of their users. They are a potent symbolic record, a secular equivalent of the great mediaeval relics, a monument in the best tradition of art to the shortness of human life, but also to its glory while it lasts. They are religious works, therefore, which, with all their other associations, are imbued with sexuality, the defining feature of those whose bodies rubbed upon these hides. Sex and religion come together entirely naturally and appropriately.[31]

If Goldstein is typical, it begins to look as if the ancient war between sex and religion may temporarily at least be at a truce thanks to the mediation of art. On the other side, the study of art is affecting some theologians' attitude to sex too. As one of our senior theologians, George Pattison, Dean of King's College, Cambridge, who has written an influential book on the relationship between art and theology over the years, puts it, 'theologians are already falling under the spell of the lust of the eye which is of the essence of a fully carnal spirituality'.[32]

7

Sex Out of This World
Men and Sex

In this chapter, we turn to a more general theme: that of how male sexuality is structured. In the following chapter, we consider women's sexuality. It should be said as strongly as possible at this point that the gender distinctions I shall be drawing here, although commonly held, are actually highly suspect.

The basic *biological* difference between men and women is becoming less clear day by day, with the discovery of, for example, women with male chromosomes and men with female hormones. Crudely, the old French joke still applies: '*Quelle est la différence entre un homme et une femme? La différence entre*' ('*entre*' meaning both 'between' and 'enters'). Even this dubious biological distinction is clothed in such a richness of differentiation that the two genders, male and female, are best seen as signposts, two poles marking the extreme points of a wide spectrum of behaviours. For the sake of clarity, we shall study principally the ends of this spectrum in these two chapters, even though in reality most people will identify more closely with the middle ground. The absolute male exists no more than the absolute female, except in fantasy.

A word of warning. Anyone rash enough to generalise about men and women, their differences and their similarities, is traversing very dangerous territory. This particular battlefield has seen, and continues to see, constant war waged between those who, on the one hand, firmly and piously believe that there is an essence of maleness and femaleness, that the two genders are as different as chalk and cheese, and those who believe that, but for accidents of culture, birth and upbringing, men and women are more or less the same.

It is not our concern here to adjudicate between these rival claims. No doubt once the human genetic structure has been fully mapped, the dispute might be at least partially resolved. Our aim is rather to try to scrutinise some of the popular views about sex current today, regardless of whether they are right or wrong. That people believe these differences exist and read books, articles and watch TV programmes about them is sufficient. And, for most of us, most of the time, differences in gender are fundamental. The first thing we notice about a person is whether they are male or female – before skin colour, before age. Someone of indeterminate gender is almost always unsettling.

It is a commonplace that when it comes to sex, men and women tend to have very different appetites, rhythms and preferences. Typical stereotypes include 'Men want sex and women want love' and 'While girls seek security, boys seek adventure'.[1] Although these stereotypes may or may not be accurate or even helpful, one cannot doubt how common they are, and it is these common perceptions, I argue, that show to what extent sexuality has become a religion.

The basic thrust of this chapter is that, for many, sexual yearnings have taken the place of more orthodox religious aspirations, and have done so in different ways for the two genders. For the male gender, the quasi-religious aspect of sex has been particularly exciting but potentially very harmful.

In brief, the particular role traditionally demanded of the male gender by society – let us call it, anachronistically, dinosaur hunting – required a denial of various important aspects of the human psyche. As long as it was important that dinosaurs were killed, or, more realistically, that wars were fought to compete for limited resources of food or habitable territory, these suppressed aspects could either be rejected altogether (with disastrous consequences) or more generally projected on to some heavenly realm.

However, increasing affluence and technological sophistication have made dinosaur hunting unnecessary, repression less important, and the heavenly realm less credible. I suggest that instead of relaxing the repression men have redirected their projections away from heaven and on to women, as we shall see. From the seventeenth century onwards, one can see a progressive displacement of religious language on to women, a process that reached its peak in the nineteenth century. Women, therefore, for several hundred years, have had to bear the suppressed parts of the male psyche. This is what gave sex its particularly religious excitement. Because sex is the reunion of the male with his dark half, with his shadow, it offers a quasi-religious fulfilment. Woman is the 'dark continent' who offers psychological completion to the strait-jacketed male, access to (his) other world. Because this dark side of the male psyche is repressed, it has taken on enormous proportions (there is nothing like repression to make something important), and so women become goddesses, divine creatures, the eternal feminine, and the simple biological act of copulation takes on an almost supernatural mystique. It should be said that this account of the male psyche sounds fantastic, but, as we shall see, it is remarkably common in many texts on male sexuality.

Naturally, this myth is as bogus as the others. It precludes good relationships between men and women, the latter becoming simply ciphers and symbols to serve the fantasies of the former, and in any case, there is no need, in a non-dinosaur-hunting world, to suppress the shadow side of the male. There is, however, I shall suggest finally, a genuine spirituality of maleness, but curiously the more genuine it is, the more simply human it becomes and the less distinctively male.

Fighting dinosaurs – fighting mother

A plain drinking glass stands on a glass shelf against a white background; in the glass, a black toothbrush, a black razor and a tortoiseshell comb. On the shelf, next to the glass, rather incongruously, a bottle of 'skin Cologne for men' – for which the picture is an advertisement. Simply and starkly elegant, the advertisement conveys a potent male sexuality whose minimal quality is actually its whole message. Here are the grooming tools of the fashionable male: simple, unadorned and stylishly black. The picture speaks of a shunning of frippery and adornment, of a concentration upon the essential. It is puritanical – almost ruthless. And there is no one there. It is detached, impersonal, powerful and rather sinister.

Such an elimination of the inessential does not come cheap. It speaks of a man (for this could not be a woman's advertisement, even though we are quite used to women's razors in advertisements) who is careful about his things, who has taste but without being soft or self-indulgent. One imagines that his life will be the same: fully under control, stylish, discreet, detached and disciplined; he will be someone able to focus his energy, to hold himself in reserve for when it really matters. Perhaps there is a schizoid quality about his life: he does not give himself immediately to every situation and is capable of maintaining reserve, not needing to be immediately liked or admired. But at what cost?

It is very difficult to do justice to the subject of male sexuality. Many of the recent books on the subject (by authors of both sexes) appear to argue that if only men were more like women, the world would be a better place, although at the other extreme there are some remarkable attempts – some very popular in the US (and increasingly over here), such as Robert Bly's *Iron John* – to conjure up a mystique of male sexuality which bear about as much relationship to the life of the ordinary male as joining a Wiccan coven has to that of the average female. It is hard to know where to turn for a sympathetic view of men's sexuality which does not just serve up either the trivial stereotype of Rambo man or a view of man as failed woman.

I propose therefore to begin with what may at first glance seem an unlikely example: an opera by Béla Bartók. The Hungarian composer wrote *Duke Bluebeard's Castle* in his thirties; it was

162

first performed in 1918 when he was thirty-seven. The one-act opera is based on an ancient Hungarian folk tale, and its story is simple. Duke Bluebeard brings his new wife, Judith, home to his castle. Judith has just left her parents, and so is nervous (having heard something of Bluebeard's terrible reputation), even more so when confronted by the great gloomy hall with its seven doors to which Bluebeard leads her. Bluebeard's castle clearly represents himself, and Judith, like many a naïve and well-intentioned girl bent on improving her man, tries to let light and air into the castle interior.

One by one, she opens the doors. Bluebeard acquiesces, but with increasing reluctance, and explains what lies behind them. The first door opens on to his torture chamber: a red light emerges, the walls are wet with blood. The second is his armoury: a bronze light pours out. The third door is that of the treasury – golden light streams out; the fourth gives on to the garden and the fifth on to his kingdom. But through each door, there are signs of blood: on the weapons in the armoury, on the jewels in the treasury, on the flowers in the garden, and in the clouds over the kingdom.

Finally, Judith insists on opening the last two doors. Bluebeard begs her to desist. But Judith persists: the sixth door conceals a lake of tears; and behind the seventh are Bluebeard's three former wives, three beautiful women who represent the morning, noonday and afternoon of his life. Judith is to be the wife of his evening: and she goes in to join the other wives, held captive now by a crown and robe taken from the treasury. At the end, Bluebeard is left once more utterly alone.

The opera, though short and stylised, is immensely strong, musically and dramatically. Most operas are based on the sufferings of women; in this work, the full pain and complexity of the masculine role are given powerful treatment. Here are the major elements of manliness – weapons, money, empire and women – and their hidden cost: the sea of tears and the loneliness and isolation they demand. A wiser woman than Judith might not have pushed so hard, might have respected the vulnerable core of Bluebeard's identity and waited to be invited in – albeit the invitation might never have arrived. But once she has forced her way in and caught sight of the lake of tears, Judith, like the other women, has to be shut away in a queenly role. At the end, Bluebeard is left alone, unable to enter into a relationship with this pretty and naïve girl. Separation and loss are the price of masculinity, the opera argues.

At the other extreme, there is what is arguably the greatest novel of the twentieth century, Marcel Proust's *A la recherche du temps perdu* ('In Remembrance of Things Past'). In the first part of the novel, Proust's narrator takes us back across many years to his childhood at his grandmother's house at Combray. He relives his childhood terrors, especially the nightly anguish of separation from his beloved mother who only allowed him the briefest of goodnight kisses, and of his distant father who thought that time spent on goodnight kisses was absurd. He recollects the one time his mother was allowed to spend the whole night in his bedroom and the unquenched tears he shed that night. He continues, 'Recently, I have increasingly begun, if I listen hard, to hear the sobs I had to make myself hold in before my father, and which burst out only when I was alone with Mama. In fact, those tears had never stopped.' That night, the one time his childhood tears were taken seriously by an adult, he describes as a *'puberté de chagrin'*, 'sorrow come of age'.

In this great novel, Proust effortlessly takes the reader back to his early childhood – and also to our own. We too, on reading it, relive our own childhood terrors, our primitive attitudes and ambivalent relationship with our parents. Written just before the acceptance of psychologists' theories about the importance of childhood to adult well-being, Proust's novel stands as a watershed at the end of the Victorian era and at the beginning of our own. Concealing the welling tears was, for a Victorian boy, part of becoming an adult male, and a thousand strategies were evolved to hold those tears in check, to provide the emotional discipline to keep the upper lip stiff.

Restraining tears is hard work; so is the 'cool' manliness of our opening picture. From where does the energy come from to sustain such an emotionally demanding lifestyle?

Various psychological explanations have been put forward with greater or lesser degrees of plausibility. An advertisement on the next page of the fashionable men's magazine that provided the aftershave advertisement ('the men's magazine with an IQ') illustrates one of them.

It is a splendid pastiche of a Degas painting of ballet dancers – in the background, a pastel wall; at the bottom of the picture, floorboards sketched in; on the floor, a row of silken ballerina-style dresses in a can-can pose. Inside each dress are not ballerinas' legs but large pairs of sewing scissors, cleverly open to look like legs, their handles just at head height. This terrifying can-can of scissor-blades (apparently advertising cigarettes), cunningly jointed just at groin height, beautifully illustrates what some would claim is the most deep-seated male fear – that of emasculation, of being unmanned.

This subliminal fear of castration, whether by your father who punishes you for getting too close to your mother (if you accept the Freudians) or by your own desire to merge back into your powerful mother from whose womb you came (if you accept the feminists), is, according to many popular psychotherapists, the motivation behind men's attempts to distance themselves from emotional relationships, to escape from fuss and decoration, to hold on to their tears. It is what drives men into such characteristically male attitudes as concentrating on achievement, working minimally and efficiently, eschewing fussiness and clutter (all redolent of the mess of the maternal body that threatens a man's separate identity – it is not only in their mouths that women have teeth). Structure and disciplined form are therefore, it is argued, the crutches that support the tottering male identity. For there is more to being masculine than simply possessing male genitals: it is, according to this theory, a whole construction, a whole mode of behaviour that is learnt with difficulty and rarely secure.

For another, more sophisticated version of the castration theory, one might turn to James Park, a popular writer on psychotherapy, who, in *Sons, Mothers and Other Lovers*, describes a boy's passage to manhood as follows:

The waters that divide the masculine from the women's realm are turbulent and his mother exerts a strong pull, but the boy's terror of being swallowed up in femininity is so great that he beats back his mother and sets out on a slow and difficult journey across the river. Far from feeling secure in their claims to power, boys scream so loudly and defend their patch so resolutely because they fear for the consequences if they were to let women get too close. Suspecting that they could not withstand a direct attack, they treat the demarcation between men and women as their Maginot Line.[2]

Park is here summarising a view whose details he goes on to criticise, stating that 'it is misleading to suggest that the boy's early condition is feminine' – he is more likely to be confused; and secondly, in 'crossing the river' '*both* sexes must prove that what mother once did for them, they can do for themselves'.[3] But he does not object to the principle, and his summary is very accurate.

Camille Paglia as usual goes for the jugular, and begins by quoting from Freud:

'Man fears that his strength will be taken from him by woman, dreads becoming infected with her femininity and then proving himself a weakling.' Masculinity [she continues] must fight off effeminacy day by day. Woman and nature stand ever ready to reduce the male to boy and infant.[4]

This is the popular explanation of the attraction of prostitutes: men can indulge their animal natures – let their testosterone have its fling – without fear of being emasculated. Niki Adams, spokeswoman for the English Collective of Prostitutes, interviewed after the British actor Hugh Grant (then in a stable relationship with model Elizabeth Hurley) had been arrested with a local prostitute on Sunset Boulevard in Hollywood in 1995, is quoted as saying: 'Famous men visit prostitutes for exactly the same reason as any other men. Because relationships are hard work, sex within a relationship is hard work and most men want sex without responsibility. When a man visits a prostitute, it's a very straightforward exchange, like a business transaction. He doesn't need to bother about taking care of someone emotionally, he can just go straight for the sex.'[5]

So, men must fight free of their mothers, like George overcoming the dragon (an image of which C.G. Jung was fond), or Perseus decapitating the Gorgon, before they can enter into a relationship with other women. As Camille Paglia points out, the Gorgon with her snaky locks is the stuff of male nightmares, a symbol of the vagina that eats the male part.[6]

But it is not only effeminacy which must be fought off, the theory goes – all emotional contact is under suspicion, even (or perhaps especially) with others of the same sex. An independent survey of two hundred men and women in the US showed that two-thirds of the men interviewed could not name a close friend, and of those who could the friend was more likely to be a woman. Three-quarters of the women could easily mention one or more close friends, virtually always a woman.[7]

There is another theory popular among what might be called the Desmond Morris school. Over millions of years, the males, the stronger sex, have been the principal fighters and defenders of their tribes; genetically, women are 'programmed' to breed from the strongest males (tribes where this did not happen would naturally soon be extinguished). When it comes to ensuring the survival of the tribe, all emotions except the most basic (loyalty to the pack) are a hindrance, and so men evolved the capacity to be able to shut off their emotional side.

The physiological differences between male and female brains have long been known, but their significance is not altogether clear. Male brains have fewer connections between the two lobes. Some would argue, therefore, that they are designed to be more focused and better able to engage in concentration. If this were the case, it would account for some of the other characteristics of the male that are generally recognised by popular writers on male sexuality: namely, that men are often alienated from their bodies; they put different aspects of life into different compartments; they tend to prefer hierarchical authority structures; they seek self-validation through clear external achievements (notably sexual intercourse); they prefer clear-cut, 'symbolic' ways of talking about unknown things (symbolism in this sense is a way of detaching from something unknown in order to analyse it). All these are symptomatic of a powerfully analytical brain that was programmed to work on a restricted quantity of data, sacrificing breadth for speed and power. Useful when hunting dinosaurs.

Woman becomes divine

Whether men are programmed to fight dinosaurs or are scared of being absorbed by their mother or castrated by their father, if this brief and necessarily general summary of common beliefs about what people believe makes men tick is at all accurate, then it will enable us to understand the extraordinary role that sex plays within male ways of thinking. In particular, it will become clear why, for most men, sex is actually the closest they come to engaging with religion. For men, sexuality and spirituality are closely and generally invisibly linked.

According to most popular psychologists, the key to understanding the male psyche is the notion of projection. Young children will delight in telling a doll or teddy bear that they are naughty when it is clearly their own naughtiness they are concerned about. Similarly, if it is true that men are able to detach themselves from their emotions and from each other, to channel their resources, to think logically and symbolically, then the parts of the self that have been repressed will inevitably bob up elsewhere. One of the great themes of almost all writers on the human psyche, from political philosophers such as Plato to Jung and Freud, is that there is a natural equilibrium which the human organism constantly tries to maintain. If one aspect of oneself is dominant, the other aspects will somehow attempt to compensate. So it would be difficult for men to achieve the degree of detachment outlined here without there being some sort of compensation elsewhere. Detachment, structure, hierarchy – all this is painful work. What happens to the pain?

The usual answer is that all the things men are detached from, what Jung referred to as the shadow (that which is not illuminated by the light of consciousness), are projected elsewhere. Unconsciously, men invest something or someone else with their own other half. This would once have been some representative in the heavenly realm – for example, the role of the Blessed Virgin throughout the Middle Ages, as Marina Warner suggests, may have been partly to take custody of this shadow side of men's projections. But now, as secularisation has deprived these divine figures of their natural habitat, so ordinary, everyday women have become bearers of these projections instead.

Thus women became for men like the dark side of the moon; they were seen as the dark continent, the unknown, the void. They were considered to be unstructured, dependent, bodily, emotional, interior and religious – all the things that have been bred out of men. Anthony Giddens, for example, is typical in suggesting that even today 'men project onto women their own unconscious reliance, dependence, quest for self-identity'.[8]

Another point follows from this. We saw in the chapter on marriage how wives became angels in the Victorian period. Now it becomes clear that women have become an entire religion substitute. If writers such as Giddens are correct, and women are saddled with men's repressed yearnings precisely because men cannot acknowledge these shadow parts of themselves, one would not be surprised to find that they take on a fantastic resonance, that they are amplified in the male mind out of all proportion – like a great shadow on the wall projected by a small point of light.

In other words, that which men are unable to accept in themselves is thrown on to some 'other', and this other is thereby endowed with religious proportions. It becomes otherworldly, out of control; it takes on a life of its own; it infects whatever is bearing it with *religious* attributes. Anything that has come to represent an 'other' world in this sense is already a religious symbol.

Of course, that which is excluded becomes attractive, and so the 'other' world from which men exclude themselves is therefore made extremely attractive by its distance and forbiddenness. At the most extreme, the woman, the bearer of man's fantasies, is the Garden of Eden for the banished male, redemption for the sinner and rest for the weary, as a thousand bad love-poems bear witness.

The claims that have been made about women by men over the years, not only but especially in the Victorian period, their excess, their imagery, their wealth of extreme forms and general unreality, indicate quite clearly that we are here on religious territory. (The reader will no doubt have his or her own favourites.) Men have elevated women to the stars and thrust them down to hell; they have set them up as temptresses privy to the foulest secrets of Mother Nature and they have made them benign, civilising influences on their unruly selves. (Charles Darwin, for example, took this line: 'The role of women is to restrain the animal urges of men which tend perpetually to threaten human progress towards civilisation and rechannel them into family life.'[9])

But then, crucially, once women have been made into goddesses, redemption is possible. Union with the divine can take place in a very male way – in sexual intercourse. One can project all one's religious fervour and yearning on to a woman and then be united with her in bliss. And so, especially over the last hundred years, sex has become the ultimate spirituality.

Today, of course, thanks to increasing affluence, things are changing so rapidly that it is almost impossible to believe some of the more excessive forms this used to take. No longer need we go dinosaur hunting. In an affluent society life is complex, success requires flexibility, and shutting down half one's psyche is a great hindrance. However, these changes are taking a long time to gain ground, although when they do they will profoundly affect men's attitude to religion in a way that will be briefly explored at the end of this chapter and at greater length in Chapter 10. Perhaps it is optimistic to expect 30,000 years' worth of male aspiration to vanish in a mere thirty.[10]

Angels and demons

I want now to illustrate these conclusions by briefly examining the work of someone who was writing in the second half of the nineteenth century, at that crucial period for the understanding of religion which has appeared in this book several times already, when for the first time in Europe for 1500 years an affluent society became secularised in almost every aspect of life, when God was going to ground and people began to transfer their desires from religion to sex.

In the example of Baudelaire (one might have chosen from many others) we have an unusually clear-cut case of the specifically religious role that women came to play in the male imagination: as whores or angels, demons and fiends or the transcendent source of *luxe, calme et volupté*.

The French poet Charles Baudelaire (1821–67) was a cradle Catholic. His father had been a Roman Catholic priest who voluntarily renounced his priesthood at the time of the French Revolution. Baudelaire was himself deeply influenced by Catholicism, but, like so many of his contemporaries, lost his faith. As Owen Chadwick puts it, 'Baudelaire lost his faith; [it was] no formal faith, no mere acceptance of another's word – he lost a vision, lost an experience which gave every sign of being real.'[11] This certainly did not prevent him using religious imagery in his poems. Rather the opposite – he took highly charged religious imagery and used it for his love-poetry. It was an inversion of the mediaeval habit of taking images of secular love and applying them to God. He borrowed the dark, heavy imagery of nineteenth-century French Catholicism and applied it to his beloved. He thus became a chief prophet of the new secular spirituality.

In 'Harmonie du Soir', for example, a poem addressed to Mme Sabatier (whom we have met before in Chapter 6), a woman with whom Baudelaire was secretly in love and whom he cast as his angel, flowers give off their evening scent like thuribles, the sky is laid out like an altar, the sun drowns in its quickening blood (a reference to the sacred heart), and finally he indulges in the ultimate blasphemy, comparing the beloved to the blessed sacrament itself: *'Ton souvenir en moi luit comme un ostensoir!'*, 'Your memory glows in me as if in a monstrance'.

It is as if the poet is saying that the angelic Mme Sabatier was his redemption; that he saw the memory of her goodness and purity as somehow actually redemptive for him in his own hellish state, addicted to opium, stricken with syphilis and in dandified poverty (he was a man of exquisite taste). This was certainly blasphemy of the highest order, but a blasphemy that would turn into the orthodoxy of our century: love, especially sexual love, brings salvation.

On the other hand, while Mme Sabatier may have been Baudelaire's angel, his personal demon was his mulatto mistress, Jeanne, of whom in one poem he has the unforgettable nightmare vision as *'une outre aux flancs gluants, toute pleine de pus'*, a bladder with sticky thighs, bursting with pus.[12] Baudelaire's depiction of his secular heaven was sublime; but his vision of hell was endowed with all the horrors of a painting by Hieronymous Bosch. The nature of Baudelaire's relationship to Jeanne was, if one may judge from the poems he wrote about her, never straightforward. Given that Baudelaire and Jeanne were lovers for years, why did he, as seems to be the case in many poems, have to frighten her into making love, or blackmail her into showing some emotion?

It seems highly likely that Jeanne was actually a lesbian. Throughout his life, Baudelaire was fascinated by lesbians – indeed the working title for his collected poems, *Les Fleurs du mal* was 'The Lesbians' – and he wrote a whole series of poems, *Femmes damnées*, addressed to them. The French scholar Dominique Rincé suggests that through his taste for lesbians, or for women who would reject him, he may have made life easier for himself:

> obsessed with the fallen, judgmental Eve, and highly suspicious of all these Venuses of flesh and blood, did the poet perhaps not prefer, finally, Sappho and her cortège of daughters of Lesbos? The spectacle of their bodies interlaced in a sumptuous sterility

must have allowed him to dream, to be amused, to sing – without getting involved except through the concupiscence of his dazzled but distant gaze.[13]

This is a classic example of someone projecting on to women all that with which he could not cope in himself. Baudelaire turned his women either into unapproachable saints (Venuses of flesh and blood) or demons (fallen Eves), and, Rincé suggests, unable to relate to either he escaped into the sumptuous sterility of lesbian fantasy. 'For Baudelaire,' Rincé continues, 'the lesbian is to the woman what the dandy is to the man', and these lesbians therefore 'were the true sisters of his poetic condition through their living on the margins, the authentic searchers after infinity'.[14] Searching after infinity is a key concept of Baudelaire's spirituality, and in 'Delphine et Hippolyte' he condemns a couple (albeit of women) in no uncertain terms because they have limited themselves:

> *Descendez, descendez, lamentables victimes,*
> *Descendez le chemin de l'enfer éternel!*
> *Plongez au plus profond du gouffre . . .*
> *Loin des peuples vivants, errantes, condamnées,*
> *A travers les déserts courez comme les loups;*
> *Faites votre destin, âmes désordonnées,*
> *Et fuyez l'infini que vous portez en vous!*

(Get down, get down, wretched victims, get down the path to eternal hell! Dive down to the very bottom of the abyss . . . Wandering, condemned, far from the living, run across deserts like wolves; fulfil your destiny, you disordered souls, flee the infinite which you bear in you!)

Such extraordinary condemnation seems hypocritical in one himself so unconventional, but the last line is important. The pair have committed Baudelaire's one unredeemable sin: by sinking entirely into each other, they risk running away from the infinite. In other words, for Baudelaire, if women betray their religious function – that of opening up infinity – they are damned!

Other women in Baudelaire get similar treatment for much less cause: '*Une nuit que j'étais près d'une affreuse Juive*', 'One night I was lying next to a foul Jewess' – whose only crime, it turns out, was not being the woman he really wanted to be next to. But this is typical. Baudelaire was projecting on to his women his own anger, fear and religious yearnings for love. Because he split his women into angels and demons, he was able to invest them with *transcendent*, religious power. They were no longer human. They were, if true to form, bearers of infinity – whether heavenly or hellish did not matter.

Whenever imagery becomes self-conscious, its end is at hand and its power waning. Baudelaire is important because he is a prophet who helped forge the vocabulary of the coming general secularisation of the European mind. As long as some overall, transcendent religious belief structure was in place, men could project their shadow side on to the divine realm without fear. But once poets could take religious language and consciously use it to express their own personal feelings for their women, the end was in sight.

Another example is the nineteenth-century French painter Courbet's celebrated work *L'Origine du monde* ('The Origin of the World') of 1866, ten years after Baudelaire wrote *Les Fleurs du mal*, which has recently been acquired from the estate of Jacques Lacan (of whom more shortly) by the Musée d'Orsay in Paris. It is simply a highly detailed, photo-realist account of a woman's lower torso, her genitals and breasts (and that is all), whose title is, in retrospect, whatever the artist's intentions, a witty commentary on the tendency of males to project religious fantasies on to the other sex and on to sex itself.

In summary, for whatever reason, women have long performed for men symbolic functions that can only be called religious. And on to the basic biological function of sexual intercourse, men have projected the highest symbolic value of all (although it is difficult to imagine anyone with these adolescent fantasies enjoying real sex with a real woman).

Men and sex

And so we come finally and explicitly to sex – and specifically to sex in its religious and spiritual aspect. If women are (or have been up to now, at least) the bearers of men's projections of their own loss, their suppressed tears, that part of themselves that is 'other' because it is such strange and unfamiliar territory, then sex is, for the male psyche, the ultimate religious act. For sex is union with all that from which the male is alienated: his body (women are often seen as essentially embodied); his emotions (again, generally associated with women). It is the ultimate self-validation, the undeniable proof of one's maleness and masculinity (something that is always a problem for men). In sex, the woman (whichever woman) can take on whatever symbolic identity is required; she can be the great goddess or the great whore – or possibly both. Sex, whether on the beach of a Caribbean island or in the back of a jumbo jet, is invested with transcendent qualities – it offers the access to another world you would expect of a religious experience. Sex is the cry for the other, union with the transcendent.

The French psychologist Jacques Lacan neatly turns this on its head with his dictum 'the cry for the Other is the cry for the Mother'.[15] Since it is boys who feel their inevitable separation from their mother the more acutely, he argues, but must repress their tears, they project their desire for the mother on to any signifier that will bear it: women, women's bodies, pictures of women, even cars, ships and unexplored continents. The woman's body is the cult image of the goddess, the ritual altar upon which men affirm their male sexuality, the screen on to which their quasi-religious fantasies of some transcendent paradise are projected – but all the time it is the mother they want.

One thinks of groups of young men in canteens exhorting each other to ogle a tabloid newspaper page-three photo to convince themselves that they are men, or of the calendars of half-naked women with breasts the size of the Willendorff Venus hanging unremarked on the walls of the barber's shop or the garage, just like the icons or popular religious reproductions in the homes of

Orthodox or Catholic peasants; or of the larger-than-life women's bodies that feature in a thousand Hollywood dolly-shots or the sinuous gyrations of a female stripper rousing a pub full of men in a liturgy of affirmation of their maleness that is perhaps as old as the world. The only surprising thing (to which we shall return) is that the religious quality of this adoration and projection still goes largely unrecognised in a materialistic era that is increasingly indifferent to religion. (Women too, of course, have their own fantasy needs, which will be explored in the next chapter. But when women seek transcendence it is generally of a different nature.)

Woman is, for the male, the land of lost content, and sexual intercourse the culmination of the long pilgrimage, the ultimate (if, alas, only temporary) possession of one's heart's desire. Sex is the homecoming become religious, the ultimate nostalgia.

Sexual prophets

Before we go on to evaluate this religion of sex, there are two special cases of projection which we must briefly consider.

First, sex offers men diachronic immortality: an immortality through time. Through a man's family, his offspring, the generations that he spawns and of which he himself is part, there is the chance of projecting himself into the future. This is certainly at present a peculiarly male matter (perhaps partly, but not entirely, because children take their father's surname). Most families have photographs of three generations of males together – grandfather, father and eldest son – that suggest the hope for a transcendence through history. The male family group portrait is an arrow flying in the face of eternity. Sex offers patrilineal immortality, a projection of linear salvation in the face of death. (Women, by contrast, it is claimed, find a synchronic immortality through the *breadth* of their family and community links, and so they do not need to project so much through time.)

Secondly, sex has always been an excuse to persecute those who deviate from society's norms. Homosexuals, particularly, have traditionally been ostracised by polite society. From this privileged vantage point, however, homosexuals have made most of the running in the exploration of male spirituality, as generally it is those outside the walls who are the freest to experiment.

The issue of the 'causes' of homosexuality is immensely complicated. It seems most likely that there is no one unitary cause, but rather a whole series of factors such as genetic predisposition, behavioural and social factors, family influence, and in some cases simple aesthetic preference.

Homosexual male culture is in some aspects a sort of parody of a religious community, a classic example of another world that provides an escape from the present one while being also a community of mutual understanding and support, and where entry is restricted to a minority. Reports of the atmosphere of, say, a New York gay bar in the pre-HIV 1970s make it clear that it was as other-worldly as it is possible to imagine, and also an interesting example of the stereotype of male sexuality at its most extreme. Most bars would have had a back room (or in some cases cellar) where patrons could lose themselves in the excitement of a completely promiscuous, anonymous and animal sexual act. This perversion of the aims of religion (losing oneself in the vision of God) is probably only the extreme version of a general male desire to lose oneself in sex with someone on to whom one can project whatever is required. The only difference in homosexual love is that it is men who are the screens on to which fantasies are projected, not women.

James Park argues that this is because many homosexual men are more familiar with the world of women than with that of their own sex, and that therefore it is the male who represents the unknown, the mysterious. For many gay men, women are all too familiar.

One plausible way of explaining why some men feel drawn towards experiencing sexual and emotional intimacy with a person of the same sex as themselves is that, because of their childhood background, such men experience the male as more 'other' than the female and therefore more intriguing, the sex they want to know about even though it is their own.[16]

Roger Scruton, as one would expect, argues that homosexuality is a perversion because the most important thing about intercourse is the complementarity of the two sexes. For him, the problem is not that homosexuality is biologically sterile but that your partner is the same as yourself. True sex is about being open to someone who is *different* from yourself. 'Precisely when most compelled to see yourself *as* a woman or *as* a man, you are confronted with the mystery of the other, who faces you from across an impassable moral divide. What you are awakening in the other is something with which you are not through and through familiar ... The opening of the self to the mystery of another gender is a feature of sexual maturity.'[17] But if Park is right, his argument would refute Scruton's strictures. For the gay male, it is men who are the other world, whom you face 'across an impassable moral divide'.

The future of masculinity: the 'crisis' of the male and the absent father

But let us get real, as the genie tells Disney's Aladdin. What we have been dealing with in most of this chapter is pure fantasy. No real woman (or gay man) is likely ever to be able adequately to bear so much metaphysical baggage.

The impossibility of finding the woman of his dreams may, of course, simply be the cause of a man moving on, as so many do, as one woman after another fails to live up to his spectacular ideals. But most men manage to give up even their most cherished illusions as they grow up; also they manage to reintegrate back into themselves those parts of their psyche that have had to be repressed. (It may be that this is in fact achieved partially through sexual intercourse.) And given that it is possible for individuals to mature into the realisation that one real woman is better than a thousand phantoms, perhaps, eventually, even societies may do the same. Thanks to the researches of feminism, it is increasingly clear that for generations women have laboured under vast, beautiful but impeding mythological clobber. Perhaps now a clearer vision is prevailing. The mythological robes can be dispensed with. So, too, women – for so long the objects of the mythological projections of males desperate to redeem that side of their nature which, like the dark side of the moon, can never be brought to light – need no longer be sold into metaphysical slavery.

This process is directly parallel to what is happening to the concept of God. In the reasonably affluent and well-defended society that is typical of most of modern Western Europe, religion is being stripped of a great deal of its mythological clutter. Just as a constitutional monarch is good for decoration and for the tourist trade, so the Victorian God of many of our Churches is useful for providing pomp and ceremony at coronations or frightening the children into good behaviour, but he has largely lost his real power. The way is clear for the development of a genuine Christian spirituality, just as in an age when men no longer have to suppress their emotions in order to hunt dinosaurs more effectively, men and women can begin to look at each other, to learn to relate, and to discover each other as they really are.

This does not prevent all those projections still being enjoyed as harmless amusement, having one's cake and eating it in a thoroughly post-modern way. Where would we be without romance? But keeping up projections for real is, as discussed at the beginning of this chapter, immensely hard work, a task requiring a vast input of energy; there is no necessity for it. While some people, when shopping on a Saturday morning in a crowded supermarket, find dinosaur-hunting skills useful, it could hardly be claimed that men really need to psych themselves up in the same way as their pagan forebears before a visit to Sainsbury's.

Projection can be imprisoning for women as well as dangerous for men. It is all very well to project one's desires on to women, to see woman as, for example, the void, the container, the matrix, the screen or the *ergasterion* (the 'workshop', in the language of

Greek Orthodox theology[18]); but it will not help one to relate to a real flesh-and-blood woman. Historically, in a violent or impoverished age, it may have been women's fate to be turned into a figure of redemption ('They [men] will come to you with their desire and you [woman] will bleed for them in return,' as R.S. Thomas wittily puts it, making a daring leap between the natural shedding of blood at menstruation and the redemptive shedding of blood at the crucifixion). But, as Marina Warner points out, being turned into a goddess is distinctly cramping.

Warner devoted the whole of her now famous *Alone of All Her Sex: The Myth and Cult of the Virgin Mary* to the intuition that the heavenly figure of Mary was being used for very human purposes: 'In the very celebration of the perfect woman, both humanity and women were subtly denigrated.'[19] This creates artificial distinctions between the sexes, as exemplified, for example, in some of D.H. Lawrence's more extreme moments, when he makes quite absurd generalisations about quasi-religious, pseudo-mythological differences. But the likelihood is that things are changing.

Some, such as Julia Kristeva, rejoice at the hiddenness of women's sexuality. Men, she argues, are so busy projecting that they have no idea about women's sexuality, and so the woman can actually take her own pleasure in her own time, unmolested by the man. But most would not agree. Religious and quasi-religious fictions are important to life, and especially when they no longer matter!

However, that a mythology has become bankrupt does not mean that it will inevitably and quickly disappear. Change is not easy. Nietzsche predicted that when Europe woke up to the fact that the heavens were empty, we should all go mad. Similarly, if men discover that women have been demythologised, how will they cope? If there are no dinosaurs to hunt, no barbarians to repel and no fantasy women to turn into goddesses, how can one prove one is a man?

The so-called 'crisis of the male' is now a commonplace in newspaper and magazine articles. Almost all the principal characteristics of maleness are under threat. Thanks to a raised awareness of what goes on inside both male and female bodies, the male can no longer be so detached from his own body, or leave 'all that sort of thing' to women. Neither can the same sort of emotional compartmentalisation be practised: the male is now expected to be fluent in the language of the emotions. Women demand men who are available in relationships, and readily divorce those who cannot offer emotional as well as physical stimulation.

What of the future for the male? One scenario for the future is that in an increasingly classless society, the heroes will be those who can negotiate the urban jungles, and they will have a different set of priorities, such as flexibility, adaptability, and the ability to blend into the landscape. The new male will be distinguished by the street cred, designer stubble, jeans and working-class or West Indian accents that have taken precedence over the bowler-hatted dark suits of Victorian bourgeois respectability. Sex will be fun and functional, but family life will need to be flexible. Religion will largely be a matter of personal superstition and private apotropaic ritual. Good-luck charms will be highly prized.

Another scenario sees a new men's movement emerging which will rekindle some of the tribal mystique of being a man. Richard Olivier, son of Laurence Olivier and organiser of the British Men's Movement, has been quoted recently as saying, 'Somewhere in the male body, there is a memory of hunting, of killing or using immense aggression in order to survive. That must be dealt with. You can't just say, if we meditate enough and eat enough yoghurt and change enough nappies, the dark energy will go away.'[20] Dark energy will presumably make for good sex, and perhaps a recovery of traditional male, corporate religious rituals. And yet it seems unlikely that men will really be able to take this new mythology of 'dark energy' seriously for a long time yet. As Anthony Giddens points out,[21] women may have broken free from the constraints of domesticity, but men haven't similarly detached themselves from their work yet, let alone found themselves able to engage in ritual drumming workshops.

A third scenario finds parallels to our situation in what happened a hundred years ago. If the male is in fact rendered powerless, is trapped in a world where he is unable to give voice to the 'dark energy', we will, some claim, enter a situation similar to that at the end of the nineteenth century, when for other reasons a whole generation of men were denied access to power and there arose the so-called Decadent movement in art and literature (which partly focused upon the dark, heavy symbolism of the unreformed Roman Catholic Church of the day).

In her entertaining book *The Sins of the Fathers*, Jennifer Birkett outlines the standard political analysis of the Decadent movement. Ms Birkett borrows the title of her book from the Roman poet Horace's great poem on decadence, which attributes the decline of Rome to neglect of religion and laxity in sexual morality – especially among women.

Birkett does not herself hold with the sexual morality theory. Rather, she blames political impotence. The decadent generation were caught in a period of transition between the old guard, 'the Fathers', still entrenched in power, and rising democratic forces not yet strong enough to pose a valid challenge. 'The decadent generation was caught between a bourgeois, capitalist and conservative Republican establishment and the new waves of socialism and feminism.'[22] On the one hand were the 'businessmen, the politicians, the military and the professions who . . . still held society in a firm grip'. On the other were the young rebels wanting nothing to do with the conformity they opposed yet conscious of their own dependence on the Fathers they despised. She concludes: 'Their hopeless dependence led to degenerate eroticism.'

As a result, they ransacked the traditions of their elders for 'forms to contain their vitality: Catholicism, the occult, pagan, Cabbalistic and Christian myth, folk and mediaeval legend, the criminal drama of modern Paris and the Riviera, the temples and forests of ancient Greece, pornographic fantasy'. For example, 'the cults of the Phallus and the Lamb come together in the scene of the Eastern Christian mass, where young men and women, painting each other's breasts with the blood of the slaughtered victim, couple in bisexual orgies'.[23]

Her analysis of a painting by Gustave Moreau, in which Odysseus, on his return home to Ithaca, shoots the suitors of Penelope, his wife, who die in decadent ecstasy, leads her to these conclusions:

Ambition for power and possession has collapsed into violence and chaos. Failure to take the queen, the symbol of the right to power, leaves only the ambition for death. The Fathers are figures to whom they [the rebel sons] owe allegiance and against whom they can only fantasise rebellion.[24]

(It might be questioned, however, whether the Decadents particularly cared about the demise of capitalism, as Birkett claims.)

Similarly today, the theory goes, failure to take the queen will lead a new generation of men to turn in upon themselves in decadent abandon; men will become powerless drones, buzzing helplessly around the dominant matriarchs who will be in control, and spending their time acting out extraordinary religio-sexual fantasies. (The sequel will presumably be a reprise of the First World War.)

A fourth scenario is less complex, and simply foresees alienated men taking the law into their own hands, and, probably in the grip of a fundamentalist religious movement, forcing women back into submission. (There are already signs of this in the United States, with the 'march of a million men' which took place in Washington in October 1995.) Sex and religion will once more clash, and a transcendent god (who will probably be very male, and anti-body) will condemn the decadence of a sexually liberated society, initiating an era of repression – perhaps similar to that envisaged by Margaret Atwood in her novel *The Handmaid's Tale*. (If so, it will certainly, as Atwood suggests, contain the seeds of its own corrupt demise.)

The emptiness of existence

Another possibility is that these celebrated differences between male and female will finally cease to matter altogether, and that people will simply situate themselves on the spectrum of gender where they feel most comfortable, regardless of sex.

But in any case, whether, at the end of the century, frustrated men turn their energy in upon themselves in fantasy or outwards in revolution, whether they make a meal of their rediscovered dark, sexual energies or manage to adapt to a new world by becoming open and flexible, whether they carry on building empires across space and dynasties across time or manage to thrive without having to colonise (empires, women, the future) and exist simply for the present, it seems likely that there will always be repressed tears behind the castle doors. But now this need really no longer be a matter of gender.

'*Le chant naturel de l'homme est triste,*' said Chateaubriand, the first French romantic writer, kicking up the dead leaves in vast Canadian forests, searching for something to fill up the emptiness of his existence ('*l'abîme de mon existence*') back in 1802. 'Man's songs are naturally sad and our hearts are like lyres which are missing some strings, so that even joyful songs have to be played in a minor key.'[25] 'Man is born to sorrow, as the sparks fly upward,'[26] said Job, plagued with boils and bowed down by misfortune. But here 'man' hardly means male.

Human life is full of sorrow, and as favourable economic circumstances roll back the hard labour that otherwise blocks them out, so the tears become more audible, especially at certain moments of emancipation, moments of '*puberté de chagrin*', when the rational adult takes his or her own internal child seriously enough to hear its weeping. As Proust puts it, 'It is only because life around me is getting increasingly quieter that I can hear my childhood tears again, like the convent bell which the noise of the street drowns during the day, so that you'd think it had stopped, but which gradually becomes audible again in the quiet of evening.'

But now we are well beyond any strictly male sexuality. This is a human matter which accepts the ecstatic togetherness of sexual intercourse as a temporary respite in the face of the great emptiness of existence, going well beyond the division into male or female gender. It is just possible that one particular model of sexuality – a particularly strenuous one that is also dangerous to bystanders, as Barbara Ehrenreich puts it – is passing and another emerging as men are becoming able to listen to their own tears without having to kiss the girls to make them cry on their behalf or to imprison them, like Bluebeard's Judith, in queenly robes.

Not everyone would agree. Mary Kenny, for example, a Catholic writer and journalist, writing in the *Guardian* in response to yet another television programme about 'the family in crisis', says: 'Young men do have to be galvanised into a sense of purpose and responsibility. It is not easy to be a man; some patriarchy is necessary. Authority and leadership there must be, if civilisation is to survive.'[27] But why this hierarchical model of authority? Life is too multifaceted to be able any longer to support this rather quaint style of leadership.

If, in some future dispensation, men and women are to relate to each other as persons and not as ciphers, sex may well play a large part in our education, as through the sensual democracy of bodily contact men and women can experiment and discover that all men are not bastards, neither are all women pure angels or rapacious demons, and that in both genders there is loss and emptiness. In the discovery of sex, this element can be acknowledged by both partners. Through sexual intercourse, we rediscover sacred space and momentarily fulfil the emptiness of existence; we create meaning in an outwardly meaningless world.

8

Regarding the Body
Women and Sexuality

Female spirituality is more difficult to talk about than that of men, partly because it has been largely ignored for two thousand years, and partly because what writing there is on the subject tends to be the result of men's projection of their own needs on to women.

When civilisation was hanging by a thread, always on the brink of plague, disaster or barbarian invasion, it is understandable that the weaker groups within society should have been at best ignored or at worst bullied by the stronger ones. And since, as noted in Chapter 2, before much was known about psychology women tended to be identified with untamed nature, that chaotic and disruptive force of which the guardians of society were afraid, women's particular and unique experience was suppressed.

However, the coming of affluence means that women's own spirituality is now being liberated. This is a particularly exciting time for women, as the pioneers of the women's movement open up hitherto secret realms of experience.

In attempting to characterise the sexuality of women and to show that it has, at its most fundamental point, some profound relationship with religious experience, one must move with extreme caution, especially if one is a male writer. In this chapter, we look at some of the common assumptions about women's spirituality, notably the suggestion, developed by many feminist writers, that women have a distinctive knowledge of and relationship to the body and its sexuality which is in some sense 'hidden' and separate from that of men. We also look at other areas in which, uniquely for women, sexuality and spirituality seem to be linked, while discussing whether this is necessarily exclusive to women.

Our bodies, our selves

The most popular assumption about the difference between male and female probably still hinges on attitudes to the body: that the male is characterised by will and intellect and tends to ignore the body, whereas women are much more in touch with their bodies and emotions. Whereas men (as suggested in Chapter 7) tend to project the shadow of their bodies on to an eternal feminine, and use the clubbable aspect of their male sexuality to buttress and reinforce their projections (this seems the most likely explanation of the often very aggressive horseplay which characterises men-only situations) women have tended to look to their bodies for ultimate meaning and identity, and find their sense of purpose in a looser, less structured network of family, friends and acquaintances.

Like all such stereotypes, this is on one level a nonsense and potentially harmful. Plenty of women are people of will and intellect; many men are in tune with their bodies and emotions. However, unlike in the early, heady days of feminism, today the differences between the genders are re-emerging. It is becoming all right to believe that there are differences between men and women after all, and that these do after all lie in different attitudes to the body. The uncomfortableness of unisex jeans was perhaps symbolic.

No one knows human nature like the advertisers. A recent

advert in the New York subway for a telephone counselling service showed three examples of people who might use their services: a man anxious about his job, and two women, one of whom was worried about dieting, the other not able to 'find someone to be happy with'. A crude analysis might indicate that women are twice as likely to seek counselling as men, and when they do, it is not their jobs but their bodies and their relationships they are worried about. Maybe life should not be like this, but advertisers know what really sells.

For a better example, let us consider a recent book of essays by women writers which is fairly typical of contemporary women's writing. Entitled *Minding the Body*, and attractively illustrated on its cover by a design of three naked women's torsos, it is a reflection on their bodies by a dozen different fashionable woman writers, and gives some insight into, in particular, the relationship intelligent and articulate women have with their bodies. This relationship might almost be called obsessive. It is not a matter of a voluntary concern for their bodies' appearances (such as male weightlifters might demonstrate) but of a lifelong struggle with the body and with how they look.

'In contrast to my grandmother's life in rural Alabama, my own control of my body seems privileged, liberated. Whereas her body was restricted by the prohibitions of her culture and class, I grew up in Middle Class America,'[1] writes the editor. And yet she still became anorexic. She continues, 'Recently I taught a class in Women's Literature at a state university and was amazed at the dissatisfaction young women felt about their bodies. "I'd rather have five pounds off my thighs than an A in this class," one woman confessed.'[2]

There is no hint here of this obsession being simply a result of women seeing themselves reflected in the male gaze, as was often alleged in the early days of feminism; rather, these essays enable us to overhear women talking to each other, and the pressures on them to conform are either internal, or come from other women as much as men. One of the more entertaining essays is by a very slim Lebanese woman, Hanan Al-shaykh, whose essay 'Inside a Moroccan Bath' recounts her sense of childhood inferiority at the steam baths, surrounded by sexily obese women. 'I feel that the bodies around me, the hills and mountains of flesh observing me, have themselves nailed the conditions of entry over the door to happiness': in other words, being plump.[3] At the other extreme, Sallie Tisdale in 'The Weight that Women Carry' longs to be thin. 'I believed that being thin would make me happy. Such a pernicious, enduring belief. I lost weight and wasn't happy.'[4]

The size, shape and contour of these authors' bodies is their constant preoccupation, because they want (as Sallie Tisdale puts it) to be rid of 'this vague discontent; then I'll be loved'.[5] For the male reader there is a sense of eavesdropping on a women's world – a world where the body is queen. What *do* women talk about among themselves? Here is the answer. Their bodies.

This is perhaps hardly surprising given the close link between women and their bodies at times of ovulation, menstruation and pregnancy. On average 70 per cent of the articles and adverts in women's magazines relate to the clothing, perfuming, treatment, care, couture and unclothing of women's bodies (whereas men's magazines have generally less than half, with cars, bicycles, beer and, above all, watches making up the running). Certainly, these adverts are reinforcing the stereotypes. But (and once again, one must remember that no one knows human nature like the advertisers) perhaps too they are appealing to real differences between the sexes.

If, as the authors of the essays in *Minding the Body* imply, the body is queen, love it or hate it, one would expect women's spirituality to be based *par excellence* upon the body. And this turns out to have a grain of truth. The subtitle of the book is 'Women writers on body and soul'. Its Library of Congress classification states it to be about 'Soul in literature'. And yet there is hardly an explicit reference to soul (or the spiritual) in the whole book. The assumption is that when women talk about their bodily preoccupations honestly and openly, they are baring their souls.

This is not a new idea. Many of the best-known women writers throughout history have used language and imagery related to the embodied soul. Admittedly, there are not many of them. When it comes to women's spirituality, we are on relatively untrodden ground. It is only recently that spiritual writers have begun to take seriously the idea that men and women might respond to the divine in characteristically different ways. Some would say that this is because the major religions have had a particular patriarchal bias against women for thousands of years, and, despite the fact that women have always been the more assiduous practitioners of religion, women's particular and distinctive experience of religion has been (deliberately or unconsciously) suppressed, perhaps being too threatening or undermining the position of men.

Such historical examples as we have, however, do seem to pay particular attention to the body. Julian of Norwich, the fourteenth-century English mystic, describes God as 'our clothing'. In one of her visions, she sees that Our Lord is 'everything that is good and comforting for our help. He is our clothing, for he is that love that wraps and enfolds us; embraces us and guides us.'[6] She imagines Our Lady (the Blessed Virgin Mary) 'in her bodily likeness, a simple, humble maiden, young in years, of the stature which she had when she conceived' – a far cry from the glorious exaltation of Mary by the Church which traditionally deprived her of almost all bodily traits. For a man, to conceive of God as 'our clothing' would be a distinctly creepy experience. Men tend to project power and might on to God rather than seeing him as a garment.

Or again, in the 'revelations' of Hildegard of Bingen (a twelfth-century German abbess and reformer, who was also a musician, artist and poet) there is a meditation upon the womb and breast-feeding which displays bodily and sexual imagery. (Julian of Norwich also has a passage dwelling in some detail on how the Christian draws milk from the breast of Mother Church.[7])

What a wonder it is
That into the humble form of a woman
The King entered . . .
Your womb contained joy
Just as the grass was infused with
Greenness, when the dew sank into it;

The fountain from the heart of the Father
Has streamed into you.
And thus Mary you are that lucid matter
Through whom the Word breathed forth everything of
   value . . .
God so delighted in you that he pressed within you
That passionate embrace of his own heart,
So that his own son was suckled by you.

Hildegard also has a splendid description of sexual desire using mainly biblical imagery which affirms, at the height of so-called mediaeval repression, the passion of both parties:

> And so, because a man still feels this great sweetness in himself, and is like a stag thirsting for the fountain, he races swiftly to the woman and she to him – she like a threshing-floor pounded by his many strokes and brought to heat when the grains are threshed inside her.[8]

But if women begin to discover that they have access to religious experience in this distinctly feminine way, through their bodies, then inevitably it will make a difference to the way that they think about God. The process is two-way. For example, an American feminist theologian, Nelle Morton, has described her discovery of quite a different sort of God from the usual male 'patriarchal' variety, an experience Morton elsewhere makes clear is bound up with her discovery of her own body.

> In 1972 at Grailville the second national conference on women exploring theology was held. One morning, its sixty-five or so women delegates gathered for worship sitting informally in semicircular fashion on the floor of the oratory. A space indicated by cushions on the floor set aside was marked off as sacred. . . . Most of us did not understand at the beginning what was taking place. I was aware early, however, that something new and different was happening to me. The climax came near the end when the leader said, 'now SHE is a new creation' . . . It was as

if intimate, infinite and transcending power had enfolded me, as if great wings had spread themselves around the seated women and gathered us into a oneness. I was not hearing a masculine word from a male priest, a male rabbi or a male minister. I was sensing something direct and powerful . . . This was the first time I *experienced* a female deity.[9]

In other words, this was an experience of God not as hierarchical and dominating, but levelling, uniting and intimate.

We will return to this shortly, but let us first complete the equation. If a woman's distinctive spiritual experience is connected with the body, then naturally sex will play an important role. The most intense form of embodiment, the time when the body is most on fire, most ecstatic, is generally held to be during sexual intercourse; and so, if the body is the basis of female spirituality, sexuality must be part of it also.

In her book *Desire in Language*,[10] and in other works, the French writer Julia Kristeva develops the concept of '*jouissance*' (the French word for orgasm) which she takes as the epitome of women's erotic experience. *Jouissance* is a sort of pure pleasure which does not partake of ulterior purposes or manipulative ends.

It has to be said that Kristeva developed the idea in opposition to what she sees as men's experience of sex, which, she considers, is concerned with domination, power and bringing things under the authority of the intellect. So that whereas men are concerned with sexual control (perhaps to ensure that their property passes from father to son), *jouissance* exists for itself alone. Just as the clitoris is the sole part of the body (of either sex) whose purpose is pure pleasure, so women's sexuality is self-contained and cannot easily be controlled. For Kristeva, *jouissance* is a sort of religious experience – as we shall see.

Paula Cooey, an American feminist theologian, suggests that for a woman, sex connects with the language of the body at the deepest level, 'one that reflects emotional, visionary and fragmentary aspects of existence'.[11] This language of the body discovered though sex is also linked to the unconscious; and so it is 'akin to music on the one hand and madness on the other'. Since men are much more interested in intellect and will than they are in music and madness – indeed, they will probably be deeply threatened by the unconscious which undermines their maleness, their being in control – then these 'characteristics associated with *féminité*, such as carnality, receptivity and emotionality, [will] challenge their patriarchal correlate',[12] i.e. the foundations of male superiority.

In other words, once the woman has experienced her body as a source of ultimate, quasi-religious pleasure, she is no longer in thrall to some 'other', 'necessarily patriarchal institution or person'. But more than that: sexual pleasure, as a celebration of womanhood, Cooey suggests, 'opens up an avenue to transcendence'. In other words, through sex, women discover not only a distinctively female bodily pleasure but also a distinctively female 'subjectivity and spirituality as well'. Through the body, and particularly through sex, women experience a religious liberation and spirituality – almost a mystical experience.

Some writers, however, would describe even this sort of language as male-tinged. They would reject any talk of transcendence as being, ultimately, a male concern, a vision rooted in an Olympian male vision of God. For them, uniquely feminine sexuality lies in refusing (male) pseudo-profundity and simply enjoying the surface. For example, we might turn to an entertaining essay in Victoria Harwood's *Pleasure Principles*, Sue Golding's 'Sexual Manners'. For Golding, sex is a matter of humorous defiance. The joke is 'the courage to refuse the Profound, and exchange it, mixed metaphors and all, for the surface of the risk'.[13] In other words, the defining character of women's sexuality is that it is *surface*: it refuses to be endowed with some pseudo-mystical sense of the Other, of the hidden depths, and it glories in the surface, in the here and now, in skin and flesh. Can such a view of the body as surface be religious in any sense?

We are so used to hearing of God spoken of in terms of profundities, of depths and heights, that this idea of surface is at first glance blasphemous, utterly denying God his (or her) natural habitat. Yet these authors are talking about the surface of the body when viewed in the light of sex, when fully charged. Sex and sensuality, the body surface responding to touch, are, it might be claimed, what reveal the latent possibilities of a superficial God. The eroticised body is holy.

This may simply reflect the different ways in which men and women respond physically to sexual stimuli. Almost every sex manual ever written explains that women experience sexual pleasure differently from men; it is less localised than for men, less committed to orgasm, more spread over their whole body, as much dependent upon kind words and a sense of security as physical stimulation. To quote from the most famous sex manual ever written, Alex Comfort's *The Joy of Sex*, 'we [women] seem to be less heavily programmed than you [men] for specific turn-ons, but once we see one of these working on a man we care about, we soon program it into our own response, and can be less rigid and more experimental because of this ability'.[14] In other words, sex and the body are more of a continuum (according to this conventional wisdom) for women than they are for men, for whom sex tends to be a discrete, localised activity of correspondingly greater intensity as it builds up to orgasm.

As Luce Irigaray, another French writer who considers that touch is for a woman the most important sexual sensation, puts it, 'Woman has sex organs just about everywhere. She experiences pleasure just about everywhere . . . the geography of her pleasure is much more diversified, more multiple in its differences, more complex, more subtle than is imagined'[15] (i.e. by men).

However, if the experience of the eroticised surface of the body is akin to religious experience, it may also reinforce Nelle Morton's view, quoted above, that women's sexuality and spirituality are so different from men's that they amount almost to an experience of a different God. For example, Paula Cooey talks of Frieda Kahlo's pictures of herself as follows: 'Her body projected into art came to represent the many different cultural voices in tension within her, these voices having in common only a refusal of any religious or political tendencies to *de-materialise human values*. Her images become no longer simulation but *flesh itself, groaning with value*.'

'Flesh groaning with value' is a wonderful description of a non-transcendent religious vision (and many contemporary theologians suggest that ultimately value and religion are intimately connected). To say that flesh is divine would be to fall into the dreadful distortions and appalling banalities of the erotic industry. But to say that flesh groans with value is another matter. Flesh is barely able to support the associations with which it is laden. It seems too frail and unreliable a substance to encompass the divine. But in sex, the leap is made.

Roger Scruton also uses sexual desire to bridge the gap between the brute animal nature of flesh and the highly precious person that is the beloved who inhabits it, who is that flesh. When you are in love with someone, they are transformed – often out of all recognition. Their body becomes totally desirable – because it is them. But there is always a strange disjunction between the infinite mystery of the person we love and their physical, animal body. Scruton suggests that erotic love is that which uniquely enables us to appreciate our partner as 'a repository of infinite value' (and that surely is a religious statement) which exists 'not in some Platonic supersphere but here in the flesh'. Thanks to erotic love, we realise that the person we love is both infinite mystery and also inhabits an animal, flesh-and-blood body, 'this infinitely precious thing actually *is* the animal'.[16] But to be lost in the body without the 'infinite mystery', the 'infinite value', is to enter hell (as we explore further in Chapter 9).

Sea of blood

As with popular views about male sexuality, many of the generalisations about women discussed or taken for granted in books and articles such as those I have summarised here are oversimplifications of the complexity of human life, or else so far to one end of the spectrum of possibilities that few women will be able to identify with them, let alone men. There is also the problem, for a male author, that much of the spirituality of women has been forged over the years by men as part of their fantasy projections about themselves, so one feels the need to tread particularly warily.

However, various criticisms can be made of some of the more extreme forms of sexuality outlined here, for example, that they take their energy from their opposition to male dominance and male views of sexuality, rather than necessarily from positive insights about women. (Two wrongs do not make a right.) 'What gives *jouissance* its liberating power lies in part in its deliberate defiance of male attempts to exert control over female sexuality,' as Cooey puts it.[17] But the suggestion that women's sexuality is so totally opposite to that of men that they cannot begin to understand it or sympathise with it is curious, and smacks of the 'all men are bastards' school of thought. It would be a strange and brutal man who had absolutely no insight or interest in what a woman was feeling – who had no interest at all in music or madness.

Indeed, almost all contemporary male literature is emphatic about the importance of a good (male) lover being able to bring his partner to orgasm and vice versa: a 'real' man is able to satisfy the woman, sexually, by being in tune with her feelings, just as (as Sally Tisdale points out in *Talk Dirty to Me*) in American pornography it is important that the woman model is depicted enjoying the experience – not as a passive (or unwilling) object, but as active participant. '[There are always] lots of close-ups of ecstatic women's faces. In fact, cunnilingus and the clitoral orgasm is a stock event in a lot of porn; part of the American obsession with lust is the goal of satisfaction.'[18]

Certainly, as noted in the previous chapter, many men tend to saddle women with a weight of religious baggage, and it must be a great relief for any woman not to have to be the goddess, angel, slut or whore of their man's fantasies. But there is inevitably something immature in sex on one's own, and autoeroticism is, ultimately, where the extreme feminist position leads. As Paula Cooey puts it, 'autoeroticism experienced as *jouissance* expresses a celebration of *féminité*, the feminine, that is tantamount to guerrilla warfare'[19] (against men). Or, as one French commentator rather smugly put it in the light of the celebrated Bobbit case in which a woman chopped off her husband's penis, 'for American women the penis is a weapon; for French women it is an object of pleasure' (thus implying that most extreme feminists are American).

There is another problem with over-investing in the body: it can ruin lives. As hinted at in the first passage quoted above from *Minding the Body* (with its deliberate pun on 'minding' – paying attention to, but also taking care of), the terrible plagues of bulimia, anorexia and self-harm loom all too easily for those who seek to overcome feelings of being unacceptable or inadequate. If you are persuaded that your body is yourself, naturally you will punish your body for your feelings of inadequacy, especially when this is reinforced by social approval – women with slim bodies almost always being held to be sexier. This highlights the role of the body – and especially that of the female body – in society at large.

Every society has a network of values. One such as ours has several immensely complicated interlocking sets of values which are difficult to analyse as they are so diffuse. But, to return to the theme explored in Chapter 4, one particular aspect of life at present seems very highly valued: to judge by the advertisements and articles in any magazine, the body reigns supreme. We see the human body dressed, decorated, adored, perfumed, coiffured, nurtured, photographed, abused, scarred, pummelled, massaged, jogged into shape; we see the body as the main expression of our power and personality and the source of its own language – so-called body language, that subtle, subliminal and particularly effective way of communicating – and as the source of our personal identity and public persona, the seat of our most important experiences. The importance of the body cannot be overestimated in today's culture.

If our bodies are, as is likely, among the most highly valued aspects of existence, then it is perfectly legitimate to suggest that the body has taken on a religious role. (The implications of this will be explored more fully in Chapter 10.) As the divine realm retreats, so the human body is endowed with divine attributes, human beings being the next thing down, in most people's scale of values, from

God, and bodies their most obvious manifestation. But just as the Old Testament was full of warnings against creating specific visual images for God – creating 'idols' to worship – such as a golden calf, much the same strictures can be applied to worshipping the body. Just as the golden calf could only ever be a partial and inadequate representation of the transcendent God, so the surface appearance of the human body can never do justice to the full depth of our humanity. Having a beautiful body is no guide to being a beautiful person, as moralists down the ages have repeatedly told us; neither does being wanted for their body ultimately satisfy anyone.

There is another area of a woman's life where reality never quite comes up to the myth. If the spirituality of women is particularly connected with the body, then there is clearly one experience unique to women that can potentially be religious – that contained in the mystique of childbirth. Some 90 per cent of women will have a child at some point in their lives.

For some, this is an unglamorous and messy time when their bodies are out of their control ('I feel all body,' as one breast-feeding mother put it), to be endured and passed through as quickly as possible with an epidural at the birth and no breast-feeding. But many women – and this is probably at present the prevailing trend – tend to glorify the business of pregnancy. Sheila Kitzinger was among the first of a long line of writers and broadcasters to popularise the notion of the earth mother, the woman who glories in the pain and mess, who finds giving birth orgasmic, as she writhes in solidarity with women throughout history, roaring at the pain in a sort of cosmic ecstasy.

'At the end of the first stage, the woman feels as if she is swimming in a stormy sea and it can be frightening, awesome, exciting, painful and joyous ... I almost heard a fanfare of trumpets as the head crowned ... Both parents ended up shouting with joy – it was all part of an intensely passionate experience ... When a mother takes her new-born baby up on to her body in flesh-to-flesh contact, it is an integral part of the sexual act of birthing, and everything she says and does then, the compassion and the tenderness, the wonder and awe, the ecstatic utterance, the laughter and tears, the often fierce possessiveness, the way she touches and explores her baby, are all part of this essentially sexual experience.'[20]

Many passages in such writers are almost mystical in their intensity: for them, this is the most real, most profound experience in their lives, in which they partake in the essence of womanhood. No disembodied mysticism this, no pale, ascetic or pious clapping of the hands in anorexic ecstasy born of midnight vigils and long fasting, but a full-blooded, earthy and creative physical agony with a sea of blood, noise and dancing to a chthonic pulse.

Naturally, just as the reality of religious mysticism in church often fails to live up to its promise, so too the actual experience of giving birth, whether in an NHS hospital or at home in a waterbath (a welcome 'advance' back to more primitive practices), is often predictably anaemic by comparison.

Much women's writing (in this country) takes the business of childbirth as the battleground in the struggle between two mythologies which puts the recent women priests debate to shame: the mythology of the earth mother pitted against that of the dominating and interfering male.

Thus the hospital becomes the temple of (male) Science. It is the very incarnation of the male mythology of efficiency, sterility, discipline and structured time. Its artificial rhythms, hushed corridors, intrusive doctors and competent and professional midwives who treat the expectant mother as a 'patient' are at the opposite end of the spectrum from the myth of the earth mother in her nest roaring in the joyful pain of delivery. Anthony Giddens talks of modern childbirth as 'a realm divested of mysticism'. The hospital is not in any positive sense an other world. It is men's way of making the human body safe by screening it off with technology. There is an artificial split between the delights of sex (the *ars erotica*) and the gory business of reproduction, so that 'the secrets of the harem certainly do not apply to the gynaecologists and the labour ward'.[21]

The great debate about home births has threatened at times to reach quasi-religious proportions, a positively mythic battle between the men trying to keep women under their control in their artificial domain, symbolised by the (until recently) general but quite unnecessary practice of shaving the woman's pubic hair before she gives birth on spurious grounds of hygiene, and women wishing to experience the birth of their child in their own bed.

The reality of the situation is more confused. Hospitals are increasingly responding to women's desire for a less clinical approach to childbirth, and women may (in theory) be attended by their community midwife rather than one on the staff of the hospital (and economically, it is cheaper to send mothers home as soon after birth as practicable instead of keeping them in for a week as was once the case).

On the other side, home births are not nearly as dangerous as doctors like to suggest. Recent research by the Clinical Standards Advisory Group shows that of women having their *first* baby (where there is generally a much higher likelihood of requiring medical intervention), only 1.4 per cent of women required a Caesarean in the second stage of labour (i.e. in extreme emergency) and 4.7 per cent in the first stage of labour. Thus the chances of requiring hospital intervention even for one's first baby are only about 6 per cent. (The same research showed that having an epidural 'was strongly associated with increasing duration of both of these stages').[22]

Here we have graphically illustrated the two extremes of the spectrum of sexuality: the clinical and objective versus the embodied and emotional. But both views are a travesty. Few women in practice find giving birth a mystical experience. No matter how many NCT classes have been attended, or how well the breathing exercises practised, few women finally relate to the descriptions of birth by the likes of Sheila Kitzinger, which in practice simply adds to the already enormous potential for feelings of guilt and inadequacy felt by many first-time mothers. And most hospitals, insofar as they can afford it, have delivery rooms designed to provide as good an ambience as possible in which the birth can take place.

But then childbirth has always been a potent source of women's spirituality. Julia Kristeva points out that the image of the maternal body has been a religious one for hundreds of years, thanks to the imagery of the Madonna and child used by the Christian

Church, imagery that has now been secularised: 'Lay humanism has taken over the configuration of that subject through the cult of the mother: tenderness, love and seat of social conservation.'[23] Conception, too, thanks partly to the widespread influence of the story of the annunciation to Mary through the ages, can be seen in quasi-religious, mythological terms (sex is the entry of the other (the male) into the woman's body).

In search of a true spirituality

Turning away from the myth and towards reality, is there perhaps a genuine spirituality of sex to be found in this area? Another fashionable distinction between men and women is that between nature and culture. The male represents culture – the artificial, civilised, that which is passed down linearly through the generations. The female represents nature. There is a good illustration in D.H. Lawrence's *The Rainbow*.

On a visit to Lincoln Cathedral Will Brangwen finds the great building, which he knows well and wants to show off to Anna his wife, profoundly resonant, and goes into a sort of swoon on entering it. (This episode is part of the battle of the sexes Lawrence describes at the start of Will and Anna's early marriage.) Anna is also initially attracted by its vast space, but soon feels imprisoned by its structure. 'She would never consent to the knitting of all the leaping stone in a great roof that closed her in . . . It was dead matter lying there. She claimed the right to freedom above her, higher than the roof.'[24] And so, Lawrence writes, 'she caught at little things, which saved her from being swept forward headlong in the tide of passion'. She points to a 'malicious little face carved in stone' and laughs at it, and succeeds in destroying Will's ecstasy, his 'passionate intercourse with the cathedral'.

Lawrence tended to stereotype men and women to an almost ridiculous extent in order to prove certain positively mythological views about the complementarity of the two genders. But this passage is an interesting illustration of the divide between the male who goes into ecstasy in a great, structured, man-made building ('He was to pass within to the perfect womb') and the woman, who prefers the sky outside. In Julia Kristeva's terms, the divide between culture (represented by the cathedral) and nature (represented by the sky) is neatly projected on to the two characters.[25] Will's yearning for the transcendent is expressed in a structured way by the cathedral – by the vertical, one might say; as the book continues, we discover that the source and focus of his wife's energy is in a horizontal direction – the very large family she and Will go on to produce. However, it is the horizontal direction of the woman's spirituality as Lawrence describes it that is important. There is more to religion than the traditional mystical encounter with a transcendent 'other': God can also be expressed through the horizontal, the surface.

It is interesting that in those pieces of women's spiritual writing which have come down to us, 'horizontal', 'superficial' images of homes and houses are a staple feature. (Some writers suggest that for a woman especially the home is an extension of the body.) The most famous example occurs in the writings of St Teresa, in which the soul is compared to a castle with different compartments and with a fountain in the middle.

Different attitudes to the home may confirm the fundamental differences between men and women (only at their most extreme, of course) that we have identified with regard to the body. It seems still to be the case that men are more detached from the home than women. The stereotype male has piles of clothes on an unvacuumed floor, the stereotype female houseplants on dusted window sills. More interesting are their different reactions to a burglary. For men, a burglary generally gives rise to anger and a desire to punish the intruder. For women, it is almost a matter of rape; it is a personal intrusion, especially if the burglar has rifled through their clothes, which, in some cases, cannot be worn until they have been washed (ritually purified).

This may be the basis of a putative differentiation of men's and women's spirituality. Perhaps there is a sort of crude distinction which, if stripped of the unpleasant associations of submissiveness and meekness to which women have been subjected over the years, does indicate a basic element of female life; that just as for men patrilineal immortality is important – vertical continuity through history – so for a woman a 'horizontal' extension in the present is the more significant. Whereas once a woman would kneel in church, awaiting a (possibly down-to-earth) mystical experience, inviting God in (in compensation maybe for the brutal invasion of herself by husband or other male), so today a secular woman opens herself to the man of her choice and affection, half investing him, perhaps, with some superhuman resonance, and possibly, similarly, half hoping for some sort of ultimate or ecstatic experience through her body.

Traditionalists would argue that this cannot be religious experience. Religious experience is simply experience of an identifiable God, preferably within, say, the Judaeo-Christian tradition, and that to call any experience endowed with unusual or unnatural importance religious is to sell the pass to liberal humanists. But while this may suit male theologians and the ecclesiastical hierarchy very well, it hardly does justice to the distinctively female experience of God explored above.

On the other hand, it is more likely that, as we concluded in the previous chapter on male spirituality, the more civilised men and women become, the more the whole spectrum of spirituality will be available to both sexes. Men can rediscover their bodies and encounter the God of the surface, and women the detachment that leads to a glimpse of the transcendent depths.

9

Come Up and Buy Me
Sex and Hell

'Pornography does not present to us a new state of grace, in which the body is admitted to heaven. Rather, the pornographer gives us his own version of hell.'[1]

Every book ever written about pornography mentions hell somewhere. When discussing pornography (hard-core porn, that is, not simply erotica, which implies a degree of mutuality between viewer and victim), it is, it seems, obligatory for every report or newspaper article to regard it as a hellish topic, the realm of the very Devil. It is hardly surprising that allegations of satanic abuse should so often be linked to pornography, especially where it affects children: 'NSPCC reports alarm at the spread of child sex rings which they claimed included witchcraft' (*The Times*, 12 March 1990) and 'blood drinking orgies' (*Sun*, 13 March 1990). Sex, hell, witchcraft, children – a potent amalgam of ingredients likely to spice up any reader's day.

Two sociologists, Dennis Howitt and Guy Cumberbatch, were recently commissioned by the Home Office to put together a survey of all the available resource material about the effects of pornography. They concluded that evidence for its effects is often minimal compared to the claims made in the press and elsewhere: 'In many ways, pornography seems to serve as a *totem* of society's ills and its convenience and tangibility as a focus makes it easy to identify as a cause of some unacceptable features of life.'[2]

When Howitt and Cumberbatch talk of pornography as a totem, they describe beautifully the role that it has come to play in society. Porn is a quasi-religious identifying symbol on to which can be projected all that is wrong with society (they mention sexual abuse of children, battered wives, sexual offenders, breakdown of the family and the disappearance of the traditional family). One has only to consider some of the more extreme statements foisted on to this totem to understand its power. For example, here are a few samples of writing on pornography:

We [women] live in cities like tame pheasants who are hand-raised and then turned loose for hunters to shoot, an activity called sport. The hunting, maiming, mutilation and murder of ourselves, our mothers, our grandmothers, our daughters, our granddaughters is the stuff of a vast inventory.[3]

In the last few decades women have been bombarded with ever-increasing numbers of pornographic images in liquor stores, book-stores and drugstores; in supermarkets; in the hands of fathers, brothers, sons, lovers, boyfriends ... The media have subjected women to dramatised rapings, stabbings, burnings, beatings, gaggings, bindings, tortures, dismemberments, mutilations and death in the name of male sexual pleasure or sheer entertainment. In the meantime, women have been increasingly and ever-more-gruesomely raped and brutalised on the streets and in their homes.[4]

[Men value and yet fear the depth of erotic power in women's lives and so] women are maintained at a distant and inferior position to be psychologically milked, much the same way as ants maintain colonies of aphids to provide a life-giving substance for the master.[5]

These are, as we shall see, quasi-religious statements, adumbrating the hellish dimension of pornography which ensnares and tortures women. From our point of view, it is hardly surprising that hell should make an appearance here – indeed, it is almost predictable. If sex is indeed a religion substitute, then naturally it must be able to interpret and do justice to the dark side of life. If sex can offer a substitute for heaven, then it must also provide a substitute for hell.

The mythological power of this blend of sex and religion cannot be overemphasised. (Although pornography is its chief focus, there are also other taboo areas, if not so accessible, which we will also examine.) It can be used for exploitation on a massive scale, or to give voice to some of the strongest and yet most incomprehensible emotions that human beings experience. In the second half of this chapter, we will examine some of these secular scenarios of hell. But first, we shall briefly consider the process of historical development of this myth and try to ascertain the actual facts behind it.

Diabolical history

If we turn to the historical background of pornography as hell, there are few surprises. Peter Michelson, in his book *Speaking the Unspeakable: A Poetics of Obscenity*, provides a helpful analysis based on the secularising effect of economic advance.

> Pornography has always flourished under the entrepreneurship of capital, for liberalism is not merely secular, it is downright profane. It is no coincidence that modern pornography developed out of the Renaissance [he quotes the example of Pietro Aretino, whose erotic *Posizioni* were published fifty years after the invention of the printing press] when the Roman Catholic church began to lose its theocratic grip, when humanism, science and technology began their offensive, when navigation got more able, the world got round and commerce went global, when

commercial printing induced a more demotic literature, when the vernacular validated itself and induced increasingly more popular literacy, when, in short, the Western world view began to be more material, various and liberal.[6]

In other words, Michelson sees the development of pornography as part of the general process of secularisation that took place as the material world began to prevail over the 'other', idealist, transcendent world of the Church.

Some writers go so far as to blame the Church itself for our current obsession with pornography. Foucault, for example, makes the extraordinary claim that the modern concept of sexuality is all thanks to the Christian Church's obsession with it since the Middle Ages. The mediaeval Church, he claims, carefully identified and catalogued every variety of sexual expression and perversion, decided what was acceptable behaviour, and through the confessional ensured that the faithful were catechised about their private lives in some detail, and thus sensitised to their sexuality. As Michelson paraphrases Foucault, 'sexuality emerged from the religious preoccupation with the flesh, and by the seventeenth century had found a form in pastoral instructions for dealing with the subject in the confessional. This established forms of discourse that are still with us.'[7] Foucault has his own axe to grind, since he believes that sexuality is simply one particular way of seeing things that might have been seen otherwise, had we been sensitised differently, and therefore he has to show how this way of looking at things began. To the nose of common sense, this has an implausible smell!

Susan Griffin, writing from a feminist perspective, also sees the Church as responsible. 'We begin to see pornography more as if it were a modern building built on the site of the old cathedrals, sharing the same foundation. And if one were to dig beneath this foundation, we imagine, one might see how much the old structure and the new resemble one another. For all the old shapes of religious asceticism are echoed in porn.'[8]

Griffin goes so far as to suggest that the agony of Christ on the cross, whipped and stripped, which has been contemplated by the

208

faithful for two thousand years, is the stuff of sado-masochism, whose basis is always 'humiliation' of one sort of another, and that this has induced an unhealthy interest among ordinary people in torture and suffering: 'all the elements of sado-masochistic ritual are present in the crucifixion of Christ'.[9] (It seems unlikely that humanity's interest in violence should be linked to one particular image, no matter how widespread.) She likes to see pornography, too, as a ritual, a sacred drama. 'The altar for this ritual is a woman's body. All the ritual which is carried out on this altar is the desecration of the flesh. Here, what is sacred within the body is degraded.'[10] So, pornography is a black mass, a perverted religious rite.

Sex, religion and hell

Whether the Church is responsible or not, pornography has developed into a secular equivalent of hell for a materialistic world. With people unable any longer to believe in an afterlife in which to locate hell, the whole apparatus of heaven and hell has been simply transferred on to descriptions of beatific happiness or violence and torture in this life – notably, in the latter case, pornography. Instead of demons with pitchforks, we have pornographers and their readers – generally men – torturing and raping their victims.

This is not to imply that women are not tortured and raped, nor models exploited. Rather, it is to suggest that the language with which pornography is described often has a peculiarly religious fervour and flavour – a reliance upon the lazy universals found in (bad) religious vocabulary. Men are turned into demons. And if men are demons, the argument runs, the particular, infernal weapon they choose for their diabolical mischief is pornography, whereby they goad each other on to keep women in their place. This, according to conservative feminists, is the sole aim of pornography – another generalisation of dubious value.

Pornography: the facts

If pornography is the object of contemporary diabolism, as a religion substitute dealing with the darker side of human nature, it is as bogus as any other that we have examined. This is not to suggest that terrible things do not happen, nor that terrible injustice has not been done, and especially to women, over the years, nor that there are no victims of the pornographic industry. However, the regular public outcries over pornography and the demonising of its personnel do not help us to deal with the facts, which are the only antidote to such satisfying but meaningless generalities as 'all men are potential rapists'.

Another problem with the mythology of pornography is the age-old one that the Devil is always a most attractive figure, and that there is a constant danger of glamorising pornography. To dignify the sordid and abominable productions of diseased minds with the notion of hell is counterproductive. By bringing religious notions into play through using that charged word 'hell', one is in danger of suggesting that there could be here some route to the 'other' world of religion. The transcendent, positive or negative, is always attractive, and if, added to the discovery of the transcendent, there is the pleasure of transgressing against what Griffin calls the 'holy prudery' of the morally unadventurous, pornography may well prove irresistible to those looking for adventure.

As Jonathan Miller sensibly puts it, 'we must identify the *genuine* risk and exorcise the phantoms. Our prurient concern with obscenity and pornography merely delays constructive social action and presents a spectator from another planet with an image as absurd as that of someone trying to adjust their dress before jumping from a burning building.'[11] In one sense, everyone needs phantoms. In this case, however, the phantoms are at risk of making attractive the merely sordid.

The facts about pornography are depressingly few. Some experiments have been carried out with students, but it is difficult to find any incontrovertible connection between pornography and, say, violence towards women. Howitt and Cumberbatch, surveying all the literature they could find in the report referred to above, concluded as follows:

1) Evidence of the adverse effects of pornography is far less clear cut than some earlier reviews imply.

2) Sexual crimes may be carried out by people who seem to have a special interest in certain kinds of pornography. However, pornography seems to be used as part (not cause) of deviant sexual orientation.

3) Variations in rates of sexual crime do not indicate any simple causal relationship with the circulation rates of sex magazines, at least.

4) Very little is known about the possible inhibiting effects of pornography on the sex crime prone individual. . . .

7) Often the findings of effects of pornography in laboratory experiments are not reflected in similar field studies.

(They note that the laboratory experiments are generally carried out on students and from a small range of universities. 'Sometimes students at Wisconsin University taking a particular course have supplied all of the available evidence for a particular view.')

9) From self-reports of women who have been abused, it would seem that pornography is associated with some forms of violence against women. However, a causal link has yet to be clearly established.

10) The use of erotic material is quite common in persons who are difficult to define as deviant . . . evidence suggests that exposure to pornography relatively later in life than normal is more likely to be associated with sexual problems.[12]

The most extreme form of pornography is also, probably, the most mythical: the snuff movie, a film in which the actor (or actress) is actually killed live (as it were). Rumours abound of such a film being available at immensely high cost, or having been made for South American drug barons. However, despite copious efforts, no researcher has ever been able to track it down. The myth, certainly, is important. The spirituality of sex demands, naturally, a materialist equivalent of hell, and this is it: someone dying on film. That is why the rumour is so believable. Reality, it seems, lags some way behind.

Much more important than these fantasies is the fate of the models who make the films and are the subjects of the photos, an aspect that does not seem to be often considered. A recent newspaper investigation into the models used for pornography elicited the following:

> Here are the women, trussed and bound, while men fill them with dildos, telephone receivers, hair dryers, knives, guns. Here is the young woman with the short blonde hair, with both hands strapped over her head to the branch of a tree, while two men in masks thump belts against her back and breasts. Here is sex with pigs, sex with eels, sex with midgets, sex with amputees with semen all over their stumps . . . Then another woman and another hand, this time with a burning cigarette making charcoal of her nipple. Who is this woman with the shoulder-length hair, pegged out on her back while a man urinates down into her mouth? Did she really give her free consent for that? Who is this woman hung upside down from her ankles, her hair tumbling on to the floor, while a fat woman in a black corset thrashes her back and breasts with a bullwhip? Or the woman with black hair, tied in knots, while endless little balloons of burning wax drop down on her skin from a candle?[13]

This is a sordid business – especially where, as often, it begins with children who have been abused and degraded at an early age, who now regard their bodies as simply exploitable.

If the models and purchasers of porn tend to be ignored by the press, the producers of such material are demonised. Many of the grounds for this, too, are fantasy. Generally, these people are businessmen who are supplying a market comparable to that of arms dealers or tobacco manufacturers. Carolyn See has undertaken some useful research on them in her book *Blue Money*, in which she paints them simply as rather shady businessmen who pride themselves (some of them) on paying their taxes like anyone else. Their living is precarious, as it depends on 'intuiting the most deeply felt American fantasies and then making them available, recognisable to the public'.[14] They may be bad, but they are not demons.

Neither is one of the models who performs sexual acts live on stage, and whom she interviews, a she-devil. Usually, after seeing friends from back home, 'wan and drawn with the effort of making it in the square world, talking timidly to her about their children', Gerri 'takes a turn or two back on stage, just to feel the breeze around her body, and picks up some guy and takes him back to her place, not for the money, she says, but to *show* him something, that other world . . .'[15]

Even sex shops, rather than being Aladdin's caves of exciting and transgressive material, turn out to be particularly restrictive, sordid and not very liberated. Michael Stein has published an anthropological survey of a sex shop entitled *The Ethnography of an Adult Bookstore*. After working unpaid for twelve months for the sake of research, he concluded that 'the entering customer is effectively cut off from the outside. The singularity and the cultural restriction . . . render the bookstore a *special* place. To enter the bookstore or to explore any of the regions therein is to move from the everyday outside world of clothed persons and general notion of sexual propriety to a place depicting and focused on the domain of fantasy, where participants engage in "dirty, nonromantic sex".'[16] Later, he comments, 'the perceived deviant or tainted quality of the purchased products rendered the store a *special* place, establishing cognitive as well as physical boundaries'.[17]

In other words, the sex shop is very likely to be a sacred place, giving access to another world. However, in the end he is forced to conclude from the very limited range of pornographic genres (senior citizens seldom appeared in titles; there were no menstruating or pregnant women, no sex as an expression of affection or for procreation, all encounters limited to lust) that 'although at first glance it may seem that anything goes in pornography, this is clearly not the case. Paradoxically pornography is circumscribed so narrowly as to suggest its own kind of prudery as regards participants and motives.'[18]

What is to be done about pornography?

Destroying a myth is not easy. If porn really does play the important role in contemporary spirituality that I am suggesting, one can understand why it will be impossible to 'do something about it'. The press and public opinion require easily identifiable targets in order to fulfil the popular longing for a hell about which 'something must be done'. But real life is not that simple. You cannot do anything about hell. Pornography itself could be fairly easily dealt with, as I shall suggest below. But hell will always be with us in one form or another, as Camille Paglia, someone for whom sex, and especially the darker side of sex, is a quasi-religious force, reminds us.

> Profanation and violation are part of the perversity of sex, which will never conform to liberal theories of benevolence. Every model of morally or politically correct sexual behaviour *will be subverted.* . . . Feminism, arguing from the milder women's view, completely misses the blood-lust in rape, the joy of violation and destruction. An aesthetics and erotics of profanation – evil for the sake of evil, the sharpening of the senses by cruelty and torture – have been documented in Sade, Baudelaire and Huysmans.[19]

We shall consider the 'aesthetics of profanation' later in the chapter.

The 'answer to porn' depends on your standpoint. Conventionally, people's reactions to pornography are broken down into three different categories – conservative, feminist and liberal. Conservatives and feminists form an unlikely alliance: both would like to keep it off the streets. For the conservatives, this is not because they are particularly concerned about women, but because they consider that obscenity is degrading, that frequent exposure to it is habituative and decreases arousal, and that it threatens basic social values such as marriage which they regard as the foundation of society. (Conservatives tend to have a low view of human nature, something they consider needs constant policing.) Their critics would argue that such attempts at social control are heavy-handed and Canute-like in an affluent society. Thanks to relative affluence and good education, people are adult enough to make up their own minds on important matters.

Feminists, by contrast, tend to believe that pornography engenders bad attitude in men. Because pornography treats women as victims of abuse, and because it suggests that women really want to be raped or abused, it therefore makes women indirectly more prone to violence in real life. This 'sexualisation of subordination and violence',[20] because it is indirect, is very difficult to prove. It is difficult to show, of any particular act of abuse of women, that it is linked to a specific experience of pornography by the perpetrator and not to some third cause of which the use of pornography is a side-effect.

Liberals, having a much higher view of human nature, believe that human beings are, once released from their chains, adult enough to make their own decisions, and that freedom of speech should never be interfered with, even if particular instances are wrong. The corrective measure they prefer is to have 'more speech' rather than less; instead of trying to ban pornography, there should be an education programme, pointing out its bad effects – for example, the evils of rape. Pornography, they say, can be harmless entertainment, and may even be cathartic, may defuse the sexual tension of those tempted to sexual violence. The problem with this view is that the free market-place beloved of liberals is never free: large publishing organisations may exercise disproportionate influence and skew the level playing field by, for example, insisting that newsagents who stock their ordinary titles should also stock pornographic material, even if they would rather not.

However, there is a fourth explanation for the particular role that pornography plays in society which, if true, would make dealing with it more manageable. Recent studies are beginning to reveal the extraordinary cocktail of chemicals which is released during erotic stimulation. It is quite clear that pornography acts as a narcotic upon its subjects, much like alcohol or nicotine. A man looking at a pornographic picture of a naked women in certain circumstances will experience a dose of a pleasant pain-relieving chemical compound. Whether the triggers that activate its release are conditioned by early experiences or are genetically programmed is not yet clear.

As Joan Timmerman puts it,

> There is no mammal who does not try by some means, physical or chemical, to alter its states of consciousness. Small animals twirl round in circles or mimic attack and escape patterns, precisely to stimulate release of varying levels of drive chemistry. The command centre in the human brain (the hypothalamus) releases varying levels of epinephrine, dopamine, endorphins, serotonin. Research has shown that it is probable that the hypothalamus is suggestible and programmable (*which also confirms what religious liturgies have always understood intuitively*).[21]

Romantic love, she claims, produces phenylethylamine, while dopamine and norepinephrine account for the powerful sensation of pleasure enjoyed after sex.

However, as with all drugs, it seems that the effects of pornography are subject to habituation: the effect wears off with use, and the body requires larger and larger doses to achieve the same effect. For an adolescent male, a picture of a woman's breasts is enough to provide intense stimulation; for a seasoned roué such as the Marquis de Sade, nothing less than murder will suffice.

Another problem with drugs is that they encourage dependency. While most people do not become addicted to alcohol, a significant number do. What begins as a temporary antidote to, say, stress or anxiety becomes a necessity. Similarly with the images of pornography: some users will become so obsessed with the stimulation they provide that they will never thereafter be able to do without them.

Alcohol and porn both cut the user off from reality. The drinker may never again be able to find a natural way within him or herself of coping with stress; the user of porn may never be able to enjoy the real thing – relationships with real people.

Most work in this area appears to have been carried out on men. Less, it seems, is known about the chemical responses of women, but it appears that female erotic responsiveness may be more learnt than that of men. On the other hand, it may simply be that boys and men are so exposed to erotic stimuli during their adolescence that they appear to learn naturally what is in fact the result of a long process. In practice, experience suggests that for a woman, although the constant reminder of her effect on men (as endlessly relayed by advertisements) can be distressing, pornography can be as stimulating and potentially as addictive as it is for men.

If this is the case, two consequences follow. Firstly, similar arguments apply to the control of pornography as to that of alcohol. Under certain circumstances, it may be that a complete prohibition on alcohol, whether voluntary or statutory, is the only solution to alcohol abuse – for example, where the whole community is hopelessly affected. In practice, such a measure tends to be counterproductive. The reason for the overdependence in the first place is likely to be that most members of the community are experiencing terrible suffering or a lack of control over their lives and are desperately in need of a viable analgesic. Suppression of something for which there is a genuine need always forces it underground, whether it be sex, alcohol or religion (as the previous communist regimes of Eastern Europe discovered), and therefore to ban porn – as with alcohol – would be counterproductive. However, pernicious habits for which no real need any longer exists rarely wither on the vine – even in a civilised society – and it is normally necessary for an enlightened government to step in to finish off something bad or dangerous.

Therefore, it follows that one should treat pornography as one would any other narcotic with dangerous side-effects: regulate its production through a well-policed licensing system and tax it heavily, but not so heavily as to make illegal production attractive. Good educational policies in schools and elsewhere explaining its dangers would also help, as would ensuring that support groups and counselling are available for those who have become hopelessly addicted.

Sex and spirituality

In the extract from Joan Timmerman's book quoted above, there was the suggestion of an explanation for certain religious practices. Religious liturgies have often capitalised on the brain's power to produce, with appropriate stimulation, psychotropic drugs. Factors such as fasting, sleep deprivation, sensitisation to one's internal states, repetition, certain types of music such as plainsong, and formalised language have always been used to pave the way for religious experience. (It is interesting that in our highly states-of-consciousness-aware society, Gregorian chant is enjoying a popular revival.) These heightened states of awareness, caused, no doubt, by internally generated psychotropic drugs, have provided the great religions with a springboard to another world. (This does not diminish the validity of the ensuing religious experience, which is as related to its physical matrix as your smile is to the lips on which it forms.) One can therefore understand how the experience of pornography might be a sort of diabolical parody of the experience of genuine contemplation, in an abusive and exploitative framework rather than in a context directed (however hopelessly) towards self-sacrifice and altruism.

There are other examples of religion and extreme sexual practices coming together. Lars Ullerstam claims that

in order to abolish the myth that the 'perverted' pleasures are of a low and tawdry nature, I intend to give a few samples of the inner experiences that these 'perverted' acts can create. Their spiritual level is often very high: practices now termed sexual offences can satisfy the same elementary human cravings as religious rites.[22]

In more orthodox vein, Susan Griffin claims that men regard the naked woman beneath the clothes as they would 'the mystery of the holy grail'.[23] And Gerri, the stripper in *Blue Money*, also gains access to God through sex and drugs:

She was stoned, bombed, freaked, her brains were frying, but she distinctly heard God breathing in the old timbers of the building. She saw fairly clearly that the boy who was with her was not just himself but her boyfriends from high school, and her father and the swarthy gent who was *really* her father and all the men she might have someday. She cried for joy, and later, when the girl came in, Gerri saw that she was part of it too, the mother who might have loved her, the sister who might have been her friend . . .[24]

Here, in the flowery plains of San Francisco in the secular sixties, God creeps in and, in a parody of mystical experience become democratic, is accessible to all who can afford the acid.

One is reminded of the French philosopher Georges Bataille, who sees the Marquis de Sade (the French aristocrat and author of pornographic novels, imprisoned under the French *ancien régime* for his vile practices and liberated in 1789 at the time of the French Revolution) as a forerunner when he draws a parallel between the demise of the French monarchy and sovereign freedom in literature. 'On the one hand, de Sade took the side of the Revolution, and criticised the royal régime, but on the other hand he profited from the unlimited nature of literature: he proposed to his readers a sort of sovereign humanity, whose privileges would no longer have to be in accordance with what the crowd wanted.'[25] In the sexual revolution, religion and sexual experience became democratic, and 'sovereign humanity' took the place of God and public opinion.

Real hell

Moving now from pornography to the dark side of sexual experience as a whole, it is perfectly possible for the negative, destructive side of sex to be incorporated into a realistic spirituality. In the rest of this chapter, we look at several ways in which sex and hell have been brought together in genuine experiences of the transcendent, whether good or bad. We consider first the connection between aggression and sex.

In real life, the experience of hell can, under certain circumstances, be acknowledged in sexual intercourse. The role of violence in intercourse is often not explored in the sex manuals, but most people are aware of the consensual violence that can occur in sex, where aggression can be owned up to and defused in play. In fact, with the current vogue for body-piercing and bondage among young people, it is almost *de rigueur*. Rousseau once said that man was born free but is everywhere in chains. Today, it seems that most people are conceived in chains.

Traditionally, it was considered that all pornography was to do with aggression, whether man's aggression against woman, man against man or a now-fashionable brand of female sado-masochism which pits woman against woman. (Occasionally a photographer will turn the tables, and the model will turn her aggression on the viewer. For example, one feminist critic notes that in the lesbian photographs of Della Grace it is the viewer who is the object of excitement and exploitation: 'We're getting off on your gaze' is the message.) For men, one way of expressing aggression is to present women as victims of their own desires. They are able to justify their behaviour to themselves as they are only giving women 'what they really want' anyway.

The Story of O, for example, is a classic pornographic text quoted by every study of pornography, perhaps because it is one of the very few traditional pornographic novels which even begins to show any psychological insight into its characters, and was (probably) written by a woman, and therefore cannot simply be written off as a male fantasy. It portrays a woman consenting to her own sexual enslavement. The heroine becomes entirely engulfed in her own body, losing her own identity in the process, because of her love for a particular man. (The novel implies that this is a voluntary act, as she has a friend who is also lured to the same place but is sufficiently self-regarding to decline to be drawn in.)

In the tradition of the Marquis de Sade, the author paints a contemporary picture of hell. The château where the novel is set is a confined location with constantly measured doses of violence, and where the women actually suffer more violence from each other than from the men. The result is that they abandon their reason and identity ('O' is tagged like an animal) and become absorbed by their bodies. Hell, in other words, is your own body. (There is a serious point here which we will consider later.)

However, although pornography presents a negative view of aggression which contrives to identify the victim entirely with their own body, there is another view which regards it as a basic component of all sexual activity if not the only component. An extreme version would be the standpoint of the psychoanalyst Robert Stoller, who argues that hostility plays a major role in generating sexual excitement: 'For most individuals, and not just for the perverted or sexually unusual, sexual excitement is produced far less often by love and affection than by mechanisms of revenge and degradation.' According to Stoller's view, dehumanising and fetishistic images are an essential part of the erotic fantasy lives of normal individuals. He considers that love 'plays a minimal role in sexual excitement'.[26]

This view is without doubt too pessimistic. Yet it is one of the few to do justice to the part played by aggression in sex. With a long-term partner to whom they are committed for reasons other than sex, many couples report that sex is the ideal arena in which to express physically the negative or aggressive sides of their personalities. Men and women act out their darkest selves, and the orgasm at the climax discharges the aggression. In good sex, it is generally reported that the 'animal' side of human beings can be very evident – and permissible. Sex with someone trusted permits a real sense of terror, of the beyond breaking through, not in a loving or sentimental fashion but, because it is part of a long-term relationship whose focus is elsewhere (such as bringing up children), in a realistic manner which pornography and commercialisation have always to deny. (Adverts, like sex shops, can never really shock their customers or step beyond the bounds of bourgeois prudery.) It appears to be important for a couple to have mutual interests outside their relationship to prevent it degenerating into obsession, as explored most famously in *Last Tango in Paris*, where the couple agree to know nothing about each other and the strain breaks them.

This element of holy terror is also a staple ingredient of good literature and film. Novelists and film-makers often use sex – sometimes very violent or apparently exploitative sex – in their examinations of human life. They are often threatened with censorship. How is one to decide whether their use of sex is justified or not?

Anthony Burgess has a useful suggestion. Pornography is bad, he suggests, because it inflames uncontrollable passions and 'when the book is closed, the inflammation still exists and has to be discharged – for example in public violence'. Good literature, by contrast, exists in the hinterland between pornography and the simple educational writing that does not arouse desire at all: 'the literary function consists in arousing emotions, even indeed arousing physical desire, but only if the *discharge* of emotions aroused is effected during the aesthetic rhythm of the work itself'.[27]

This is probably more a matter of wishful thinking than of reality. Few works achieve such catharsis. The problem is one of the attractiveness of transgression: authors naturally always wish to push the boat out ever further, to taste forbidden fruit. Transgression is one great source of energy – the source of the desire to pioneer, to explore the further realms of the human spirit.

Peter Michelson takes the argument further by suggesting that what he calls 'obscene poetics', the use of obscenity in art, literature and film, far from being a tame product of the affluent society as most pornography is ('*pillules aphrodisiaques pour vieux messieurs*', as was said of the erotic drawings of Félicien Rops), is really engendered by a poetic nostalgia for the transcendent world that our materialist society has now made obsolete, the 'nostalgic appeal of vestigial idealism in the face of decentering materialism'.[28] Obscene poetics, he claims, evolved out of the philosophical preoccupations of the eighteenth century; from de Sade onwards, the great literary pornographers have targeted conventional good taste as 'an idol of the mind', aiming to puncture conventional erotic titillation by revealing the Devil grinning through the chinks. Artistic pornography is concerned with 'speaking the unspeakable'.

Even *The Story of* O, Michelson considers, can be interpreted in a moral fashion, because it is the record of both men and women being overtaken by self-destructive elements inside themselves. It uses the paraphernalia of pornography (whips, chains, torture, sado-masochism, masculine power, feminine submission) to explore the depths to which men and women respectively can descend once they give themselves to Eros. Some women can be so completely dependent upon another for their sense of self-worth that, like the eponymous heroine, they will undergo any torture for the reassurance of being loved. Men, similarly, will always be tempted to destroy the thing they love in order to be sure of possessing it: the men in the story all forgo any genuine relationship with women for the sake of control. Michelson concludes:

The story of O is anarchical at a deep and distressing personal level: it is a cultural suicide note, articulating the obsessive masculine need for the security of possession and an obsessive feminine need for the security of love. Masculinity can only prove itself by destroying what it most desires: need carries the seed of its own loss. And woman is at once gratified and destroyed by it.[29]

For Michelson, therefore, 'Porn is the risky side of the story teller's art'.[30] In the religion of sex, storytellers are the new preachers; just as a good sermon should disturb the congregation's sense of security by dangling them over the pit and then restoring them to grace, so a pornographic film or novel exposes its audience to the hell within and sends them out chastened and in control back into the world.

Unfortunately, this is today the current orthodoxy in the arts, so that it is positively expected of a painting or novel that it will shock its readers. Excrement art is high fashion; just when one imagines that artists have exhausted the different ways of shocking their public we are assaulted by an even grosser display. Perhaps this is especially the case in England. If it is true that the English are one of the least naturally religious races, as is often claimed, then this may explain why English obscenity is so lacking in seriousness. Even in Victorian times as Michelson puts it, 'when the English got obscene they merely got smutty'.[31]

Nonetheless, in the work of those few who have the courage truly to confront the demonic, one finds a vision of hell that is entirely genuine; and authors like Georges Bataille are correct in suggesting that true pornography can be the vehicle to a real encounter with the transcendent – not some masturbation fantasy about exploiting a dream-maiden, but the truly terrifying discovery of the appalling nature of the human spirit at its worst. The transcendent can be glimpsed through transgression, and, as in the case of great art, its effect is not to encourage any sort of exploitation but to open the mind to its own huge and terrifying dimensions.

For some, this sense of hell is actually their reason for believing in God; for example, Anthony Giddens points out that the 'Sadean universe discloses possibilities of its opposite'.[32] But this is a cop-out. Real pornography of the sort that Michelson describes is a Custer's last stand against the progress of materialism, heroic yet tragic because ultimately always defeated; for one drowning in matter, self-laceration against the enclosing darkness is a straw to grasp at, pain voluntarily accepted to defeat the numbing anaesthesia.

10

Glimpsing Paradise

From the marshlands and swamps of purgatory we climb now up the mountain of human experience towards the higher slopes. The valley beneath was full of sulphurous fumes, but the top of the mountain is also hidden by cloud. Perhaps there are things there which are beyond the power of words to deal with. For fear of the angels, we must tread carefully.

We begin by looking at a book that charts a similar journey, although less explicitly connected with sex. It moves from the appalling destruction wrought upon the human body by torture and war, and from this goes on to produce a whole theory of creativity which will be of immense importance to us when, at the end of the chapter, we attempt to formulate more precisely the relationship between sex and religion. Later in the chapter, we explore what has happened to the concept of God – especially if sex has become the religion substitute of our day. But first we must look a little more systematically at the process of secularisation that has occupied most of this book in more general terms. Once the importance of the body has been clarified, it will be even clearer why it is that sex, rightly or wrongly, is as supremely important as it is today.

The body in pain

The book is Elaine Scarry's *The Body in Pain*,[1] a long, difficult but exhilarating study of the connection between pain and the imagination. The workings of the imagination, Scarry claims, have always excited curiosity. What is it that looses these bubbles that lie at the bottom of the mind's oceanic depths, and which burst to produce images that are in some way linked to our very being? How is imagination connected to creativity? How do we create the human world in which we live?

Scarry begins with Amnesty International documents of the sort with which most people will be familiar, detailing some of the particularly terrible things human beings do to each other. For example, in a leaflet headed 'This leaflet will bring tears to your eyes', Amnesty recount how 'in the hands of the torturer, everyday things such as bottles, pins, sticks, water and electrical power become capable of causing the most extreme torment and suffering. The use of exhaust pipes to burst a victim's lungs, water forced into the stomach, eyes gouged out with pencils, women raped with bottles, children disfigured with hot irons . . . Electricity is unsurpassed in its ability to inflict pain . . . with skilful application of the current, your blood will literally boil.'

The effect of torture, Scarry demonstrates from Amnesty's evidence, is to shrink the world of the victim, to remove all those props and supports that human beings rely on to remain human, and leave the victim *all body* – in hell, in the sense explored in the previous chapter. Not only that, but pain is fundamentally isolating. No one else can ever really imaginatively share your pain. We may say, 'I know how you must feel,' but of course we don't. The acuteness of pain is mercifully forgotten the moment it stops. The torturers may hasten this process of deconstruction by, for example, deliberately using familiar objects to create pain: a bed or a bath or a lavatory, which customarily *relieve* us of pain by taking our weight or relieving us of cold or of a stomach ache, are deliberately perverted to *cause* pain.

If the torturers are successful, Scarry argues, the world of the victim shrinks simply to the confines of their body – which is why, as Amnesty document, the discovery by a prisoner of even a one-word note smuggled in with their bread is the most valuable thing in the world, because it instantly recreates the world the torturers have destroyed. It relinks the victim with their humanity; they are no longer alone.

The aim of torture is rarely the extracting of accurate information – when in pain, one will say the first thing that comes into one's head without regard for accuracy. Rather, it is a battle for power. The torturers need to be able to humiliate their victims, and thus to rubbish the particular aspirations or demands (for example, for human rights) that led to their arrest in the first place. Triumph comes, as at the end of George Orwell's *1984*, when the victims accede to the world view, to the power, of the torturers, and can therefore be despised as they will from now on despise themselves. (Amnesty never ask people whether they have confessed.)

Scarry also has a whole chapter on the purpose of war, to which she attributes a similar end: that of *enfleshing* through wounding a particular self-understanding, but this time of a nation, not just an individual.

Studying these documents made Scarry turn the question round. If the aim of torture is to destroy the world of the victim by destroying their defences against pain, might not pain under more normal conditions be responsible not for destroying the world but for constructing it? And from this basic intuition about the body in pain, she has gone on to construct a philosophy that will help us understand not only where God has disappeared to in our affluent society, but also why it was practically inevitable that this should happen.

Her argument goes roughly as follows: the whole of human history is dominated by bodily pain, and ways of avoiding it. For all of recorded time, bodily pain has been the primary stimulus upon human beings to create an imaginary world, a world other than the present one, a world where there is no pain.

But then, Scarry continues, human beings have the capacity over time to turn these imaginary worlds into reality – to create *artefacts* which act to relieve the particular pain that led to their being dreamt up in fantasy in the first place.

As a result of these reciprocated wishes, we have gone on to create, for example, clothes, medicines, spectacles, aeroplanes. The artefacts we create to dispel our pain are not just concrete things but also, and perhaps more importantly, abstract concepts. The gods and the concept of the afterlife (for example) are, she argues, imaginative responses by the body to its pain.

Because Scarry is a philosopher, she ignores what seems to be a perfectly straightforward biological explanation of this – that the body in pain produces natural painkillers, which not only kill the pain, but also stimulate some gland in the brain responsible for the imagination. Even if superficially true, this theory cannot explain the value we give to the products of the imagination. The imagination can link us more closely to reality and make it possible not just to escape reality but to restructure it – for example, to dream up democratic alternatives to oppressive political conditions.

Thus, she argues, pain and the imagination are inextricably linked. Pain gives rise to counterfactuals, imaginary ideas, and then these are reciprocated into reality, back onto the human body which was in pain in the first place, and they can then act to relieve the pain.

Our culture is thus like a great cloak with which humanity covers itself as a protection against pain. All artefacts (which collectively make up our culture) are extensions of the body to protect it from its susceptibility to pain. Our work, for example, is a sort of pain voluntarily entered into. But the effect of work is to create greater pain relief for ourselves and for others; and the most important point about work is that (generally) it is pain voluntarily endured, and – unlike the acute pain of say a stomach ache which isolates the sufferer – it may be shared.

The forms pain relief may take will vary according to who we are. John Keats may write an ode to autumn, thus restructuring the painful sensations of death and decay that we experience in autumn, reshaping them, giving them positive meanings by association; whereas Mildred Keats, by contrast, may make a winter coat to keep out the cold of autumn. Curiously (and this is important), although Mildred Keats's coat may be more practical, John Keats's poem will turn out to be much more long-lasting, and will be taught in schools all over the English-speaking world long after Mildred Keats's coat has been disposed of. Strangely, in our culture, many abstract forms of pain relief are actually more highly valued than sensible, sensate ones!

So, to conclude this brief summary of Scarry's argument, the human body's susceptibility to pain is intricately connected to the human imagination.

Investing in artefacts

As a worked example, I shall look briefly at the monumental African Exhibition that took place at the Royal Academy in London in 1995. This was a stunning collection of exhibits collected from all over the African continent. Each item was taken from a different community with differing values and traditions; together, they presented a richness of cultures that it was impossible to assimilate at once.

To take three very different examples, Bocio figures from South Benin are stylised representations of the human figure. They link the visible world to the invisible; their primary function is to trap evil forces by causing them to mistake the sculpture for a real person's presence. The direction in which the figure looks is the one from which evil might come. Although some are beautifully carved, others can be just 'minimal transformations of a log, and all the accidents linked to the growing of a tree can be animated by the carver'. But there is another factor involved in their creation: 'permanent exposure to the elements continues the carving process'.[2]

The Akan people of South Ghana, who mined gold in the forest and traded it in North Africa, developed no less than four different series of weights, based, according to the use of their trading partners, on the Islamic ounce, the *mithqhal* (one sixth of an Islamic ounce), the Portuguese ounce and the Dutch ounce. The four series were combined into one traditional table of about sixty different units of weight – and a huge variety of different decorated 'goldweights' were created to weigh all these units, some in geometric form, others in the shape of a human figure. 'In the Akan world,' said the catalogue, 'the weighing of gold was a complicated and time-consuming art.'

In the Congo, *nkondi* identify and hunt down unknown wrong-doers such as thieves and those who cause sickness and death by spells. The *nkondi* are generally contained within a wooden figure, of which there were some truly terrifying examples in this exhibition. To persuade these forces to go to work, the catalogue told us, 'they were both invoked and provoked: invocation, often in extraordinarily bloodthirsty language, spelled out the problems . . . To provoke the *nkondi*, gunpowder might be exploded in front of the container, insults might be hurled at it, but above all, nails, blades and other hardware were driven into it.'

However, fascinating as these glimpses of other peoples' lives were, the most interesting thing about the exhibition was that it enabled the visitor to evaluate the role of the artefact within his or her own world. By visiting another culture, by removing ourselves from the familiar, we can better understand the role and purpose of culture as a whole.

Naturally, there is always the risk with an exhibition of this type of attempting to bring anything strange into one's own European purview. Several hundred artefacts spanning the whole course of human history, from the earliest discovered tool and from all over a continent that has always acted as Europe's shadow (Africa, Cornel West suggested in the catalogue, has always been associated with the exotic and the transgressive, with 'hypersexual criminal abstractions'), are, inevitably, just by dint of appearing in the Royal Academy, going to be subject to a form of cultural imperialism. These artefacts laid out for us represent a rainbow juxtaposition of signs, symbols, sacred objects and humdrum tools from myriad groups of people, none of whom, until very recently, had either a word for 'art' or a concept of Africa. However, allowing for these reservations, if we were to compare the power of these marvellous artefacts with those of our own time, we would probably find our own artefacts (material and non-material) to be quite etiolated by comparison. Why should this be?

Scarry's general principle can be extended. Surely the impact of an artefact is in direct proportion to the pain of the artist and culture that produced it. A materially affluent culture, because there is less pain around, does not produce such dramatic forms of pain relief as were to be seen in the exhibition. (No doubt this is what Picasso found in African art, for all his talk of demons: a way of dealing with pain that he could understand and assimilate.)

But not only is there less pain around in a materially sufficient society; its investment in artefacts against pain can be so widely diffused that no one object in such a balanced portfolio need be invested with the supernatural power with which there can be no doubt many of these African objects were invested. And so, while our own Western power objects (as fetishes are now called) – a mobile telephone, a judge's gavel, a Speaker's mace, a teen idol, a medicine cabinet – also participate in a richness of connections and meanings, as much as the African ones, none of them have the simple power of an object in which the whole psychic investment of a community is stored, and thus they may seem very drab by comparison.

The human race, like any sensible institution engaging in risk management, has spread out its activities as broadly as possible, each one taking part of the strain and all of them together making an immensely complicated and powerful network of values. The interesting thing about the African exhibition was the extraordinary power of many of the artefacts, due, as I argued above, to the fact that they were invested with power in a very condensed way, taking up vast physical human resources, and representing something of immense symbolic importance to the human imagination of the time. That today we have masses of these power objects, each with much less individual significance, is surely, a matter for rejoicing on all grounds except aesthetic ones. In a memorable image Scarry talks of the massive, continuous and ongoing repair work performed, almost unnoticed, by the human imagination, as being 'like a watchman patrolling the dikes of culture by day and by night'.

Gods as artefacts?

We move now on to the second and more important part of the argument. What are the implications of all this for religion? Scarry, as a philosopher, is quite happy to regard gods as artefacts produced by the imagination to enable human beings to escape from their bodies, 'to relieve bodily engulfment'. (Another of her findings about the way artefacts work is that the more important the symbol or artefact is to a culture, the less is its nature as artefact appreciated.) She has a whole chapter on the Old Testament view of God – and although her reading of the Bible is clearly that of someone brought up in the North American Protestant tradition, and her treatment of Old Testament texts historically cavalier, it is an interesting illustration of her argument. For her, the Scriptures 'are the record of the imagination's aspirations towards disembodiment and of its origins in pain'. In the Old Testament, she argues, God is entirely disembodied, while human beings are entirely embodied. Any attempt to embody God by making an idol such as the golden calf results in punishment; God can have no material body, for he is the primary and ultimate creator.

Scarry turns this round, to interpret the Old Testament vision of God as being the ultimate symbol of human beings' ability to escape their sensitivity to pain, their embodiedness, through the imagination, through self-extension, through creating artefacts. God is the summation of the human being as creator, the ultimate artefact.

However, she also traces in the Bible a countervailing pattern; there is a constant desire that God be enfleshed, that the disembodied products of the imagination be reciprocated into matter.

The energy required to keep God separate and holy began to be dissipated as the people of Israel became more settled. Scarry charts the process – gradually in the Old Testament and rapidly in the New – of God acquiring a body, and, corrrelatively, man acquiring a voice.

There was a difficult moment when the transcendent and holy God, originally a helpful concept which gave a moral basis for the apparently random pain inflicted by the universe, changed roles and was now seen to inflict pain in an immoral way in order to make people believe in him. 'The artefact invented to relieve bodily engulfment now itself requires bodily engulfment to confirm its "realness".'[3] But at this point, his end was already in sight. For example, later in Old Testament times, the Jewish Law (an institution that was more clearly a human artefact) came to take on an importance equal to God's.

Finally, in the New Testament, God becomes totally embodied, and whereas, for example, the Old Testament prophet Jeremiah[4] can mock pagan idols (representations of God's body) as being like scarecrows in a cucumber field, now God dies on a cross outside the city gates looking as much like an idol as Jeremiah's scarecrow.[5] In the Christian version, God is embodied and (arguably) in pain.

In other words, a more affluent society such as that of the New Testament cannot envisage God simply as a disembodied and transcendent power object; already the creator is being fused with the creation, the artefact is becoming reciprocated on to human beings. Just as human beings long dreamt of being able to fly, and finally invented an aeroplane in which to do so, so we dream of being untroubled by bodily pain and discover a god who lives a pain-free existence, a being who finally inspires humanity to discover ways of living that, thanks to medicine, technology, democracy, the law and the other great Western institutions, are (just) beginning to make life pain-free for a slender majority of people at any one time. The dream of Eden is being fulfilled (as it has throughout history): through the religious vision that stems from the Judaeo-Christian tradition, men and women are inspired to reciprocate an escapist transcendence back into reality.

Abiding truths and principles

To move on, then, to the contemporary world, I would suggest that we live in a hugely affluent society where we have reciprocated our power objects so thoroughly and invested our pain relief so widely that no one artefact can possibly have enough power to do the work that was once done by God.

Naturally, this does make life difficult for religion. Most traditionally religious people like the capacity religion has to invest artefacts with simple and enormous power – whether the Bible or the eucharistic host, the Pope or the Archbishop of Canterbury – and therefore regard our present society as godless because power is so widespread.

The previous Archbishop of York, Lord Habgood, for example, in his 1995 Priestland Memorial Lecture, attacked our modern 'information culture' in general, and the Internet in particular, because, he claimed, it was in danger of disorienting people with an explosion of information, and creating a culture of contempt where knowledge was just 'an endless succession of human opinions and where there are no abiding truths and principles'.

But in fact our society has a highly complex and amazingly comprehensive network of truths and principles. It is precisely because our investments are so wide, because they no longer 'abide' in just a few specific power objects, material or non-material, that they are less visible.

However, this still leaves the burning question: where is God in all this? Can we be content to see God sunk so deeply into culture, so profoundly embodied, so perfectly secular that he/she is invisible to the naked eye? Can we be content to know that the energy and fervour with which human beings used to worship their gods are now disseminated through thousands of different channels?

This, at last, is where sex enters the argument. For not all channels are of the same importance. I would like to suggest that there are peaks and troughs in the great sea of culture. Although the waves of fashion may be fickle, there is one image in particular that is predominant, and which still has 'religious' power in the traditional sense: that of the human body itself.

The modern concept of the body is probably as much an artefact as anything else. If the human body in pain is, as Scarry suggests, the source of all culture, it is logical that the body itself should become the ultimate artefact, that it should become divine, and in sex, as this book has argued, the human body should be uncovered at its most profoundly resonant. The human body is paramount – it is our most important artefact – it is in a sense divine, and sexual intercourse its sacrament *par excellence*.

To explain. We have already seen how in the arts today the exploration of the human body is at the forefront. Artists are no longer concerned to idolise or falsify it, as traditional nudes, for example, used to, but rather to penetrate its reality and complexity. In 1995, for example, the Tate Gallery in London exhibited Geneviève Cadieux's installation *Broken Memory*, a huge glass cube with sloping sides in an empty room, itself empty except for snaking wires, with four loudspeakers giving out voices of disembodied pain. The piece was riveting, haunting and profoundly disturbing. One's natural instinct was to try to comfort the voice – but you cannot comfort a disembodied voice. The viewer was made acutely aware of the body by its absence.

This is one small example among thousands of how entirely secular artists attempt to explore the complex resonance – one might almost use the word 'sacredness' – of the human body. And not only in the arts, but in almost every aspect of life which matters, the human body is generally to be found in pole position. Many people sense that in our secular, non-sacramental culture, the language of words is too flat, too limited, to be up to expressing such an exalted vision (and the uncomfortableness of these very words simply proves the point); and this may explain why the language of the visual arts, for example, is frequently used instead to express this intuition of depth and resonance. Yet works such as Cadieux's are certainly esoteric, and probably seen by fewer people than attend church services, and so this is why, when trying to express this sense of richness, of strangeness and complexity of the body, most people tend to use the language of sex, for it is when the body is viewed in the light of sex that its richness of meaning is most easily perceived. This is why sexual intercourse is the ultimate sacrament, often explicitly celebrated in surprisingly religious language. To put it another way, as Roger Scruton neatly phrases it, 'through the sexual act, the body is transformed from a prison to a home'.[6] More than that, in sex, even in a secular age, the body promises near-sacred ecstasy.

For fear of the angels

And yet even with all the pain relief in the world, the body – that constant reminder of our animality – will always demand a certain degree of sublimation, of imaginative projection, that cannot (at present) be reciprocated: the cure for HIV or cancer; clean nuclear energy; time travel; colonising space; eliminating poverty in the Third World; preventing suicide or murder. There is still a constant need to project – and rightly so. A society that had lost this vital capacity to create new worlds would have become incorrigibly decadent.

Even today, especially in the civilised countries of the West, that terrible disease which Durkheim first identified all those years ago as *anomie* still lurks just beneath the horizon: the sense that nothing is worth fighting for, that nothing can impede the worlds' revolving 'like ancient women gathering fuel in vacant lots'. It seems that human beings still require a certain minimum quantity of suffering to spur them on to live productive and active lives. Curiously, a society where the lion lies down with the lamb is likely to be moribund. Fortunately, even in Eden, there will always be a snake. This is not for a moment to suggest that there is any sense in which human beings are justified in causing pain to each other – one does not need a particularly sensitive imagination to realise that there is always enough suffering without needing to add to its total.

The human body is essentially precarious, and the grander our aspirations the more precarious it becomes. The body may be wonderful, but the greater our sense of wonder and the more sensitive we become to the sense of the richness, complexity and transcendence that it unclothes for us, the more we come to respect the ambivalence, the potential for both creation and destruction, of those angels glimpsed at moments of heightened experience such as sex.

There are a huge variety of different expressions of sex, some of which we have explored in this book, and all of which are different ways of reciprocating the image of God back into matter, of exploring the richness, that quality of infinity, of the human being. But all are capable of abuse. If sex is unreal, if the expectations of its possibilities are too great, if it is controlled or manipulated, if it is used in a way that cannot in any sense be ultimately 'reciprocated' back into the present, then, like bad religion, it will be immensely damaging. It will lead to physical pain and exploitation and murder. If, on the other hand, sex is real, then like good religion it can indeed give access to another world.

Mystical union

In the closing chapters of the Bible, there is a visionary description of the heavenly Jerusalem coming down to earth at the end of the world. In this paradisial city, there is, according to St John, its author, no temple.[7] 'And I heard a great voice from the heavenly throne saying, "Behold, God's tent is among human beings, and he will pitch his tent with them, and they shall be his people; and God himself shall be with them. And he shall wipe away every tear from their eyes; and death shall be no more, nor sorrow, nor crying, neither will there be any more pain: for the former things have passed away" . . . And I did not see any temple in it, for the Lord God, the pantocrator, is its temple.' (The tent referred to is the tent that housed the Ark of the Covenant in the Old Testament – the Bible's ultimate sacred space.)

And so, even in the Bible itself, there is an image of God so completely present among his people that there is no need for any specific sacred space. This seems to be the perfect illustration of Scarry's philosophy. Although, clearly, to consider the present world as perfect would be the ultimate blasphemy, nevertheless this passage has set an agenda that the human race is relentlessly pursuing. Is this blasphemy or an accurate description of the way things are?

The sense that there *is* another world, a genuine source of discovery found not in escape from but in exploration of this one, applies not only to the body. Like physicists opening up the structure of the atom, astronomers that of space and biologists that of the cell, one may be continually surprised by the complexity of reality. Certainly, sex is sacramental: it opens up the deep structures of life and, rather than providing an escape, actually roots people in the present; the 'Other' world actually turns out to be the most real aspect of this one which can be glimpsed, when sex is used well, within a fuller perspective, and in its full beauty, danger and complexity. But sex and the body are by no means the only route. For not just the body, but the whole of reality would finally turn out to be sacramental – if only we had the language in which to express such a magnificent intuition.

Fifty years ago, prophetic writers such as Teilhard de Chardin predicted that matter would soon be seen to be sacramental, that people might expect to find God therein. If so, sex is where matter and mind, body and spirit, meet; sex is thus the spirituality that reveals the sacramental richness of matter. Through sex, we find that all of matter is 'groaning with value' – that all reality becomes erotic.

Conversely, just as some find that sexuality at its best puts us in touch with reality, so others find that reality at its best is erotic. Physicists, scientists and astronomers report being drawn by contact with matter to the perception of the sacredness of life itself. As Don Cupitt puts it in *Radicals and the Future of the Church*: 'The real, for us human beings, is indeed close to the erotic, in that for there to be any "reality" at all we must be enticed. Our interest has to be aroused by something still concealed, ambiguous, questionable, teasing, duplicitous, provocative, puzzling and tempting.'[8]

That these expectations of sex are not entirely unfounded is shown by the glimpses of the mystical aspect of sex found in literature and the arts. We lack a proper mystical vocabulary in our flat world, and so must rely upon borrowed clothes to make up for our lack – those of the visual arts, poetry, ritual, dance and drama.

One of my favourite examples is Yeats's poem, 'Leda and the Swan'. Leda was, in Greek mythology, the girl raped by Zeus in the guise of a swan who thus became mother of Helen of Troy. Yeats pictures her caught up 'by the brute blood of the air' and wonders 'Did she put on his knowledge with his power/Before the indifferent beak could let her drop?' The poet captures the sense that there is, in sexual ecstasy, potentially a moment of almost mystical timelessness, a moment in which past and future come together, that perhaps enabled Leda to see momentarily through the divine eyes of her lover the course of history unrolling before her. The perception at a charged moment of the richness of human existence, of the vast multitude of connections and networks in which even the most humble life participates, extends to the depths of time, of past and future.

Or, as Rollo May puts it in *Love and Will*:

In sexual intercourse ... there is the point where the lovers are carried beyond their personal isolation, and when a shift in consciousness occurs which they experience as uniting them with nature itself. There is an accelerating experience of touch, contact, union to the point where, for a moment, the awareness of separateness is lost, blotted out in a cosmic feeling of oneness with nature ... This seems to be a normal part of the momentary loss of awareness of the self and the surging up of a sudden consciousness that includes the earth as well.[9]

We too, on occasion, climb back up into the mountains with which this book began, to re-establish contact with the sacred, to revisit the simple, powerful religion of the great white peaks, to escape the endless 'packages of predigested information and culture'[10] supplied on radio and television and in the press – to re-experience the sublime tragi-comedy of the two different planes, the transcendent and the human, coinciding.

But life on the mountain is uncomfortable, and most of us make our way back down to the valley sooner or later, though glad that there are always some to keep the old rites going, some who have seen angels and lived to tell the tale. As Owen Chadwick puts it at the end of his work on secularisation, 'once the human race has an experience which it has found in part to be authentic, it does not let go'.[11]

So we return to daily life, putting our clothes back on, limiting our consciousness to the immediate concerns of the everyday, but always hesitantly, taking care not to make false or imperious demands of life or of God – for fear of the angels.

Notes

Introduction – Landscapes of Desire

1 Robert Bates, *Sacred Sex* (London: Fount, 1993), 220f
2 Valerie Kelly, *How to Write Erotica* (New York: Crown Publishers, 1986), 14
3 John Donne, 'On Going to Bed'
4 Roger Scruton, *Sexual Desire: A Philosophical Investigation* (London: Phoenix, 1994), 14
5 Georges Bataille, *L'Érotisme* (Paris: Les Éditions de Minuit, 1957), 13
6 Anthony Giddens, *The Transformation of Intimacy* (London: Polity Press, 1992), 180
7 Michel Foucault, *History of Sexuality*, Vol 1 (London: Penguin, 1990), 7
8 Sue Haines and Chris Wright, *Sexuality and Religion* (London: Lion Educational, 1991), 18

Chapter 1 – Entering the Garden – Sex and Childhood

1 Humphrey Carpenter, *Secret Gardens: A Study of the Golden Age of Children's Literature* (London: Allen & Unwin, 1985), ix
2 Carpenter, 67
3 Asa Briggs, *A Social History of England* (London: BCA, 1983), 227
4 Carpenter, 13
5 Peter Gay, *The Bourgeois Experience*, Vol 1 (New York: Oxford UP, 1984), 304
6 Carpenter, 220
7 Carpenter, 222
8 Bryan S. Turner, *The Body and Society: Explorations in Social Theory* (Oxford: Blackwell, 1984), 131
9 Bruno Bettelheim, *The Uses of Enchantment* (London: Penguin, 1991), 128
10 I differ from Bettelheim in regarding this point as important

11   Bettelheim, 187
12   Bettelheim, 187
13   Thomas Traherne, *Centuries of Meditation*, from *Third Century*: 1, 2, 3
14   Charles Baudelaire, *Mœsta et Errabunda*
15   D.W. Winnicott, *Playing and Reality* (London: Penguin), 108, quoted by Peter Fuller in *Art and Psychoanalysis* (London: Writers & Readers, 1980), 202
16   Fuller, 166
17   Sigmund Freud, *On Sexuality* (London: Penguin, 1991), 120
18   Iona and Peter Opie, *Children's Games in Street and Playground* (Oxford: OUP, 1984), 15

Chapter 2 – Poaching the Gamekeeper – Sex and Nature

1   Wordsworth himself later in life showed growing veneration for the English Church in his *Ecclesiastical Sonnets*
2   Other highlights of this translation include:
    The palace of Pentheus the rash
    To the quaking ground in ruins shall crash
3   Euripides, *The Bacchae*, edited with an introduction and commentary by E.R. Dodds, second edition (Oxford: Clarendon Press, 1960), 97
4   This interpretation of *The Bacchae* is partly derived from Camille Paglia, *Sexual Personae: Art and Decadence from Nefertiti to Emily Dickinson* (London: Penguin, 1992), 104ff
5   Mary Daly, *Gyn/Ecology: The Metaethics of Radical Feminism* (London: Women's Press, 1991), 88
6   Bryan Turner, *The Body and Society* (Oxford: Blackwell, 1984), 132 quoting H.R. Trevor-Roper, *Religion and Social Change* (London, 1967)
7   Arthur Miller, *The Crucible* (London: Penguin, 1968), 40
8   *The Crucible*, 39
9   Richard Weismann, *Witchcraft, Magic and Religion in Seventeenth Century Massachusetts* (Amherst: University of Massachusetts Press, 1984), 88, 76
10 Weismann, 78
11 Weismann, 79
12 Weismann, 89, (my italics)
13 Weismann, 42
14 *The Crucible*, 127
15 Weismann, subtitle of Chapter 10
16 Weismann, 183
17 C.H. Dodd's phrase

18 Weismann, 53 (my italics)
19 Weismann, 56
20 Gerard Manley Hopkins, *God's Grandeur*
21 D.H. Lawrence, *Women in Love* (London: Penguin, 1960), 256
22 *Women in Love*, 259
23 *Women in Love*, 124
24 For the symbolism of the railway engine and horse, compare *Introduction*, 8f
25 Eric James, *A Life of Bishop John AT Robinson* (London: Collins, 1987), 92ff. James continues, 'The bishop added "lower case" under his breath, but most papers reported him as saying Holy Communion (upper case).'
26 D.H. Lawrence, *Lady Chatterley's Lover* (London: Penguin, 1960), 180f
27 *The Guardian Weekend*, 4 February 1995
28 Foucault himself comes to a similar conclusion in *History of Sexuality* Vol 1

Chapter 3 – Into the Ring – Sex and Marriage

1   Lawrence Lerner, *Love and Marriage* (London: Edward Arnold, 1979), 112
2   Rollo May, *Love and Will* (New York: W.W. Norton & Co, 1969), 328 f.n. 10
3   Noel Annan, *Leslie Stephen* (London: MacGibbon & Kee, 1951), 75
4   Lerner, 141
5   Lerner, 142
6   Quoted by Asa Briggs, *Social History of England* (London, BCA, 1983), 240
7   Don Cupitt, *Sea of Faith* (London: BBC, 1984), 22
8   D.H. Lawrence, *The Rainbow* (London: Penguin, 1989), 131
9   *The Rainbow*, 302
10 *The Rainbow*, 134
11 Peter Berger, *Facing Up To Modernity* (London: Penguin, 1979), 57 (my italics)
12 Anthony Giddens, *The Transformation of Intimacy* (London: Polity Press, 1992), 197 (although this is not in the context of marriage)
13 Niklas Luhmann, *Love as Passion* (London: Polity Press, 1986), in the Introduction to the English edition
14 Roger Scruton, *Sexual Desire: A Philosophical Investigation* (London: Phoenix, 1994), 242 (italics original)
15 Diana Leonard, *Sex and Generation: A Study of Courtship and Weddings* (London: Tavistock, 1980), 266f

16 Quoted by Giddens, 24. Compare, too, Rollo May in *Love and Will*, 46: 'The Victorian person sought to have love without falling into sex; the modern person seeks to have sex without falling into love'

17 *The Rainbow*, 184

18 Lerner, 159

19 Janet Reibstein, Martin Richards, *Sexual Arrangements: Marriage and Affairs* (London: Heinemann, 1992), 202

20 Reibstein, 162

21 Berger, 46

22 *Sexual Arrangements*, 16

23 Statistics quoted by the *1+1* marriage research charity on a BBC *Panorama* programme about the future of marriage, 13 November 1995

24 Adrian Thatcher, *Liberating Sex: A Christian Sexual Theology* (London: SPCK, 1993), 96f

25 Jeffrey Weeks, *An Unfinished Revolution: Sexuality in the Twentieth Century* in ed. Victoria Harwood, *Pleasure Principles: Politics, Sexuality and Ethics* (London: Laurence & Wishart, 1993), 1–17

26 Scruton, 271

27 Leonard, 256

28 Giddens, 196

29 L.J. Weitzman, *Legal Regulation of Marriage: Tradition and Change* California Law Review 62 (4) July 1974

30 BBC *Panorama*, 13 November 1995

31 Jack Clemo, 'Intimate Landscape' from *Selected Poems* (Newcastle-upon-Tyne: Bloodaxe Books, 1988), 45

32 Weeks in ed. Harwood, *Pleasure Principles*, 17

Chapter 4 – Feasting on Flesh – The Shock of the Nude

1 Georges Bataille, *L'Érotisme* (Paris: Les Éditions de Minuit, 1957), 24

2 Julia Kristeva, *Of Word and Flesh*: an interview with Julia Kristeva by Charles Penwarden in *Rites of Passage* catalogue (London: Tate Gallery, 1995), 24

3 Anthony Giddens, *The Transformation of Intimacy* (London: Polity Press, 1992), 180f

4 Bataille, 35

5 Camille Paglia, *Sexual Personae: Art and Decadence from Nefertiti to Emily Dickinson* (London: Penguin, 1982), 20

6 James Park, *Sons, Mothers and Other Lovers* (London: Little, Brown & Co, 1995), 130

7 Roger Scruton, *Sexual Desire: A Philosophical Investigation* (London: Phoenix, 1994), 280

8 Jan Moir, *My Body, My Self* (London: *Guardian Weekend*, 24 September 1994), 42

9 Anne Hollander, *Seeing through Clothes* (Berkeley: University of California Press, 1993), 86

10 Margaret Miles, *Carnal Knowing* (Tunbridge Wells: Burns & Oates, 1992), 124

11 Sigmund Freud, *The Interpretation of Dreams* tr. J. Strachey (London: George Allen & Unwin, 1954), 244

12 Scruton, 277 (my italics)

13 Scruton, 281 (my italics)

14 Scruton, 280

15 It is important, however, that at times of bereavement one *should* be able to believe this (as the film *Truly, Madly, Deeply* made beautifully and sympathetically clear)

16 Sallie Tisdale, *Talk Dirty to Me: An Intimate Philosophy of Sex* (London: Pan, 1995), 9f

17 Tisdale, 10

18 Valerie Kelly, *How to Write Erotica: Turn Your Fantasies into a Fortune* (New York: Crown Trade Paperbacks, 1986), Appendix D, 282

19 Kelly, 294

20 Kelly, 287

21 Kelly, 79

22 Kelly, 90

23 Kelly, 84

Chapter 5 – Unfrocking the Priest – Sex and Religion

1 'Bishop Turnbull had recently endorsed the Church's official view that self-proclaimed homosexuality was "incompatible with full time stipendiary ministry".' *The Guardian* 26 September 1994

2 Even when he is not gay

3 All these quotations are taken from interviews in the BBC *Everyman* programme first screened on 26 November 1995

4 Emmanuel le Roy Ladurie, *Montaillou: Cathars and Catholics in a French Village 1294–1324* (London: Penguin, 1980), 167

5 Ladurie, 158

6 Ladurie, 155

7 Ladurie, 156

8 Georges Duby, *The Knight, the Lady and the Priest* (London: Penguin, 1985), 111

9   Edward Said, *Orientalism* (London: Penguin, 1991), 190

10   Said, 188

11   Said, 118

12   Said, 122 my italics

13   Said, 120 my italics

14   Said, 121

15   Said, 190

16   *The Love Plan: Sex from the Heart* written, produced and directed by Adam Cole, Safe Productions, London, SFH01 (no date)

17   David L. Snellgrove, *Indo-Tibetan Buddhism*, (London: Serindia, 1987), 259 ff

18   Snellgrove, 201

19   Geoffrey Parrinder, *Sex in the World's Religions* (London: Sheldon, 1980), 240

20   Janie Gustafson, *Celibate Passion* (Harper Collins, 1978) in ed. James B. Nelson, Sandra P. Longfellow, *Sexuality and the Sacred: Sources for Theological Reflection* (London: Mowbray, 1994), 280

21   Jack Dominan, *Sexual Integrity* (London: DLT, 1987), 88–105, reprinted in Nelson & Longfellow, 273

22   Peter Gay, *The Bourgeois Experience*, Vol 2: *The Tender Passion* (New York: OUP, 1986), 258

23   Paul Ricoeur, *Wonder, Eroticism and Enigma* in Nelson & Longfellow, 84f (originally appeared as *Sexuality in the Modern World*, in 'Crosscurrents', Spring 1964)

24   Mircea Eliade, *Images and Symbols – Studies in Religious Symbolism* (London: Harvill Press, 1961), 14

25   Dominian, 267

26   *Song of Songs* 7:7–9 (NJB translation)

27   Robert Bates, *Sacred Sex* (London: Fount, 1993), 209, (this is a very loose translation)

28   Bates, 154

29   *Ezekiel* 23:11–30 (NJB)

30   The phrase is Jill Lloyd's from the preface to her *German Expressionism* (London: Yale UP, 1991), *vii*

Chapter 6 – Painted Flesh – Sex and the Fine Art Tradition

1   Peter Gay, *Art and Act* (New York: Harper & Row, 1976), 224

2   Sigmund Freud, *On Sexuality* (London: Penguin, 1977), 124

3 Paula Cooey, *Religious Imagination and the Body: A Feminist Analysis* (New York: OUP, 1994), 48

4 Camille Paglia, *Sexual Personae: Art and Decadence from Nefertiti to Emily Dickinson* (London: Penguin, 1982), Chapter 1 *passim*

5 *Letters of Vincent Van Gogh*, ed. Mark Roskill (London: Flamingo, 1983), 121

6 Kenneth Clark, *Civilisation: A Personal View* (London: BBC and John Murray, 1969), 212

7 G.K. Howes, *Secularisation and Religious Art*, a paper delivered to the American Society for the Study of Religion, Chicago, 1986

8 Howes' intention in his paper is to show that it is not easy to draw straight parallels between art and religion; he is not responsible for my interpretation of his findings

9 G.K. Howes, *Religious Art versus Religious Experience*, a paper given at St Alban's Centre, London, 24 April 1995

10 Peter Gay, *The Bourgeois Experience* vol 1 (NY: OUP, 1984), 392

11 Gay, 394

12 J. Russell, *New York Review of Books*, 5 April 1979, 29

13 Russell, 29

14 Letter to Theo, 8 September 1888

15 Quoted by L. Hanson and E. Hanson: *The Post-Impressionists* (London: Cassell, 1963), 132

16 Quoted by R. Pickvance: *Van Gogh in Arles* (New York: Abrams, 1984), 19

17 Quoted by Russell, 32

18 Letter to Theo, end September 1888

19 Quoted by Meyer Schapiro, *Modern Art* Vol II (London: Chatto & Windus, 1978), 96

20 Letter to Theo, early September 1888

21 Schapiro, 94

22 From Munch's literary diaries of the 1890s

23 Peter Gay, *The Bourgeois Experience* Vol 1 (New York: OUP, 1984), 207

24 Peter Gay, *The Bourgeois Experience* Vol 2 (New York: OUP, 1986), 417

25 *Emil Nolde* (London: Whitechapel Gallery, 1995), 18

26 Technically, the immaculate conception was what happened to Mary's mother, St Anne, but it seems that Nolde intended to refer to Mary here

27 *Emil Nolde*, 33

28 *Emil Nolde*, 96

29 Peter Fuller, *Art and Psychoanalysis* (London: Writers and Readers, 1980), 225

30 Quoted by George Steiner, *Real Presences* (London: Faber, 1989), 228

31 Goldstein recounts with satisfaction how a lady wearing a mink coat (another dead animal skin) ran screaming out of his exhibition, 'unable to endure so naked a display of male sexuality at the point where it becomes spirituality'.

32 George Pattison, *Art, Modernity and Faith* (Houndmills: Macmillan Academic, 1991), 176

Chapter 7 – Sex Out of this world – Men and Sex

1   Quoted by Janet Reibstein, Martin Richards, *Sexual Arrangements: Marriage and Affairs* (London: Heinemann, 1992), 74f (from a report of 1965)
2   James Park, *Sons, Mothers and Other Lovers* (London: Little, Brown and Company, 1995), 47, 56
3   Park, 49 (my italics)
4   Camille Paglia, *Sexual Personae: Art and Decadence from Nefertiti to Emily Dickinson* (London: Penguin, 1982), 27
5   Anita Chaudhuri, *Oh Hugh, How Could You?* (London: *The Guardian* 2, 28 June 1995), 5
6   Paglia, 47
7   Anthony Giddens, *The Transformation of Intimacy* (London: Polity Press, 1992), 125
8   Giddens, 60
9   Andy Metcalf, Martin Humphreys, *The Sexuality of Men* (London: Pluto, 1985), 93
10 The earliest drawings of female genitalia (presumably in a religious context) go back to about 30,000 BCE
11 Owen Chadwick, *The Secularization of the European Mind in the Nineteenth Century* (Cambridge: CUP, 1975), 255
12 Charles Baudelaire, *Les Métamorphoses du Vampire*, 20
13 Dominique Rincé *Baudelaire et la Modernité Poétique* (Paris: PUF, 1984), 61
14 *ibid*
15 Quoted by Wendy Holloway in edd. Sue Cartledge and Joann Ryan, *Sex and Love: New Thoughts on Old Contradictions* (London: Women's Press, 1985), 133
16 Park, 131f
17 Roger Scruton, *Sexual Desire: A Philosophical Investigation* (London: Phoenix, 1994), 306 (italics original)
18 Julia Kristeva, *Desire in language: A Semantic Approach to Literature and Art* (Oxford: OUP, 1980), 251
19 Marina Warner, *Alone of All her Sex* (London: Penguin), *xxi*
20 Victoria McKee, *Drum and Drummer* (London: *The Guardian* 2, 14 June 1995), 5
21 Giddens, 149

22 Jennifer Birkett, *The Sins of the Fathers: Decadence in France 1870–1914* (London: Quartet Books, 1986), 14
23 Birkett, 17
24 Birkett, 6
25 François-René de Chateaubriand, *René* (1802)
26 *Job* 5:7
27 Mary Kenny, *The Nuclear Explosion* (London: *The Guardian 2*, 1 November 1995), 6

Chapter 8 – Regarding the Body – Women and Sexuality

1   ed. Patricia Foster, *Minding the Body* (New York: Anchor, 1995), 3
2   Foster 7
3   Foster 204
4   Foster 19
5   Foster 19
6   Julian of Norwich, *Revelations of Divine Love*, tr. Clifton Wolters (London: Penguin, 1973), 67f
7   Julian, 170
8   From Hildegard of Bingen, *Causae et Curae*, quoted in *Sisters of Wisdom: St Hildegard's Theology of the Feminine*, Barbara Newman (Berkeley: University of California Press), 136f
9   Nelle Morton, *The Journey is Home* (Boston: Beacon Press, 1985), 155–7 (italics original)
10 Julia Kristeva, *Desire in Language: a Semiotic Approach to Literature and Art*, (Oxford: OUP, 1980), *passim: jouissance* defined (by Léon Roudiez) on page 15
11 Paula Cooey, *Religious Imagination and the Body: a Feminist Analysis* (New York: OUP, 1994), 22
12 Cooey, 23
13 Harwood, *Pleasure Principles: Politics, Sexuality and Ethics* (London: Laurence & Wishart, 1993), 88
14 Alex Comfort (ed), *The Joy of Sex* (London: Quartet, 1972), 63
15 Quoted by Cooey, 22; from Luce Irigary, 'Ce sex qui n'en est pas un', transl. in edd. E. Marks and I. de Courtivron, *New French Feminism: An Anthology* (Amherst: University of Massachusetts Press, 1980), 103
16 Roger Scruton, *Sexual Desire: A Philosophical Investigation* (London: Phoenix, 1994), 251 (italics original)
17 Cooey, 56

18 Sallie Tisdale, *Talk Dirty to Me: An Intimate Philosophy of Sex* (London: Pan, 1995), 95
19 Cooey, 22
20 Sheila Kitzinger, *Birth at Home*, Rev'd edn (Oxford: OUP, 1980), 137–144
21 Anthony Giddens, *The Transformation of Intimacy* (London: Polity Press, 1992), 174ff. Jeffrey Weeks makes a similar point about the secularisation of sex in his essay in Harwood
22 Clinical Standards Advisory Group, *Women in Normal Labour* (London: HMSO, 1995), 22f
23 Julia Kristeva, *Motherhood According to Bellini*, in *Desire in Language: A Semantic Approach to Literature and Art* (Oxford: OUP, 1980), 237f
24 D.H. Lawrence, *The Rainbow* (London: Penguin, 1989), 245
25 Kristeva, 237ff

Chapter 9 – Come Up and Buy Me – Sex and Hell

1 Susan Griffin, *Pornography and Silence* (London: Women's Press, 1981), 24
2 D. Howitt, G. Cumberbatch, *Pornography: Impacts and Influences* (London: Home Office Resources and Planning Unit, 1990), 95 (my italics)
3 Marge Piercey, "An Open Letter" in *Take Back the Night: Women on Pornography* ed. L. Lederer (NY: Bantam, 1980), *ix*
4 L. Lederer, *Take Back the Night*, 2
5 Audre Lorde, *Take Back the Night*, 295
6 Peter Michelson, *Speaking the Unspeakable: a Poetics of Obscenity* (new York: State University Press, 1993), 6
7 Michelson, 19
8 Griffin, 14f
9 Griffin, 47, 68
10 Griffin, 79
11 In ed. M. Yaffé, *The Influence of Pornography on Behaviour* (London: Academic Press, 1982), 45
12 Howitt, 94f
13 Nick Davies, *Dirty Business* (London: *The Guardian Weekend*, 26 November 1994), 14; *Red Light for Blue Squad* (London: *The Guardian 2*, 29 November 1994), 7
14 Carolyn See, *Blue Money* (New York: McKay & Co, 1974), *xi*
15 See, 180
16 M. Stein, *The Ethnography of an Adult Bookstore* (Lewiston, New York: Edwin Mellen Press, 1990), 42 (my italics)
17 Stein, 43 (my italics)

18 Stein, 68
19 Camille Paglia, *Sexual Personae: Art and Decadence from Nefertiti to Emily Dickinson* (London: Penguin, 1982), 24
20 Daniel Linz, Neil Malamuth, *Pornography* (London: Sage Publications, 1993), 44, from which other aspects of this analysis are also taken
21 Joan H. Timmerman, *Sexuality and Spiritual Growth* (Crossroads) 1992, reprinted in edd. J. Nelson, S. Longfellow, *Sexuality and the Sacred* (London: Mowbray, 1994), 102 (my italics)
22 Quoted by Michelson, 25
23 Griffin, 29
24 See, 172
25 Georges Bataille, *L'Érotisme* (Paris: Les Éditions de Minuit, 1957), 185
26 This according to Arthur J. Mielke, *Christians, Feminists and the Culture of Pornography* (Lanham, Md: University Press of America), 1995, *xiv*
27 Anthony Burgess, *Obscenity and the Arts* (Valetta, Malta, 1973), np
28 Michelson, 7
29 Michelson, 59
30 Michelson, 64
31 Michelson, 17
32 Anthony Giddens, *The Transformation of Intimacy* (London: Polity Press, 1992), 202

Chapter 10 – Glimpsing Paradise

1 Elaine Scarry, *The Body in Pain* (New York: OUP, 1985)
2 All these quotations are taken from ed. Tom Phillips, *Africa: The Art of a Continent* (London: Royal Academy of Arts, 1995)
3 Scarry, 184
4 *Jeremiah* 10:3–6
5 Scarry, 228
6 Scruton, 71
7 *Revelation* 21:22
8 Don Cupitt, *Radicals and the Future of the Church* (London: SCM, 1989), 163
9 Rollo May, *Love and Will*, (New York: W.W. Norton & Co, 1969), 316
10 Grey Gowrie speaking on BBC Radio Three, 4 January 1995
11 Owen Chadwick, *The Secularization of the European Mind* (Cambridge: CUP, 1975), 265

Acknowledgements

Thanks for help with this book are particularly due to Jennifer Kavanagh and Roland Phillips, whose unflagging enthusiasm for the book and its subject sustained me through the long months it took to complete; and to all those who graciously consented to be interviewed, gave of their time and advice, or read chapters in draft. Thanks, too, to members of the Athenaeum and Millennium groups who kindly submitted to early versions of several chapters and offered stimulating comments and criticism; and to the staff of Catford Library, unfailingly helpful and resourceful, who never once betrayed their professionalism by so much as the raising of an eyebrow; similarly, to the staff at the British Library. I am particularly grateful to Anne Baker, John McDade and latterly Tim Noble at *The Month* for their support and encouragement over many years, and to all the parishioners here at St Laurence's, one of the most diverse and stimulating parishes in the Church of England, for their patience and understanding; also to my colleagues Anthony Braddick-Southgate and Sheila Cameron, but for whose dedicated assistance in the parish writing a book would have been out of the question. Finally, to the book's dedicatee, whose tolerant understanding alone made the whole enterprise possible, I offer this small token of gratitude and love.

Acknowledgement is due to the copyright holders for permission to quote the following extracts:

Beacon Press, Boston, for an extract from *The Journey is Home* by Nelle Morton; The University of Massachusetts Press for extracts from *Witchcraft, Magic and Religion in Seventeenth Century Massachusetts* by Richard Weismann; *Les Éditions de Minuit, Paris*, for extracts from *L' érotisme* by Georges Bataille; Crown Publishers Inc, New York, for extracts from Valerie Kelly's *How to Write Erotica*; the editor of *The Month* for permission to use extracts from several of my articles over the last few years, and the editor of *Theology* for permission to quote from my articles in the May 1986, July 1990 and July 1992 editions; and Bloodaxe Books, Newcastle, for part of a poem by Jack Clemo.

Index

and reality 95–6; male attitude to 97, 167, 188, 204; as a *memento mori* 96–7; and the mind 132, 133; naked 93, 94, 97, 100–103, 104, 140; and pornography 105; as precarious 236–7; and redemption 46, 96; sacredness of 104, 105; sex, nature and 50; sex, religious experience and 47; suffering of 105; women's bodies 175–6, 188–96, 198, 199

Body and Society, The (Turner) 24, 55
Body in Pain, The (Scarry) 226–9
body language 198
Book of Common Prayer 77
Bourgeois Experience, The (Gay) 22, 140
Brain, Reverend Chris 113–15
brain, male/female 167–8
breast-feeding 18, 24, 32, 191, 192, 199
Briggs, Asa 20
British Men's Movement 181
Buddhism, Tibetan 120–23
Burgess, Anthony 222
Burke, Edmund 138
Burnett, Frances Hodgson 19, 27
Burton, Sir Richard 119
Byron, George Gordon, Lord 124

Cadieux, Geneviève 235
Calvin, John 135
Calvinism 24, 135
capitalism 71, 76, 182, 183
Carpenter, Humphrey 18–21, 23, 25, 28, 30, 40, 43
Carroll, Lewis *see* Dodgson, Charles Lutwidge
castration theory 165–6, 168
Cathar heresy 116–17
Catholic Church 54, 70, 115, 116, 123, 135, 182, 207
Centuries of Meditation (Traherne) 34–6
Chadwick, Owen 171, 240
Chamberlain, Richard 115
Chateaubriand, François, Vicomte de 184
Chesterton, G.K. 71
child abuse 18, 21–3, 205, 206, 212
childbirth 199–201
children/childhood: and Arcadia 17, 18–26, 30, 37–8, 43, 44, 134; Calvinist view of children 24; child development 17–18, 23, 40, 43; childhood as a locus of the sacred 11; child's bodily contact with mother/carer 17; innocence 17–18, 34, 35, 36; and middle class 17, 18, 20, 21, 24, 25, 26; myth of the protected child 25, 34, 43–4; object relations

theory 39–40; and paradise 17, 20, 26, 32, 46; and pornography 205; and a sacred space 18–21, 36–8, 39, 41–2, 43; sexuality of children 26–34, 41, 43, 44; spirituality of childhood 27, 34–40; Victorians/Edwardians 17–24, 26
children's books 18–21, 23–34, 37–8
Children's Games in Street and Playground (Opie and Opie) 42
China 122, 123
Christianity: becomes one religion among many 10; boys' religious phase 42; children's authors and a crisis of faith 19; decreases in influence 20–21, 43, 65; and infidelity in marriage 86; and the Orient 118; and resurrection 104; and sensual art 140; sex, nature and the body in 50; and witchcraft 59
Church Commissioners 112
Church, the: decline in importance of central institution 76; and homosexuality 112; and inner life 110, 130; and marriage 77–8, 88; middle class alienation from 10, 26–7; and peasant society 8; and pornography 208; and the Reformation 53; and religious abuses 103; repressive stance on sexuality 51–3, 55, 56, 113; and sacraments 16; and science 60; and sex 110–11, 114, 127; and sexuality 208; as a very human institution 10; and witchcraft 57
cinemas 154–5
Civilisation and its Discontents (Freud) 51
Clark, (Lord) Kenneth 137
Clemo, Jack 90–91
clergy, sex and the 111–17, 124–6, 127, 132
Clésinger 140
Clinical Standards Advisory Group 201
coitus reservatus 122–3
Cole, Adam 120
Comfort, Alex 46, 195
conception 201–2
Conrad, Joseph 119
conservatives, and pornography 214–15
Cooey, Paula 133, 193–4, 195, 197
Cotter, Jim 5
Courbet, Gustave 174
courtly love 123
creation, the 10, 73–4
'crisis of the male' 180
Crucible, The (Miller) 55–6, 58–9
Cult of Art, The (Gimpel) 152–3
culture, and nature 202–3